New Activism and the Corporate Response

New Activism and the Corporate Response

Edited by

Steve John

and

Stuart Thomson

First published 2003 by
PALGRAVE MACMILLAN
Houndmills, Basingstoke, Hampshire RG21 6XS and
175 Fifth Avenue, New York, N.Y. 10010
Companies and representatives throughout the world

PALGRAVE MACMILLAN is the global academic imprint of the Palgrave Macmillan division of St. Martin's Press, LLC and of Palgrave Macmillan Ltd. Macmillan® is a registered trademark in the United States, United Kingdom and other countries. Palgrave is a registered trademark in the European Union and other countries.

ISBN 1–4039–03115 hardback

This book is printed on paper suitable for recycling and made from fully managed and sustained forest sources.

A catalogue record for this book is available from the British Library.

A catalog record for this book is available from the Library of Congress.

Editing and origination by
Curran Publishing Services, Norwich

10   9   8   7   6   5   4   3   2   1
12 11 10 09 08 07 06 05 04 03

Printed and bound in Great Britain by
Creative Print & Design (Wales),
Ebbw Vale

Stuart would like to dedicate this book to Alex, Mum, Dad and Iain

Steve would like to dedicate this book to his Gran

CONTENTS

LIST OF FIGURES

LIST OF TABLES

LIST OF BOXES

Contributors

Svein S. Andersen

Svein S. Andersen (born 1952) is Professor and Dean of Doctoral Studies at the Norwegian School of Management. He is former director of ARENA (Advanced Research on the Europeanisation of the Nation State), University of Oslo. He holds a Ph.D. in sociology from Stanford University. He has published 12 books and numerous articles. Working within the area of comparative institutions and institutional theory his empirical studies have focused on issues relating to EU institutions and EU lobbying, as well as the regulation of the oil and gas industry. He also has an interest in research methods, focusing on the possibilities for generalising from case studies. His last book *Making Policy in Europe* (2002 with K. A. Eliassen) was recently published in Chinese. He has been a visiting professor at several European and American Universities; among them Centre des Hautes Etudes in Paris, UC Berkeley and UC Santa Barbara.

Martin Caraher

Martin is Reader in Food and Health Policy at City University. He originally trained as an environmental health officer in Dublin. While working in health promotion and community development in the northwest of Ireland he developed an interest in the public health and health promotion aspects of the work.

He has written extensively on issues related to cooking skills, local sustainable food supplies, the role of markets and co-ops in promoting health, farmers' markets, food access and poverty, retail concentration and globalisation of the food chain. Current research includes the role of local food projects in promoting health and the relationship between the state and locally/regionally funded food projects in England.

Antonio Carmona Báez

Dr Antonio Carmona Báez holds a Ph.D. in Political Science from the University of Amsterdam, the Netherlands. Originally from Puerto Rico, Carmona Báez is currently a Senior Researcher in the New Politics Project of the Amsterdam-based Trans-National Institute, a think tank and global network of scholar-activists. Carmona Báez is the author of *Global Trends and the Remnants of Socialism: Social, Political and Economic Restructuring in Cuba* (Pluto, 2003) and several other published articles concerning labour conditions in Cuba, new forms of political engagement for progressive social movements and scholar-activism.

Graeme Chesters

Dr Graeme Chesters is based at the Centre for Local Policy Studies at Edge Hill University College. He holds a Leverhulme Trust Special Research Fellowship to research global civil society, democracy and governance. He is co-editor of the book *We Are Everywhere: The Irresistible Rise of Global Anti-Capitalism* (Verso) and is currently writing a book on the alternative globalisation movement for Pluto Press.

Kjell A. Eliassen

Kjell A. Eliassen is a Professor of Public Management and director of the Centre for European and Asian Studies at the Norwegian School of Management – BI, in Oslo and Professor of European Studies at the Free University in Brussels.

He was formerly professor at the University of Aarhus, Denmark, and a visiting professor at several European, American and Asian universities, and is an Honorary Professor at the Fudan University in Shanghai and at the Jiaotong Xian University.

He has published 15 books and many articles on European and Asian Affairs. His latest books are *Making Policy in Europe* (2002) and *Global Telecommunications Liberalisation* (in Chinese) (2003).

Justin Greenwood

Justin Greenwood is Professor of European Public Policy at the Aberdeen Business School and a Visiting Professor at the College of Europe in Bruges. He has led 11 book projects in as many years on his subject specialism, interest representation in the European Union, the latest of which, a single-authored book of that title published by Palgrave Macmillan, was launched by European Commission Vice-President Kinnock at an event in Brussels in May 2003.

Mark Hatcher

Mark Hatcher is a member of the Global Regulatory and Professional Affairs Board of PricewaterhouseCoopers, the world's largest professional services organisation. He works with the firm's leadership in managing issues of public and regulatory policy impacting on the firm's business in 142 countries. He also consults with clients of the firm as a member of its European Policy Advisory Services team, based in Brussels.

A lawyer by training, Mark worked in government in the United Kingdom before joining the Strategy, Policy and Economics group of PricewaterhouseCoopers where he founded the firm's public affairs consulting practice. He takes a particular interest in world trade issues and corporate responsibility. He writes and lectures on various aspects of global public affairs practice.

He is writing here in a personal capacity.

Steve John

Steve John is a director of the government relations practice of the international law firm DLA. He has extensive experience of managing government relations and public affairs programmes involving high-level political campaigning, issues management, strategic advice and media relations.

As well as being a senior associate on a National Audit Office VFM study, he has also worked as a politics and finance producer for ITN and a political analyst on the Channel Tunnel project. He has worked for a number of political consultancies in London. He has a Ph.D. in Political Science from the London School of Economics. In 2002 he was the author of *The Persuaders: When Lobbyists Matter*, published by Palgrave Macmillan. He lectures and writes regularly on business and politics.

Grant Jordan

Grant Jordan, Professor of Politics at the University of Aberdeen, has written extensively on British policy making and interest group influence and membership questions. His books include *Shell, Greenpeace and the Brent Spar* (Palgrave, 2001, with W. Maloney), *The Protest Business* (Manchester University Press, 1997), *The British Administrative System* (Routledge, 1994) and *The Commercial Lobbyists* (ed.) (Aberdeen University Press, 1991). He is currently working on an ESRC-supported study of participation through interest group membership.

Charles Miller

Charles Miller worked in Whitehall and the House of Commons before becoming a policy analyst in the City and in industry. A lobbying consultant for over 25 years, he has written and broadcast widely on the subject, with books including *Lobbying: Understanding and Influencing the Corridors of Power*; *Politico's Guide to Political Lobbying*; and *Winning Friends, Influencing People*. He was also a contributor to *The Commercial Lobbyists*. He is currently managing partner of Policy Analysis Group, a regulatory and political risk management company, and is director of the Regulatory Best Practice Group of the European Policy Forum.

George Monbiot

George Monbiot was born in 1963. He is the author of *Captive State: The Corporate Takeover of Britain*, and the investigative travel books *Poisoned Arrows*, *Amazon Watershed* and *No Man's Land*. He writes a weekly column for the *Guardian* newspaper.

He is Honorary Professor at the Department of Politics in Keele, Visiting Professor at the Department of Environmental Science at the University of East London and formerly Visiting Fellow at Green College Oxford and Visiting Professor at the Department of Philosophy, Bristol.

In 1995 Nelson Mandela presented George Monbiot with a United Nations Global 500 Award for outstanding environmental achievement. He has also won the Lloyds National Screenwriting Prize for his screenplay *The Norwegian*, a Sony Award for radio production, the Sir Peter Kent Award and the OneWorld National Press Award.

He has been involved in protests against road building, mahogany imports and genetic engineering. He helped to found the land rights campaign The Land is Ours.

Nick Nichols

Nick Nichols is a founder, Chairman and CEO of Nichols–Dezenhall Communications Management Group Ltd. With over three decades of experience in the communications business, he is an expert in crisis management, and specialises in environmental, food, drug and product safety controversies.

Nick began his career as an investigative news correspondent before moving to Washington, D.C., to become senior media spokesman for the Cuban–Haitian Task Force under the Carter and Reagan administrations, where he focused on crisis communications following the 1980 Mariel boatlift.

He has appeared as a spokesperson on numerous television network news programmes including ABC's *Nightline*, NBC's *The Today Show* and the *CBS Evening News*.

Nick has become a frequent lecturer on the topics of crisis management, environmental extremism, eco-terrorism and the need for greater transparency by tax-exempt activist groups. He has addressed trade associations, academic institutions, corporations and policy groups, including the American Legislative Exchange Council and the State Legislative Leaders Foundation. Nick has authored a series of publications including the book *Rules for Corporate Warriors*, which was published in October 2001.

Duane Raymond

Duane Raymond is Oxfam GB's e-campaigns (e-activism) manager. He has an M.Sc. in Responsibility and Business Practice from the University of Bath School of Management. He has worked with UBS as a corporate social responsibility advisor, with Cap Gemini as an e-business consultant and AIESEC International as a director. He is currently setting up an ethically-based business which will turn activists' concerns into insight to help corporations prevent and resolve contentious issues. He is Canadian and has lived and worked extensively around the world.

Nick Robinson

Nick Robinson is Lecturer in Public Policy at the University of Leeds. He has published widely on the politics of the car, agenda-setting theory and the role of direct action within contemporary politics. He is author of *The Politics of Agenda Setting: The Car and the Shaping of Public Policy*, and is presently completing a book on the politics of the common transport policy of the European Union.

Robert H. Salisbury

Robert H. Salisbury is Souers Professor of American Government at Washington University. His most recent work has involved various aspects of American pluralism. He is particularly expert on how local community groups, religious institutions, the arts and sporting bodies operate in American society, past and present.

He has twice been Chairman of the Department of Political Science at Washington University and authored or co-authored four books. He has written dozens of academic journal articles and book chapters on subjects including interest groups, policy analysis, lobbying and political theory.

Linda Stevenson

Linda Stevenson, Research Fellow at the University of Aberdeen, has worked on local government, public policy, interest group and social capital projects and is currently working on a Leverhulme-funded study of the dynamics of national and regional identity as part of the Nations and Regions programme, and an ESRC-funded project examining the extent of policy divergence and/or convergence in a devolved United Kingdom as part of the Devolution and Constitutional Change programme. A co-authored book with Michael Keating on policy making and Scottish government will be published by Edinburgh University Press in 2004.

Chris Thomas

Chris Thomas has spent his entire career in the media intelligence industry. Previously a director at Observer Group company Media Works, and currently head of research with online reputation consultants Infonic, he has held a variety of analytical, consulting and management roles. The larger part of his experience has been in the design and implementation of measurement programmes for corporations, in order to help them better understand their image, reputation and the success of their communications activities. Chris has specific expertise in corporate reputation measurement, and works mainly towards the global healthcare and technology markets.

Stuart Thomson

Dr Stuart Thomson is a communications and public affairs consultant with DLA Upstream, part of the international law firm DLA, advising on media relations, political campaigns and issues management. He is also an Honorary Research Fellow in the Department of Politics and International Relations at the University of Aberdeen.

His publications include *The Social Democratic Dilemma: Ideology, Governance and Globalization* (Macmillan, 2000) and *Dictionary of Labour Quotations* (Politico's, 1999). He is an associate editor of *Renewal: The Journal of Labour Politics*, and has also contributed articles to other political and business publications.

Preface

As the editors of this book we find the issue of activism interesting and thought provoking. While we have differing views on activism and the corporate response, we nevertheless hope that this book is stimulating and interesting to a number of different people. Undoubtedly as the problems the global economy faces continue apace and societal changes demand different and varying actions from corporate players, activism will become an increasingly important element in day-to-day lives. In many ways activism signifies the way in which individual citizens are finding their voices. We would, of course, like to thank all of those who have submitted chapters to this book. Without them there would be no *New Activism and the Corporate Response*. We did approach activists from a range of different backgrounds and sectors, some of whom were happy to contribute either in written form or informally through telephone conversation or e-mail while others were wary of putting their thoughts down on paper. We fully respect their position and hope that they will find the finished product of interest to them in any case.

Acknowledgements

We would like to thank many people who have helped in the production of this book.

First, we thank Stephen Rutt, our commissioning editor at Palgrave. His interest in this book has driven us forward and ensured we delivered within the timescale.

All our contributors have been diligent, and met our demands with good humour. Our copy editor, Chris Carr at Curran Publishing Services, has also been highly professional (and very helpful!).

We both work for DLA Upstream, the public affairs and communications practice of DLA, one of Europe's largest law firms. The environment in which we work has always been innovative and challenging. Our Chairman, Lord Tim Clement-Jones, has been supportive and enthusiastic, and despite being an extra-curricular interest, this book was completed under his watch. Another colleague, Matthew Davies, has kept us constantly up to speed with developments, and his take on life has provided us with new ideas and fresh thinking. All of our colleagues have supported us in our endeavours.

On a personal level, Stuart Thomson would like to thank Alex Ricks for giving him the support, encouragement and help needed to complete this book and also his mother (Maureen), father (Bill) and brother (Iain) because without them none of this would ever have been possible.

Steve would like to thank his grandmother, Anne John, for her enduring love and support.

We hope that you enjoy reading this book as much as we have enjoyed putting it together.

In Chapter 11, the press release of 'The Great Betrayal' is reproduced by kind permission of Dr Vandana Shiva, and lyrics of Richard Thompson's 'Fast Food' by kind permission of Beeswing Music.

Acronyms

ABPI	Association of the British Pharmaceutical Industry
ACE	Alliance on Beverage Cartons and the Environment (EU)
AFL–CIO	American Federation of Labor and Congress of Industrial Organizations
AGM	alternative globalisation movement
AHI	Aviation Health Institute
AI	Amnesty International
ALF	Animal Liberation Front
ARENA	Advanced Research on the Europeanisation of the Nation State
BIA	Bioindustry Association (UK)
BITC	UK Business in the Community
BMA	British Medical Association
BRF	British Roads Federation
CAP	common agricultural policy
CBI	Confederation of British Industry
CEI	Competitive Enterprise Institute (US)
CEO	chief executive officer
CESR	Committee of European Securities' Regulators
CHD	coronary heart disease
CI	Consumers International
CJ&POA	Criminal Justice and Public Order Act (UK)
COE	Corporate Observatory Europe
COLIPA	European Cosmetic, Toiletries and Perfumery Association
CPRE	Council for the Protection of Rural England
CSR	corporate social responsibility
DALYs	disability adjusted life years
DDT	insecticide: dichloro-diphenyl-trichloroethane
DETR	Department of the Environment, Transport and the Regions
DTI	Department of Trade and Industry (UK)
DVT	deep vein thrombosis
EDF	Environmental Defense Fund
ELF	Earth Liberation Front
EPA	Environmental Protection Agency (US)
EPC	Environmental Policy Centre
EPE	European Partners for the Environment
ERT	European Round Table of Industrialists
ESF	European Services Forum

ETUC	European Trade Union Confederation
EZLN	Zapatista National Liberation Army
FAO	Food and Agriculture Organisation
FDI	foreign direct investment
FTAs	free trade agreements/Freight Transport Association
G8	Group of Eight
GATS/GATS2000	General Agreement on Trade in Services
GATT	General Agreement on Tariffs and Trade
GMO	genetically modified organism
HLS	Huntingdon Life Sciences
ICO	International Coffee Organisation
ILO	International Labour Organisation
IMF	International Monetary Fund
IOSCO	International Organization of Securities Commissions
MEAs	multilateral environment agreements
MNCs	multinational corporations
NAFTA	North American Free Trade Agreement
NCPP	National Coal Policy Project (US)
NFU	National Farmers Union (UK)
NGOs	non-governmental organisations
NHS	National Health Service (UK)
OECD	Organisation for Economic Cooperation and Development
PACs	political action committees
PETA	People for the Ethical Treatment of Animals
PGA	People's Global Action
RHA	Road Hauliers Association
RTS	Reclaim The Streets
SAPs	structural adjustment programmes
SHAC	campaign to Stop Huntingdon Animal Cruelty
SOGAT	Society of Graphical and Allied Trades (UK printworkers union)
TABD	Trans-Atlantic Business Dialogue
TNCs	trans-national corporations
TNI	Trans-National Institute
TRIPS	Trade-Related Aspects of Intellectual Property Rights
TUC	Trades Union Congress (UK)
UK BCC	UK Breast Cancer Coalition
UNCTAD	United Nations Conference on Trade and Development
UNICE	Union of Industrial and Employers' Confederations of Europe
UNICEF	United Nations Children's Fund
WHO	World Health Organisation
WSF	World Social Forum
WSSD	World Summit on Sustainable Development
WTO	World Trade Organisation
WWF	World Wide Fund for Nature (formerly the World Wildlife Fund)

Activism is Dead: Long Live Activism

Steve John and Stuart Thomson

Capitalism and corporations are under more pressure now than at any time since the Great Depression. At that point governments in the West worried about the rise of organised labour and about socialist ideas coming to the fore. With millions unemployed in each country, social security systems, welfare states and active support policies were devised.[1] This proved sufficient to ensure the continuation of the prevailing economic orthodoxies, especially the central position of the market. Since this time, many argue, corporations have grown ever more powerful at the expense of democratic institutions. International bodies have been established that set the needs and desires of corporations above those of citizens. Governments are mere tools of corporations, and have been provided with the ideal excuse for pursuing the policies that favour them: the rise of globalisation.

Arguably, this system is now under pressure. The decline of powerful corporate actors such as Enron and WorldCom amid allegations of fraud and corruption appears to be both a symptom and a cause of this pressure. Recent bankruptcy filings in the United States include K-Mart, US Airways, Consolidated Freightways, Global Crossings, United Airlines and Conseco. In addition, there have been allegations of wrong-doing around Tyco, Martha Stewart Living Omnimedia, Rite-Aid, Kwest Communications and Dynegy. Credit Suisse First Boston was fined £4 million by the UK Financial Services Authority for allegedly 'systematically lying to financial and tax regulators' (*Observer*, 22 December 2002) while Merrill Lynch have also been fined (around $100 million). To these we must add those tainted by involvement in collapses such as Enron's, including JP Morgan Chase, Citigroup and, of course, Andersen. Governments have been forced to show that they still have a role and can protect their citizens. Yet more important, and often high profile, is the citizen fight-back: the rise of the new activist.

This book looks to develop thinking on activism and how those being attacked react. It argues that we are witnessing a generational shift in how governments, businesses, interest groups and citizens interact.

Many in society are now more aware of the role of activists and the impact, whether positive or negative, that they have. It is often noted that citizens are no longer active. The days of mass participation in political movements have ended and instead citizens prefer not to be involved. To judge from the election statistics in democratic countries many cannot even be bothered to vote. Admittedly, some do realise that this alienation can be a problem, leading to the rise of extremist political parties, rejection of laws and so on. The 'PlayStation Generation' is often seen as the way of the future.

This view, however, is simply not credible. Just look at the increasing number of people who are involved in politics in all its forms across the globe. This involvement extends beyond purely political parties but engages with the full range of government, labour and local events, as well as with corporations and the capitalist system.

The wider awareness of the role of activism may have come about because many of the activities are high profile, as with the violent protests against capitalism/globalisation. Just look at any opinion poll and the fact remains that people are now less trusting of government and corporations; this feeds the ability of activists to have an impact and also provides a great deal of opportunity for them. There is also a clear understanding on the part of activists of the need to vary tactics. Whereas political parties still find it very difficult to move away from embedded decision-making processes or monthly meetings, activist groups recognise the need to be mobile, to use new technologies, to shift tactics if one set does not work, and to know when to keep the pressure up and when to turn it down.

Younger people are often more clued up to issues that they believe are important and relevant to them, particularly the environment. A strong argument can be made that they are more perceptive than generations of the past, possibly aided and abetted by the proliferation of the media. What is noticeable, though, is their failure to see the relevance of existing political institutions, particularly political parties. Maybe this has to do with their parents' declining attachment to political parties, itself a reflection of the decline of class and religious allegiances among other factors.[2] Instead citizens focus more narrowly but more definitively on the issues which mean most to them and excite them more.

It is worth remembering that in September 2000 the darkest hour of the first term of the British Labour Government came not from a well-organised opposition or an over-mighty media, but from a rag bag of irate lorry drivers and hauliers complaining about the price of fuel. The fuel protestors, much like the anti-globalisation movement, represent a new type of dissent. They are decentralised, operate in networks or cells, and make extensive use of information and communications technologies in both their organisation and execution of tactics.

Some may well argue that activists have always been around. This would be quite true. However, one may draw a similar analogy to the globalisation debate. Some ask whether globalisation really exists. Another view is often that globalisation has always been around and it is merely the speed at which it is taking place that marks it out as different from before. Others, although this is becoming less and less common, say that it is a new phenomenon primarily facilitated by technological developments. A debate around activism can be conducted along similar lines. Is activism new? No. What is clear, however, is that there are new ways of organising, more flexibility in shape and size, and new tactics available, again using technological developments.

The Activist Debate

This book intends to use activist and activism as generic terms. We, of course, realise that this means that we treat a diverse set of actions in a similar way. Yet it remains important to have an easily understood term that can be applied across both the range of activities described in this book and also the range of tactics employed. We take activist to mean one who is engaged in an activity against a perceived wrong, whether that be perpetrated by a government, a corporation or an individual.

Much of the activist debate has come to be dominated by the anti-globalisation movement. This, for many years, has symbolised the activist movement. While targets and tactics varied, anti-globalisation became a byword for activism. It also appeared to be something that bound activists together. This is no longer the case. Since September 11 cracks and disagreements have emerged in the activist movement. Primarily the fissure has appeared between those who saw the terrorist attacks as helping to undermine globalisation and those who saw it as an attack on a democratic country and on democracy itself. The anti-terror campaign being led primarily by the US Government has therefore had an impact on the activist community and its attitude towards war. In this sense it initially helped governments, as it has taken the focus away from globalisation and placed the spot light firmly on terrorism.[3] But the agenda has shifted. Activists have succeeded in switching the focus. The US-led military action against Iraq in Gulf War II was protrayed by activists as being the consequence of the US's thirst for oil. Despite all the 'evidence' presented by politicians about Iraq's failure to comply with UN resolutions, its possession of weapons of mass destruction and its appalling treatment of its own citizens, few trust the motives of the coalition leaders and support for a war was limited. This meant that activists have once again been able to unite: you can be both anti-war and anti-corporate.

Politicians and governments have often used foreign policy to deflect attention from domestic problems: normally a faltering economy. It so happens that many of President Bush's domestic problems are to do with corporate failures. A war on terrorism helps to deflect attention away from these failures. It has been suggested by many authors, primarily Michael Moore (see *Stupid White Men and Other Sorry Excuses for the State of the Nation*), that the president has extremely close links with many corporate actors, especially in the energy market. For instance, Enron was for many years a major donor to Bush's campaigns. This link, of course, also assists the activists in depicting the war against Iraq as motivated by factors other than defence. This perception of a very close link between politicians and corporates has not been helped by several developments. In the National Homeland Security Bill introduced by President Bush, a clause was inserted that protected the drug manufacturer Eli Lilly from lawsuits by the families who believe their children have been poisoned by a mercury-based vaccine preservative. Eli Lilly contributed more than any other drug company to the Republicans in recent campaigns, and of their total contribution of some $1.6m (£1m), around 80 per cent went to the Republicans. Bush's plans for corporate governance and accounting following the Enron collapse have also been criticised by many for being too weak and making merely a token gesture. A recent case filed by the General Accounting Office at Congress asked that the courts force the president to reveal details of those who had assisted in formulating energy policy. The judge, a Republican appointee, was of the opinion that the president did not have to reveal these sources. This again does not enhance the credibility of politicians or the trust that citizens have in them. It undermines politics and politicians.

If one looks at the United Kingdom, then again corporate actors appear to enjoy a great deal of freedom. In a recent review of taxation, the Hartnett Review, the Inland Revenue noted that it wanted to be 'supportive of business' and that they would work with the corporations in 'a relationship of mutual trust'. According to estimates, corporates who trade in the United Kingdom avoid payment of around £20 billion in UK tax each year (minutes of an internal Inland Revenue meeting quoted in *The Observer*, 17 November 2002), and the Inland Revenue only uncovers around a tenth of this. Meanwhile large companies have been invited to help the Inland Revenue form new policy. It has been claimed that large corporations have not had big penalties imposed on them for breaches. Add to this concessions made recently to British American Tobacco, General Motors, ICI, Rolls Royce, SmithKline Beecham and Unilever, and you have the appearance of a taxation system geared to the needs of corporate players. (See Nick Davies' article in the *Guardian*, 23 July 2002.)

Citizens are also confronted with an increasing role of corporations in society. Corporates not longer merely supply services or sell products; they are increasingly involved in every part of daily life (see Monbiot's chapter in this book). As companies extend their involvement, people are increasingly worried. As governments continue to cut state involvement and funding and look to lower taxation, additional opportunities are provided for corporates to step in and fill the void. A prime example of this is in schools where companies provide teaching materials to fill the gaps in state provision. Many critics have examined such materials and claimed that they give a very biased view in favour of the company and slant history to put the company in a better light.[4] Look at the links between organisation such as the United Nations and corporates. World Children's Day is actually a trademark of McDonald's but was supported by Kofi Annan in a drive to help disadvantaged children across the world.

The mistrust of politicians and governments combined with the ever-increasing role of corporations, leads to the increasing reliance on activism for fear of otherwise being powerless.

The Range of Activism

On many occasions this book refers to activism being undertaken against corporations. Again, while it is realised that this is only part of the debate, these are often the best examples and highlight 'best practice' adopted by activists. It is nevertheless imperative that we do not become blinkered by seeing activism merely as an anti-corporate movement *per se*. Activists are engaged in struggles across a range of different areas, across different countries and against different actors: governments, world organisations, individuals and, on occasions, other activist groups.

Huntington Life Sciences (HLS) will be an example familiar to many, especially those in the United Kingdom and United States. The company tests products, as is required by law, on animals. It has been the subject of attacks from many groups, primarily Stop Huntingdon Animal Cruelty (SHAC), for many years. The premises owned by HLS, key staff and increasingly those who provide support to the company have all been attacked, not just verbally but many also physically. Intimidation and violence are increasingly used. Politicians who support the company are targets, and insurers, brokers and bankers have also all been targeted.

SHAC has set up demonstration camps near employees' homes to intimidate, and are vocal in targeting individuals. The private addresses of executives of both HLS and those who support them, in the widest possible sense, are targeted. It has got to the stage where the UK Government has stepped in so that the Department of Trade and Industry provides insurance cover and the Bank of England has provided banking facilities.

Just think about the range of different activity that takes place throughout society at the present time. There is, of course, the very obvious and high profile anti-globalisation movement but others can be more subtle and also open to a far wider range of citizens. The chapters contained in this book provide a much fuller description of the range of different activities being undertaken. However details below highlight some of the ways in which activism is developing.

Boycotts

While the 1970s may have been seen as the heyday of boycotts, these are again becoming increasingly popular. Nestlé decided to call in a £3.7 million debt from Ethiopia at the end of December 2002. The company has for many years been the target of activist attacks, primarily because of the marketing of breast milk substitute to developing countries. It may seem that Nestlé, perhaps more than any other company, should be better aware of the demands and thinking of activists through all these years of experience. However, calling in of the debt shows that this has all gone to waste. Calls for Nestlé's products to be boycotted led the company to reverse its decision on the debt. If one were to organise a boycott nowadays it would be easy to refer people to a companies website to check their full list of products. Nestlé has, however, shown great resilience and its 2002 profits showed an increase of more than 13 per cent to £3.68 billion.

Activist action is littered with examples of boycotts. The rejection of new Coca-Cola in 1985 forced the company to reverse its policies (this boycott was because of the drink's taste rather than any breach in ethical behaviour). The 'Stop Esso' campaign by Greenpeace continues to gain support. In February 2003 Greenpeace used groups of volunteers in small mobile teams to chain themselves to petrol pumps and also targeted the company's headquarters and caused it to close down (activists abseiled from its roof). The activity took place across 17 countries.

Other campaigns are also taking place at the time of writing. Among others, there is a US boycott of French wine, because of the French Government's opposition to war in Iraq; pensioners in Minnesota are boycotting GSK as it attempts to stop its drugs being sold at the same cheaper prices as in Canada; in the Arab world both Coca-Cola and McDonald's are subject to boycotts (Islam, 2003). The number seems endless.

Gap has also seen calls for its products to be boycotted as groups such as Africa Forum and Unite have accused the company of making use of sweatshop labour. The Burma campaign has put forward a list of around 70 companies who are said to help finance the military dictatorship in Burma that has perpetrated some of the worst human rights abuses of recent years. While this produces media coverage and gives people an easy way to become activists, it can also be a boost to those companies not tainted. The Burma campaign, for instance, also publicised those firms that took a deliberate decision not to work in the area.

Music

While we have for many years been used to high profile songwriters and bands using their position to put forward political ideas, what is more unusual are those such as Radio Boy who create songs and sounds through the destruction of products. On CD and in live concerts Radio Boy, aka Matthew Herbert, destroys crisp packets, video tapes, Coca-Cola cans and Happy Meal packaging to protest against corporate activity.

People Power

Simply getting people involved may not be enough. However, getting them to do something shocking or unusual may help the cause. A group of around 600 Nigerian mothers and grandmothers protested against Chevron Texaco and forced them to promise jobs, electricity and other improvements to villages in their area simply by threatening to take their clothes off.

Getting large numbers of people involved in a campaign can provide a huge influence. In the United Kingdom 1.5 million people took part in a march against the imminent war against Iraq, and similar marches took place across the world on the same day. Large numbers of people can also be of great use in various other types of campaign; for instance, see the earlier discussion of boycotts.

Lobbying

While politicians and corporates may have been lobbying for years, this has less often been the case for activists and charities. There is an increasing understanding that the traditional and political processes can be used for the benefits of an activist's aims. The UK Breast Cancer Coalition (UK BCC) has been at the forefront of using patients as advocates in lobbying the UK Government. They approach Members of Parliament, get involved in various committees and generally favour mass lobbying (Gaines, 2002). This type of technique has been used in the United States but is relatively new to the United Kingdom for charities and activists.

Shareholders

For many years it was taken for granted that shareholders would support the board of a company. Yet as the activity of companies appears to move away from the needs of society, as the rewards given to board members – and especially chairpersons – have less and less to do with the economic performance of the company, the shareholders are fighting back. Various organisations now exist to help shareholders organise themselves and understand the processes fully, to inflict defeat on the boards and have their say in the ways the company should be run. The Trades Union Congress (TUC) in the United Kingdom launched a campaign in February 2003 to increase shareholder activism by pension funds to tackle excessive executive pay and failings in corporate governance.

Advertising

This has traditionally been the stronghold of the corporate sector. Recent examples, however, have shown that activists know how to use advertising for their own means. International Buy Nothing Day aimed to encourage people to have one day when they would think about excessive consumption and inequalities between rich and poor countries. Adverts were placed on TV, along with the usual ones, which had a talking pig encouraging people to buy nothing. The day was created by Kalle Lasn of the Media Foundation, which also publishes the magazine *Ad Busters*. Lasn's provocative, clever and often humorous perversion of the use of corporate ads has provided an extremely useful weapon in the armoury of activists.

There are, however, examples of corporates playing this game as well. Increasingly, guerrilla tactics are being used to capture the imagination of the public. Two male streakers used a rugby match to advertise Vodafone. Corporates are using 'beautiful people' to encourage the use of their products: carefully selected individuals are chosen to use the product in appropriate locations. This is used by clothing manufacturers as well as companies that develop and need to encourage the use of products such as electronic equipment. Viral marketing, the creation of the activists, has also been taken up the corporations as they recognise its power in helping them to sell products.

Legal Action

The law is being used by both activists and corporations to attack and defend. One only has to look at some recent examples to see that this is most definitely a device that is being brought into play by both sides. Greenpeace launched a High Court case over a loan to British Energy, McDonald's is being sued for failing to warn that its food can lead to obesity, Greenpeace (again) lost a case over illegal timber and – this time on the receiving end – Greenpeace and Npower were criticised by a regulator, the Advertising Standards Authority, for appearing to claim that the 'green' electricity they suplied at a higher tariff came from windpower. Even the New York Police Department has gone to court to try to overturn a legal ruling that limits its ability to spy on political activists.

Electronic Communications

The spread of electronic communications, its various forms and its impact on activism is dealt with in several chapters in this book, including Duane Raymond's. However, it is important to note that its availability has shifted the landscape for both activists and corporations. Activist groups of all sizes now effectively have more power: smaller, more radical groups have increased in importance and influence, while larger groups have been able to internationalise still further.

We are intrigued, as we hope others are, by new activism and the corporate response.

New Activism and the Corporate Response

We hope, from the above, that it is obvious that new activists are using a range of increasingly sophisticated and diffuse tactics involving the media, the Internet, telephones, direct action and good old fashioned 'people power'. Grassroots cells can be coordinated by a hand full of dedicated, often anonymous, believers who can bring a corporation to its knees with terrifying speed. Groups engage in a multi-headed attack on workers, shareholders and customers. Corporations, individual brands and individuals, among others, can all be subject to attack.

Look across the range of media, the types of materials produced by companies, the actions of government, the establishment of new activists bodies and the like, and you will see a shift.

Politicians have begun to accept the power of communities; if we take the United Kingdom as an example, the main political parties are all advocating policies that shift the emphasis from a powerful central state towards devolved powers to local communities. It must, however, be said that some countries, especially in mainland Europe, are well ahead of the United Kingdom on this issue. There is still too great a reliance on elections to enable people to have an influence, but simply having elections does not 'prove' that democracy exists.

In many cases it is now easier for the citizens to become involved in new forms of activism. You can simplistically attribute this to technology – the rise of the Internet and e-mail as both information source and tool – but you need also to consider the failures of government, the 24-hour media, the expansion of corporations into all parts of people's lives. When you do this you begin to see why a change is taking place. Corporations are coming under increasing pressure and scrutiny from citizens; governments no longer have all the answers. Activists are trying to hold the corporations to account.

These new forms of radical activism are destroying some corporations, placing others under increasing strain and hitting shareholder value. That is, of course, the aim of many and they can thus claim great success. Corporations are often caught staring like rabbits at the headlights of an oncoming campaign hurtling towards them. The activist groups themselves will also face choices about whether to adopt insider or outsider status. This book will argue that while the older, more established groups have opted for insider status, involving themselves in governments and corporations, this has acted as a motor for the smaller, more radical activist groups.

Few books have attempted to look at the new activist environment, *New Activism and the Corporate Response* is an attempt to rectify this. It seeks to look at what motivates activists and examine their tactics, while also looking at the reaction of corporate actors and the options open to them.

Contributors to this book come from across a range of disciplines and represent viewpoints that can broadly be described as coming from the activist, academic and business communities. This represents an attempt to bring all the groups together so that they learn more about their different perspectives, but also so that the reader can gain a greater depth of understanding. It has also been important, given the nature of the subject, to adopt a trans-national – even global – perspective where possible, to ensure that the book is not skewed towards any particular locality or political system. The contributors come from across Europe and the United States and make reference to examples and case studies from around the world.

The broad heading of new activism in the title of the book is a deliberate attempt to catch all the various groupings, targets for attack, reactions and tactics involved. The contributors refer to anti-globalisation and anti-capitalist movements as well as particular groups and it should be stressed that the book seeks to include all of these. Salisbury begins proceedings by setting the theoretical backdrop and framework to the discussion.

The earlier reference to the splits in the anti-capitalist movement shows the importance of scholar-activism in providing concrete ideas about the way forward. Báez in his chapter details some of these ideas and the importance of scholars in the new environment. It is no longer adequate to be merely anti; instead ideas about new forms need to be at the fore of the debate.

There are similarities across some of the chapters even though they are coming from opposite perspectives. In particular, Monbiot's examination of the corporate takeover and Miller's assertions that there is no real change in how business and government deal with each other have some echoes. Miller tries to advance a 'business as usual' perspective, believing that businesses are dealing with the obstacles being put in their way and that the impact of the activist movement is limited but actually helpful. Nichols argues much more strongly that corporate actors can and should fight back, and provides a detailed checklist of how they can achieve this. Monbiot shows that the very notion of powerful corporations is an explanatory factor behind the growth of activism. Although largely using the example of the United Kingdom, his chapter also brings in examples from the United States. Chesters provides some interesting pointers as to why activism arises, traces the development of the anti-globalisation groups and assesses their impact on governments.

The book tries to highlight forms of activism that may not have traditionally been viewed as such. Greenwood looks at the role of trade associations and makes a case for their use in defending the position of an industry against activist action. Hatcher looks at the development of the business environment, especially in the global context, detailing the options open to corporations for action. Andersen and Eliassen similarly look at the increasing importance of the European Union.

Caraher's chapter on food protest is many ways encapsulates the notion of the over-powerful corporation, but also warns that reliance on direct action by activists can mean that the real issues are missed. A misplaced emphasis can mean that the real problems are not addressed: activists are not always right. This point is endorsed from the corporate perspective by Nichols.

Jordan and Stevenson look at the issue that arise when activists become insiders and work with corporations. They highlight some of the drawbacks, such as the alienation of members, and prefer to see it as a tool in the armoury of activists rather than the be all and end all. This is further supported by looking at the example of Shell. Although Greenpeace has worked with the company since the Brent Spar incident, environmental campaigners continue to exert pressure on the company for what they claim is its 'shocking' pollution record. However, some of the ultimate insiders in the United Kingdom, such as the NFU (National Farmers Union), the BMA (British Medical Association), and the Law Society, are coming under pressure to reform and to have less of a role. They are no longer the all-powerful voice that once they were.

There is no doubt that some corporations are thinking about the way in which they do business and are becoming more *honest*. A company's corporate social responsibility (CSR) initiative is often used to demonstrate their ethical standpoint. It is imperative that companies do not see such a CSR activity as merely a public relations exercise: it has to be part of the way in which the company does business. Even so, pressure will still remain. Nike and Adidas continue to be criticised for having failed to stop sweatshop abuses. Timothy Connor (in 'We are Not Machines') states that 'Nike and Adidas have not done enough to address the concerns of human rights groups, consumers and workers themselves'. 'Those improvements which have occurred are commendable, and demonstrate that positive change in response to international pressure is possible. Unfortunately they fall well short of ensuring that Nike and Adidas workers are able to live with dignity' (see Richard Lloyd Parry, 'Nike and Adidas Have Failed to Stop Sweatshop Abuses'). Even Nike realise that they have more to do, as they state in their own CSR report.

Robinson details a case study of the fuel protest movement in the United Kingdom, as mentioned earlier, finding that while the activities of this group were not new *per se* they were in the context of UK politics, marking an important shift.

The chapters by Thomas and Raymond both deal with the use of electronic communications, by the corporate sector and by the activists respectively. Thomas has looked at the opportunities presented to the business community while Raymond looks at the development of communications as part of the range of options open to activists.

Overall

There were other areas such as shareholder activism where we, as the editors, could have looked for contributions. With limited space, we wished to include as much as possible but had to make some omissions. Activism can take so many forms that it would not be possible to give them all space in this book.

The events of September 11 have made it even more imperative to understand new types of activism. Terrorist activity is the most extreme example of a way in which 'activists' seek to exert pressure and to get their way. These violent actions are another area that is not examined in detail in the book.

The book's conclusions bring together the themes and findings of the various chapters and attempt to summarise them in a way that all groups, both activist and corporate, can understand and learn from.

Notes

1. Although the form and timings of these institutions varied, there was a definite trend towards governmental support.
2. For a full exploration of the evidence and theories surrounding the decline of class and other factors in elections see S. Thomson, *The Social Democratic Dilemma.*
3. For a fuller examination of the emerging split in the activist community see Johann Hari, 'Whatever Happened to *No Logo*?' *New Statesman*, 11 November 2002.
4. In particular see N. Klein, *No Logo.*

CHAPTER 1

The Modern Interest Group

Robert H. Salisbury

Introduction

There can be no doubt that in the contemporary world of politics, especially but by no means exclusively in democratic systems, there is a vast
array of what we call interest groups or lobbies at work, trying to influence
what governments do. Sometimes and in some places these organisations
seem to dominate the processes that determine who gets what, when and
how, while elsewhere they seem more often to be supplicants hoping for a
favourable nod or lamenting their lack of success. In general, however,
most of both the winners and the losers in the decision-making struggles
we call politics are interest groups, non-governmental organisations
advocating particular policy preferences and trying to persuade those with
official standing and authority to support their position.

This chapter explores the existing literature looking at the development
of the modern interest group: their attitudes, opinions and actions. This will
provide the setting to the book as its contributors explore the recent development of activism, from the rise of the anti-globalisation movement
through to small, Internet-based organisations. Without an understanding
of the historical perspective any examination would fundamentally undermined and would be unable to address issues such as whether the actions
are 'new'.

Interest Groups

Throughout the history of democratic politics the impact of interest groups
on governmental decisions has been regarded by many as a serious normative issue. The classic statements of democratic theory provided no place
for interest groups, standing as they did between individual citizens and
governmental authority, the principal components of traditional concern.
Apart from the English pluralists of the early twentieth century, groups
were generally regarded as divisive forces, allegedly reflecting selfish and

partial views that made it more difficult for policy makers to reach decisions that optimised benefits for the whole society. Journalists and academics alike have looked upon 'special' interests as a major source of corruption of the body politic, not just because they often utilised nefarious techniques like bribery but more generally because they were thought to demean the processes of public debate and decision, reducing them to base considerations of narrow self-interest.

By the end of the nineteenth century business corporations and labour unions had grown to great size and power and, especially in the United States, a host of other organisations had emerged to articulate values and points of view, calling for reforms, regulations, subsidies and restrictions across a vast expanse of potential governmental action. At the same time, the growth of government, at national, state and local levels, had considerably enlarged its impact on people's lives, and had also come to offer opportunities to the enterprising to extract something of value from what public authorities did. Accordingly, at every level of government, scandals were uncovered and reforms demanded, and organised interest groups played major roles on every side of every question.

In many aspects of the American culture this period – roughly from the Gilded Age of the 1870s through the Progressive Era that ended in 1914 or so – evoked what has sometimes been called 'critical realism', as in the novels of Norris, Sinclair and Dreiser, or the 'revolt against formalism', as in the philosophy of William James and John Dewey. Standard formulations of governmental matters had generally been expressed in terms of legal norms and official institutions – and, indeed, continued to be so in textbooks for several decades to come – but in the hands of 'muckraking' journalists like Lincoln Steffens and academics like Charles Beard the 'realities' of political life, past and present, began to receive closer attention. For some this involved looking at psychological factors affecting political behaviour, or at the impact of mobs and crowds that defied the usual 'rational' explanations of how people behaved. In any case, by shifting the emphasis away from the abstract formalities of governmental action and reporting the observable behaviours of people both in and out of office, a fundamental and far-reaching change in perspective and understanding was accomplished. Despite the lively work in the early years of the twentieth century, however, it took several decades for this intellectual sea-change fully to work its way into political science.

One book from this era came eventually to serve as a major inspiration to those interested in studying interest groups and their impact. This was Arthur Bentley's *The Process of Government*. Although the work was published in 1908 it received scant attention from the scholarly community at the time, and it was not until it had been republished in 1935 that it began to be read. Bentley insisted that groups were the fundamental units of observable action in the political world, and that if they were adequately mapped one would have all that was needed for a full characterisation of the political process. Bentley's groups were not, however, synonymous with pressure groups or any other form of organisation. Rather they were conceptual labels for patterns of all the activity, from whatever source derived, that was directed toward some common purpose or, if you prefer, some interest. Bentley refused to separate the group from its interest; they were simply different aspects of the same phenomenon and defined by the observed activity. All those acting in a common policy direction, regardless of their position or the form of their action, were part of the 'group', and every action – every speech, every vote, every judicial opinion, every newspaper editorial, every academic treatise – that worked toward the same objective represented that interest and was part of the group.

The effect of Bentleyan analysis was to demystify, even to deconstruct, politics. He argued that the underlying meaning of every political act, no matter what its apparent form might be and however abstract its language, was the representation of some interest, the advantaging of some group and its purposes. At the same time, however, his prescription was not readily adapted to the needs of empirical research. It was all very well to say that everything should be understood as representing particular interests, but Bentley offered little guidance as to what those interests might be or what forms of action might most often be employed in their pursuit. For the generations that came after Bentley the study of interest groups, while deriving some degree of encouragement from Bentley's strictures against the 'ghosts' of formalism, had to draw on other sources for advice about how to proceed.

From the late 1920s on, American political scientists occasionally undertook case studies of interest groups, examining particular organisations like the Anti-Saloon League (Odegard, 1928) and the American Medical Association (Garceau, 1941), or larger arrays of groups (Herring, 1929; Childs, 1930; Schattschneider, 1935; McKean, 1938), but the subject remained on the periphery of professional concern. Not until the publication of David Truman's *The Governmental Process* (1951) were interest groups brought into the core of what political scientists thought important. Truman paid homage to Bentley's work, and his title quite consciously employed the same words Bentley had used. Moreover, Truman was able to find a substantial array of scholarly work, and bring it together to form a coherent, theoretically informed analysis of interest groups in American politics. Despite the linguistic parallel with Bentley, however, Truman was pursuing a different objective. Bentley had been trying to 'fashion a tool' for the analysis of any political situation. He proposed to interpret all forms of observable activity in terms of the interests represented, the groups advantaged. Truman, on the other hand, after offering a theory of his own regarding the formation of groups, went on to describe the ways in which non-governmental associations sought and used access to governmental officials in order to influence their decisions on public policy. Where Bentley proposed a generic way of thinking about politics, Truman offered an analysis of an important, but partial, feature of the process as it worked in the United States.

Truman's perspective has dominated both the scholarly and the popular conception of the role of interest groups in politics. That is, they are generally understood to be non-governmental organisations that seek *access* – Truman's key concept – to governmental authorities in order to influence policy decisions. The research agenda that follows from this perspective has focused on such questions as which groups have access and how they get it, to what extent access translates into policy influence, and what alternative sources of influence over policy decisions are at work. To each of these empirical issues there has generally been a normative companion asking whether, whatever the present reality may be, it constitutes an acceptable state of affairs in a democratic polity, and, if not, how improvements might be introduced.

In Truman's analysis, and in virtually every other discussion of interest groups, it was assumed that groups were a more or less inevitable consequence of the development of what might be thought of as 'value communities'. That is, as certain sets of people were similarly affected by social or economic developments – farmers, for instance, or railroad workers – they would join together to form organisations to express their common interest, and if that interest was adversely affected by some other group – meat packers, say, or railroad companies – they might try to persuade government to legislate some remedy. This commonsense view of interest group politics seemed to fit the historical record reasonably well, and Truman offered a substantial list of the dynamic factors like technology, war, and various forms of social change that had given rise to the creation of interest groups in the United States and, presumably, elsewhere in the world.

Collective Action

In 1965, however, an economist, Mancur Olson, presented a fundamental challenge to this basic assumption. In *The Logic of Collective Action* Olson argued that in most cases it was not rational for individuals or firms to join an organisation in order to lobby for favourable governmental action. The benefits that might accrue from that action would not be denied a non-member, and one person would have little effect in determining whether the organisation's efforts succeeded. Thus, farmers, workers, environmentalists, small business owners, and a host of other potential 'groups' could not be expected to organise effectively simply because they had values in common. At the same time it was obvious that there were, in fact, many voluntary associations that had somehow overcome the 'free rider problem'. Olson argued that they had done so by providing members selective benefits, such as cheap insurance or technical assistance, that were not available to non-members. Having recruited members with *selective* benefits, the organisation could lobby for advantageous public policy as what Olson called a 'byproduct' of its membership strength. Olson did not claim that his theory applied to every type of interest group, and it could readily be shown that, although there were many free riders in the world, there were also a good many people who joined interest groups without worrying whether it was the strictly 'rational' thing to do. None the less, Olson had moved the question of why people become group members from the status of assumption to that of a research question.

Salisbury (1969) shifted the argument, suggesting that individuals joined associations in response to incentives offered by 'entrepreneurs' who, having invested the necessary capital, presented them with a combination of three types of incentives: material, solidary, and expressive. Olson had focused on the use of material incentives such as cheap insurance or marketing advantages, but neglected the potential appeal of social interaction among group members and, especially, the willingness of people to pay the cost of group membership in order to express support for a cause they believed in. The latter might well involve issues of public policy so that, in effect, the members of expressive groups would, *contra* Olson's position, be joining in order to support an effort to secure government action; often, indeed, an action from which they personally would derive no direct benefit. Salisbury's formulation left considerable room for leadership initiative in determining what policy-related actions to take. The relationship between group leaders and their members was seen as problematic, with the leadership constrained but by no means always controlled by the policy preferences of group members. The latter could thus be viewed as constituents who might sometimes exercise their 'voice' within the organisation and sometimes choose instead to 'exit' (Hirschmann, 1970).

Salisbury's emphasis on entrepreneurial initiative as necessary for the establishment of a voluntary association called for attention to be given to the conditions under which entrepreneurs would emerge, raise their initial investment resources, appeal to a 'market', and institutionalise a stable support base. Truman's broad historical sweep had provided some leads, suggesting, for example, that many organisations were formed in a kind of 'wave-like' sequence. The effects of war, say, or technological change might destabilise a system of economic relationships, creating an imbalance of bargaining power. New structures would be created to counter this change and create a new equilibrium. This 'homeostatic' hypothesis seemed roughly appropriate to the late nineteenth century rise of big business organisations and the countervailing emergence of labour unions and farm organisations. An alternative, though not mutually exclusive, hypothesis of interest association formation stressed the 'proliferation' of organisations when increasing social and economic complexity generated more and more differentiated values and policy concerns that could serve as bases for voluntary associations. Jack Walker (1991) emphasized another factor, calling attention to the importance of cross-organisation subsidies in providing start-up capital for new associations. In particular, Walker showed that the substantial upsurge of non-profit 'citizens' organisations after about 1960 had received vital assistance from wealthy donors and charitable foundations.

This intellectual evolution has led to the recognition that voluntary associations are not some sort of spontaneous formation springing up out of shared values, but rather are created by organisers who invest money and effort in formulating a set of benefits that they hope will attract enough members to establish a viable enterprise. Within this framework there are a number of important empirical questions to be raised regarding any particular association. Who are the organisers, and where do they come from? Where do they get their initial investment capital? What is their market of potential joiners? What benefits are offered and with what success? Notice, however, that these same questions might be asked about any voluntary group regardless of whether it had ever been involved in the political process. A local quilting society can be examined within the same framework as Common Cause or the Anti-Saloon League. For a political scientist, therefore, an additional question must be raised. Why did a particular group get involved in the processes by which public policy decisions are made: that is, in politics? Before we speak further to that issue, however, we must look beyond the ranks of what interest group scholars traditionally took as their primary field of action: voluntary associations.

In 1984 Salisbury pointed out that in fact many of the organisations actively seeking to influence public policy were not voluntary associations but what he called institutions: organisations that did not need constantly to recruit members or defer even nominally to the policy preferences of their 'members' but whose leadership could operate with a longer time horizon and take a more flexible view of what political strategies to adopt. Thus business corporations, hospitals, universities, local governments and religious institutions are all active participants in the effort to influence what government does, and any sensible conception of interest group politics must obviously include them. Like voluntary associations, however, not all institutions try to affect political outcomes, so we return to the issue of why organisations enter the political arena.

The obvious answer is that they believe there is something of value to be obtained from the exercise of authority by the institutions of government. That something may be positive or negative, getting a good or blocking a bad, and it may result from governmental decisions at any level or jurisdiction. It may involve some direct material advantage such as a contract, tax break or subsidy, or it may be more indirect, involving the kind of future potentialities created by a change in the rules governing bankruptcy or naming a new justice to the Supreme Court. The stakes at issue may be more symbolic than material, involving the expression of moral values, ethnic or religious group attachments, or some other matter that people care about deeply enough to seek governmental action to further the cause. What is critical is that groups perceive some form of governmental authority as a relevant means by which to advance the valued objective.

This seemingly obvious point has an important consequence; namely, the volume of interest group activity in a democratic society depends upon the range and scope of governmental authority. The bigger the government, the more extensive the interest group activity. And there is a reciprocal point: the more extensive the group activity, making demands for assistance and defending gains already achieved, the larger the scope of governmental authority is likely to be. The growth curve is not infinite. There are groups whose advantage is served by reducing the scope of public policy. But the vast array of organised groups abounding in the modern democratic state must be explained in part, as both cause and effect, by the expansion of state authority.

It is vitally important that we recognise the differences among institutional arenas in their potential for affording advantages to particular groups. In a democratic society, interests with little wealth but broad popular support may well expect that their votes can overcome the resistance of the economically powerful, and so the 'have nots' of society have often turned to political action to redress their economic distress. But in a predominantly middle class society it is not at all clear that the poor have a broad enough base, and what numerical advantages they might have are seldom effectively mobilised. They may do better to call for a consumer boycott or conduct a campaign on college campuses to change public sentiment. Shifting the strategic emphasis from economic bargaining or campaigning intended to change societal attitudes to political action is rarely an easy or obvious decision, and in fact many groups, to the extent that they can muster the necessary resources, try to advance their claims wherever they can. Nevertheless, the points of effective access and leverage vary according to the institutional targets chosen, and so also do the resources of greatest value: numbers, money, social prestige, verbal skills, organisational efficiency and so on.

The Arenas of Politics

The arenas of politics themselves present important differences that affect the strategies and tactics employed by interest groups. In the United States the combination of federalism and the separation of powers creates an extraordinarily complex array of institutional targets, differing in their authority to make meaningful decisions and in their responsiveness to various types of group efforts to persuade. For some groups – builders and property developers, for example – local governments are the arenas of primary importance as they control matters of zoning and construction requirements; building trade unions may similarly emphasize local politics. In the steel and auto industries, on the other hand, both corporate and labour interests give more attention to national politics. These organisations operate throughout much of the country and engage in nationwide economic bargaining, and the main governmental decisions affecting their interests are made by Congress and the president. Some industries, such as oil and gas, are heavily involved in politics because they are affected in virtually every phase of their business by governmental decisions, while furniture companies and jewellery makers are not. Groups involved in education have been primarily concerned about what happened at the state and local levels of government, where the main decisions affecting funding, teacher training and curricula are made, and are more peripherally involved in national politics.

Interest groups may find that they have a comparative advantage in one governmental arena as compared to another. Until the 1960s, for example, civil rights groups found themselves unable to make any headway against state or local segregation policies in the South and, given the strength of Southern members of Congress, were frustrated at that level also. They turned to the courts and, by skilfully mustering persuasive constitutional arguments, gradually secured more favourable policies. The Supreme Court ruling that racial segregation was unconstitutional gave civil rights groups better leverage in other institutional settings, so that protest marches and sit-ins could more effectively bring about change at every level. Groups may of necessity focus their lobbying efforts on institutional arenas where they have the greatest likelihood of success, but they must also recognise that some of those arenas have far more power than others to bring about the desired result. College students opposing American involvement in Viet Nam or apartheid in South Africa protested on the campuses because, even though the universities had only the most marginal influence over national policy, that was where protest could be effectively mobilised.

We must recognise that the structure of authority and rules of procedure governing the political process *always* give advantage to some groups and work against others. The degree of centralisation or decentralisation will be a factor in interest group success. Enhancing the power of legislative leaders to control the agenda will work to the benefit of some groups and not others. And, as we noted above, the extent to which the courts play a significant role in determining who gets what from government can be a major factor. Moreover, any significant reform of the prevailing institutional arrangements will alter the pattern of group advantage, which is why reform proposals are controversial. There are groups on both sides with interests at stake.

We tend sometimes to think of interest group activity as primarily a matter of demand, of groups seeking (or trying to block) some kind of policy from government. We should also recognise that once policies are enacted they generate interests, establishing advantages that groups will seek to defend (or alter) as time goes on. Thus when a programme of national defence establishes military bases and acquires weapons systems, it creates interests in the districts where those bases are located and the weapons are manufactured. Elected officials from those areas are alert to defend the maintenance and growth of the programmes, which quickly take on the characteristics of vested interests and become difficult to change politically. Similarly, programmes of support for scientific research provide funds for the leading research universities, and while those institutions organise to defend their largesse, other, less prestigious, schools try to expand the scope of scientific support in order to attract some of the funds. In an era when American governmental budgets have reached trillions of dollars, there is an enormous array of interests vested in established programmes, but at the same time alterations, even at the margins, constitute appealing targets of opportunity for groups throughout the society.

As we have said, the enormous expansion in the scope and impact of modern government is both a cause and an effect of the growth of interest groups in both numbers and influence. That relationship is not a simple one, however. A number of other factors are involved. One is the increasing complexity of society as economic and social differentiations divide people into more and more combinations with distinct concerns. Another is affluence, which has enabled more organisations to attract members and to invest more heavily in efforts to affect public policy. Improved means of communication, from the coming of the railroads and the mass media to jet travel and the Internet, have enabled people to join together more readily and to mobilise in support of causes they believe in. And since interest representation succeeds in part as a result of effective techniques of advocacy, the growth and diffusion of professional expertise in these arts over recent decades of lobbying experience have contributed to the prominence of interest groups in every facet of public life.

The Actions of Interest Groups

Let us now look more closely at what interest groups actually do. What kinds of activity do they undertake? The question might seem a simple one, and indeed there is a rather simple answer, but before long it leads us to more complicated considerations. The simple answer is that interest groups advocate particular proposals for governmental action. They try to persuade public officials to support their position and offer reasons for so doing. The methods may range in form from abstract philosophical discourse to bribery, from arcane statistical analysis to *quid pro quo* bargaining, from appeals to moral sentiment to threats of mob reprisals. The kinds of reasons offered may reflect the values of a group's membership. An organisation like Common Cause, supported by well-educated middle-class citizens committed to the values of 'good government', would hardly countenance watching its representatives engaging in the earthier forms of vote trading. But arguments must also conform to the rules and expectations established by the institution in which they are presented. What is suitable before a congressional committee might not work either in a courtroom, on the one hand, or in a party convention, on the other. Much of what interest groups do, therefore, is to formulate the arguments they will present in their efforts to persuade officials to do one thing rather than another.

It is often assumed that the policy agenda advocated by an interest group is derived more or less directly from the desires of its members. While there is usually a connection between member preferences and group advocacy, it is often quite complicated. For one thing, as Olson pointed out, many people join interest groups to enjoy benefits that have little to do with the public policy positions the group may endorse. Furthermore, many of the specific policy objectives pursued by interest groups are developed by the leadership or staff as political circumstances produce changing threats or opportunities that affect organisational values. The members may know nothing about these matters, and group agents spend much of their time monitoring the governmental process and figuring out what positions to espouse. They may need to inform their members and persuade them to support the chosen position, a process sometimes called 'farming the membership'. Interest group advocates thus face in two directions at once: toward the officials who are the primary targets they must try to persuade, and their own members whose support is necessary to make their advocacy credible.

As noted, much of the group advocates' time must be spent in monitoring the complex processes of government. Patrolling the corridors of power and touching base with critically positioned actors is part of this; perusing the vast amounts of relevant literature, ranging from the daily press to technical studies and official documents, is another part; checking up on the activities of allies and adversaries is yet another necessary component. But intelligence gathering is not enough. Interest group representatives must also devote time and resources to the formulation of policy positions and the crafting of arguments in support of those positions. They must stipulate the provisions of law or the appropriation of funds they seek or support, and present reasons that not only justify their position but, they hope, persuade others to agree with them. Moreover, they must develop plans and strategies by which to negotiate their path through the institutional mazes of government: making acquaintances, cultivating contacts, and building coalitions. Much of this work, we should note, takes place well away from the lobbies of governmental authority, in organisational offices and conference rooms.

Often, of course, both the policy goals and the patterns of interest group support and opposition have been clearly established. Even so, however, there may be much uncertainty as to the precise strength of the contending forces, and group representatives must keep close watch on the process so as to spot both dangers and opportunities. Part of this uncertainty stems from the complexity of the process. In the United States the authority involved in making public policy decisions is highly fragmented, with the divisions among the different branches and levels of government compounded by further subdivisions of power and complexity of procedure within each branch. The need to know how this system works, as well as what policy substance is at stake, creates imposing challenges to interest group representatives, and they must learn how best to conduct their business. Accordingly, as one major study found, those who advocate group interests tend to be veterans of the policy wars, serving the same organisation for twelve years on average (Heinz *et al.*, 1993). Further, that study showed that while it is helpful to have personal contacts within the government, it is more important to have command of the substantive issues. And because so many different units are typically involved in making policy decisions, lobbyists must maintain contact with several different parts of the governmental apparatus.

There are occasional examples of dramatic lobbying campaigns in which new stratagems are employed or highly focused pressures are brought to bear, and now and then a sudden entry of previously inactive groups may capture attention. The broader trend, however, has been for interest groups to establish a more or less continuous presence close to the seats of governmental power, bringing to bear all the techniques their resources will allow. If one organisation pioneers with grassroots mobilisation of support, as the US Chamber of Commerce did in the 1970s, others soon follow if they can afford it. In 1939 the NAACP established the Legal Defense Fund under Thurgood Marshall as a non-profit organisation to pursue legal challenges on behalf of civil rights. More recently, conservative groups have followed that example on the other side of the issue. Interest groups learn over time, growing more sophisticated and skilful and generally avoiding the cruder forms of pressure. Groups tend to employ whatever techniques they can and try to establish sympathetic working relationships with officials throughout the political system. At the same time, of course, no organisation brings unlimited resources in money or personnel to the fray, and at any particular point in time competing groups may not be fully equal in talent either. As a consequence of these inequalities the outcomes of most public policy contests continue to be uncertain.

Finance

We cannot disregard the potential significance of interest groups' financial contributions to political parties and candidates for office. Groups are not the only sources of political money, to be sure, but in the aggregate they contribute very large sums to what is thought, by almost every observer, to be an outrageously vast amount of election spending. The question, of course, is what the groups get for their cash. The general assumption is that, at the least, they buy access: a receptive and friendly ear to receive their complaints and demands. Accordingly, a large proportion of campaign contributions goes to incumbents, officials whose past electoral success and accumulated power indicates that they are particularly worth talking to.

Other groups, however, devote most of their money to candidates who agree with their positions and, if successful, will support those interests in office. Some groups are quite pragmatic in their use of campaign money while others are driven by partisan or ideological commitments. And, just as the pattern of interest group giving displays motivational diversity, so does the impact of that investment.

There has been extensive research into the question of how much influence campaign contributions have on policy outcomes, and the answers are very mixed. There is no doubt that interest group political action committees (PACs) have helped make campaigns the occasions for heavy spending, but whether that spending has greatly distorted the policy decisions of governmental officials is not so clear. Most officials are eager to serve their constituents, not only to get re-elected but because that is what democracies expect them to do. Interest groups are composed of constituency segments, sometimes quite small ones but sometimes representing broad components of the public. If somehow all the organised groups were eliminated from the political process, it is not at all obvious that the resulting patterns of public policy would more accurately represent values approved by popular sentiment. In any event, the groups are there, they make contributions, they seek access, and they hope for influence. The chances of group success vary from one issue to another, from one electoral period to another, and from one group to another. Any generalisation regarding interest group influence must be phrased with great caution.

It is important to recognise that, while there are notable and sometimes dramatic exceptions, most policy issues do not just suddenly appear on the public agenda. Many are perennial, involving essentially the same disputes over authority and appropriations every year. Others, like farm policy, may recur only every three or four years but are matters of constant attentive concern from the groups affected and the officials with jurisdiction over the programmes. This means that monitoring and advocacy are ongoing and, as we noted earlier, this makes it advantageous to have experienced and knowledgeable people in place to represent group interests. It also means that over time groups will seek out and develop cooperative relationships with other like-minded organisations, sharing information and often collaborating in the planning and execution of influence strategies. Some of these connections have evolved into formal coalitions with names and office suites, while others remain more informal as working groups. A particularly vigorous policy dispute, such as the struggle over the Clinton health care proposal in 1993, may trigger the appearance of ad hoc alliances to sponsor TV campaigns and coordinate the lobbying effort, but many networks of group interaction are durable players in the policy process and lend a degree of simplifying structure to the cacophony of contemporary advocacy that results from the presence of so many thousands of interest group representatives.

In advancing their claims and justifications for governmental support interest group advocates produce an enormous amount of verbiage. Written and oral testimony, legal briefs, advertisements, research studies, editorials and a host of other materials compete for attention along with more mundane items such as lavish entertainments or campaign contributions. Many have argued that, in addition to the 'social noise' generated, the net effect of all this activity is to bias the processes of government in favour of those interests with the greatest resources. Schattschneider's formulation (1960) is the best-known version of this position. He contends that interest groups make claims on behalf of constituencies that are narrow in their policy concerns and ignore the interests of the large but unorganised portions of the public. Political parties, on the other hand, in order to win electoral majorities, must appeal to a broader range of interests and thereby pay more heed to the unorganised and the less affluent segments of society. It is certainly true, almost by definition, that interest groups, taken one at a time, appeal to rather narrow segments of the political spectrum. It is not so clear, however, that in the aggregate groups are more inclined to 'sing with an upper class accent'. The concerns of society's 'have nots' are surely represented more eloquently by organised groups like the Children's Defense Fund than by political party platforms. And if we include under the heading of interest groups all the non-governmental advocates of particular policies – the editorialists and media commentators, the think tanks, the academic experts and so on – there may still be substantial bias in the system, but the overall balance is not entirely obvious, and its calculation is certainly not simple.

Conclusion

Interest groups are often perceived primarily as the bringers of pressure upon officials. They have their policy demands and they try to persuade those with the power of government to accede to them. Obviously, there is much truth in this image, but it is far from a full picture. For one thing, although the general outline of its priorities may be reasonably constant, many of the policy specifics on an interest group's agenda emerge as the days and weeks of each political year reveal new implications and possibilities, new threats and necessities. Indeed, it is the need to recognise in a timely way these emergent concerns that makes it so important for groups to monitor closely the policy processes.

The image of groups as instruments of pressure is misleading in another way also. To a substantial extent they are better understood as the bearers of information, conveying to policy makers the needs and concerns of their members and reporting to their members the developments in the policy world that might affect them. This two-way flow can clearly be of great importance in building a foundation of rational understanding for both policy makers and group members. The difficulty arises when the group universe is too small and the information flows too restricted. Thus the impressive growth in recent decades of citizens' groups has arguably expanded democratic potentialities far more than traditional electoral processes alone could have done. In any case, it is difficult to see how in a democratic society the shortcomings of interest group politics can be addressed except by means of expanded interest group activity.

Much of the existing literature does not address this growth and impact of new citizens' groups. This book, by bringing together various perspectives from across the academic, business and activist communities is an attempt to redress this current imbalance. If these groups are to remain a part of democracy then they have to be more fully understood – both their actions and motivations. If western democracies continue to witness a decline in electoral turnout then the future may well be dominated by interest group activity.

CHAPTER 2

Beyond Win–Lose Processes?

The Potential of Group Co-operation Strategies

Grant Jordan and Linda Stevenson

Some groups have begun to bypass government altogether by working directly with the polluting industries, as in the 'New Direction' partnership in which selected environmental and corporate representatives are directly and voluntarily negotiating emissions standards.

(Phillips, 1994, p. 74)

From Demonisation and Direct Action to Dialogue?

Andrew Rowell (2001) reported on the protest in Genoa by anti-globalisation organisations such as the Rising Tide coalition and Ya Basta (enough is enough) against the annual summit of the G8. He quoted claims that this represented a battle for legitimacy between multinationals and civil society. He pointed to the claim that business was reacting by seeking to 'frame' protest in a particular way. 'While the language heats up on both sides, it is the protestors [portrayed as non-legitimate] who are being labelled as violent, even though the majority of the violence could be from the Italian authorities [which is portrayed as being legitimate].'

This sort of confrontational practice and analysis can be labelled win–lose politics. It assumes antagonism in group/corporate relations but, as indicated at the head of this chapter, there are now numerous examples of groups and companies in dialogues with win–win aspirations. Increasingly corporations are talking the language of corporate citizenship. In parallel many groups are pursuing dialogue rather than direct action. Hartman and Stafford (2001) note how the New York-based Environmental Defense Organization reinvented its 'Sue the Bastards' image via its 'Waste Reduction Task Force with McDonald's'. They noted Greenpeace's Greenfreeze campaign with business to replace destructive refrigerants. The one-size-fits-all confrontational campaign style has been supplemented by other approaches such as 'critical co-operation'.

We are dealing here with an idea 'in good currency'. Covey and Brown claim that what we are dealing with is a new form of engagement between business and civil society.

> Critical co-operation offers opportunities for social society actors to recruit the capacities and resources of business in the services of social problem-solving, and for business actors to mobilize the commitment and grassroots reach of civil society actors in the mobilization and protection of their business goals.
>
> (Covey and Brown, 2001, p. 13)

The process relies on mutual benefit, mutual reinforcement, and mutual legitimation.

The dialogue device has elements of the assumed benefits of *deliberative democracy*: that some superior outcomes are possible when there is mutual learning and exchange. There are hints that these enhance civil society in an era when confidence in traditional party-based decision making is eroded. The increased volume of these sorts of exercise at least raises the question of a transformation in group/corporate relations (but the partnership idea is patently *one style* of group relations rather than the only, or even a dominant, style). In modern variegated democracies there is a smorgasbord of democratic devices, a multiplicity of arrangements that overall can be seen as ensuring democratic responsiveness. The proliferating dialogues and partnerships are broadly democratic in 'feel', but that is not to say that even numerous examples mean they are anything other than a minor part of the democratic patchwork. Their importance should not be exaggerated: they are part of a democratic story not the single device. Certainly in part they seem stimulated by the globalisation idea that since governments have only weak levers on companies, groups should try direct influence. Even if generally useful, this does not mean that there cannot be scepticism about the motivation for some of the exercises.

An Institute of Public Relations publication (Deegan, 2001) describes how (past) reactive approaches to dealing with activists may have had limited or detrimental results and instead the volume 'discusses a way forward that involves proactively working with activists to avoid conflict'. This new conventional wisdom advocates 'two-way symmetrical communications' and a 'two–way dialogue with . . . a view to working together on an ongoing basis to reach a situation that benefits both parties' (Deegan, 2001, p. 35). Among the advantages claimed for this approach are that, 'activists, on the basis of experiencing the organisation's openness and efforts to improve performance, are more likely to trust companies in the event of an emergency such as a chemical spill'. Deegan says that the inter-action has benefits for the groups. It secures a commitment to deliver by the company; it allows the group to facilitate improvement; it is less resource-intensive than campaigning; it is potentially a fast route to improvement. Moreover the group can retreat, without having expended great resources, if there is no progress.

In a volume published in 1997 with the pointed title *In the Company of Partners*, John Elkington of Sustainability Ltd noted that, 'few types of partnership are as challenging for business as those some companies are beginning to develop with their erstwhile enemies, the non-governmental organisations (NGOs)' (in Murphy and Bendell, 1997, p. vi). He argued that there was a development of 'strategic alliances between companies and selected NGOs', and presented the phenomenon as 'mutual reprogramming of mindsets' (ibid, p. ix). He said, 'growing numbers of businesses are seeking to move beyond confrontation to forge more productive relationships with NGOs'. Indeed he saw a possible shortage of NGOs with the capacity to work alongside business – and thus possible 'first mover' benefits for organisations setting up early relationships.

Murphy and Bendell (1997, p. 3) noted that after the Rio Conference a number of businesses and environmental groups started on collaborative relationships. This partnership approach they describe as 'third wave environmentalism' (1997, p. 56). They present a rich source of examples of a 'good company': the Bread for All scheme based on Del Monte and Migros, a Swiss retailer; Gap and the National Labour Committee (human rights organisation); Fairtrade Foundation involving Sainsbury's and the Co-operative Wholesale Society, World Federation of Sporting Goods Industry and Save the Children; the 1995 Group that involved the UK wood product trade and WWF-UK; Marine Stewardship Council and Pollution Probe. Rowell (2001) noted that the Swiss-based World Business Council for Sustainable Development has also stepped up its use of 'stakeholder dialogues'. The Council includes Du Pont and Dow, BP and Shell, Aventis, WMC and Rio Tinto. He quoted the Council's chair, Björn Stigson: 'The ability of companies to manage and contribute to multi-stakeholder partnerships is a new business asset'.

In 1996, Greenpeace launched the magazine *Greenpeace Business* with a flyer complete with business testimonials: 'Calor Gas has a policy of always working with the experts and there is no doubt that as environmental specialists, Greenpeace is the world leader' (John Harris, Director of Calor Gas). It is now a commonplace to find business represented at events such as the Greenpeace Business Conferences in the United Kingdom:

Rowell (2001) quoted the Environment Council's chief executive, Steve Robinson: 'A fruitful and mutually rewarding dialogue with stakeholders is possible'. His organisation (a sort of facilitating agency in the field) describe their aim as going 'beyond compromise: building consensus in environmental and planning decision making'. They define 'consensus-building' as 'a process in which people work together to create mutually beneficial solutions to their problems'. They contrast their procedures with those of the adversarial public inquiry system, which they claim actually encourages disagreement. They say that in inquiries positions often become fixed, entrenched and ferociously defended. The system, they say:

- encourages conflict between groups and generates anger
- forces people into entrenched positions
- makes one group suspicious of the motives of another
- leads to very long delays, or in some cases stagnation, in decision making
- requires arbitrators and legalistic decision making
- imposes a 'solution'
- is expensive in itself and in its effects.

The Council processes are claimed to seek trust between participants by the use of mediators rather than arbitrators. The role asserted is not to judge between competing propositions, but to help the participants to find agreement. At an Environment Council organised conference – 'Getting Engaged' in 2001 – Andrea Spencer-Cooke, former editor of the *Tomorrow Magazine* for green business, argued the business response to environmental activism should be to 'include, listen, cooperate, emulate, re-invent and match any market campaigning with corporate activism' (quoted in Rowell, 2001).

It is questionable whether dialogue between NGOs and business is a *new* phenomenon. As Church (1999) points out, environmental groups and business were interacting with Friends of the Earth as early as the 1970s in discussing RTZ's plans for an open-cast copper mine in Snowdonia, and they were involved in dialogues over whaling and nuclear issues that produced industry concessions. It may not have been as sophisticated a process as is it today, but it still took place. Bosso (1988) in an article significantly entitled 'Transforming Adversaries into Collaborators' described how, 'after more than a decade of sharp conflict, environmental and chemical industry lobbyists sat down in direct, private negotiations of reforming pesticides regulatory policy'. But the practices now seem widespread and are causing fairly profound reconsideration in group rankings on best practice.

The Central Bargain: Reputation Management for Solutions Campaigning?

Certainly such developments may be inspired by a tactical desire by companies to defuse opposition, but the claim by advocates is that this is not simply protest management. There is at least some interest on the corporate side in 'good citizenship'. There is a specific and not disreputable benefit for business however. Bendell discusses why stakeholder dialogue has become so popular:

> Northern retailers of products from southern countries are particularly in need of credible information to reassure consumers, while southern producers require credibility for their social and environmental claims in order to access ethically or environmentally sensitive markets in the North. . . . People believe NGO campaigners more than spokespeople in industry or government.
>
> (Bendell, 1999)

Credibility is linked to marketing, as is the concept of 'reputational capital'. When companies like Shell and McDonald's are enmeshed with NGOs they are essentially trying to 'borrow' the good reputation of their partners. As Bendell (1999) also points out, 'Traditionally corporate legitimacy was conferred by the nation-state and legality within a system of state law. With globalisation, the assumptions and value systems are changing . . . [and] these changes are affecting the way corporate legitimacy and reputation are produced.' As a result multinational corporations are acknowledging that 'the successful company of the future will need to demonstrate year on year progress towards greater openness and involvement of key stakeholders'.[1]

On the interest group side there is a widespread feeling that it is time to engage in specific *solutions* rather than simple opposition.[2] As early as 1994 the international director of WWF was arguing that 'the time for protest alone is over. . . . Conservationists today must develop practical solutions to environmental issues' (Murphy and Bendell, 1997, p. 51). They talk generally about a move among groups away from a blame culture towards a solutions culture as a result of a 'public cry-wolf fatigue' (1997, p. 53).

Greenpeace's shift to run conferences to further business co-operation was described as underlining the organisation's shift from a 'narrow confrontation-at-any-costs agenda . . . to market oriented solutions – and working with key industry players – to implement them' (Warshal, 1996). This change of approach within Greenpeace has led observers to identify a tension between the 'fundamentalist' and 'collaborationist' wings. Grant

(2000, p. 31) has discussed Greenpeace as a good example of a group deserting an 'outsider' influence strategy and moving, at least partially, to a more mainstream insider role. Though some would disagree, there is at least some mileage in Grant's assertion that the 'lounge suits' have defeated the 'rubber suits'.

As early as 1994 under the headline 'We'll Agitate, Not Capitulate', Chris Rose (then Greenpeace's UK Campaigns Director) conceded that in *some* ways Greenpeace *had* been changing its spots. He argued that in the 1970s and 1980s the important role was agenda setting in getting environmental issues recognised. The fact that governments now at least acknowledged the problems was, he said, a positioning problem for environmental groups as their past 'outsider' role was overtaken by the success of the redefinition of the importance of the environment. Accordingly, he said, Greenpeace had to change its style, while retaining its core aims and values. He argued there was now a need for more than direct action. 'We have already drawn attention to problems; now we must follow through and force solutions into practice.' He underlined the importance of the Greenpeace involvement in the development of the 'green fridge'. He said, 'our new strategy relies on forcing solutions, conducting investigations, challenging science, changing politics and communicating directly'. He added that 'we are even changing the way we communicate. We are children of the media, but now we must communicate directly with those who create problems' (*Independent*, 21 November 1997).

Upstream (23 April 1999) quoted Lord Melchett (then chair of Greenpeace) making the similar point that 'taking direct action is not something we could forsake, although I think demonstrating with banners outside AGMs is a little unsophisticated'. He argued that '*stop-that* campaigning . . . may not be the best way of dealing with the complex issues of policy'.

Peter Wilkinson, an ex–board member of Greenpeace, has noted that as Greenpeace has survived it has also evolved from a marginalised 'outsider' body to a 'ready-made, viable and respected organisation. . . . Latter-day Greenpeacers . . . could find their employment a test bed for a career in politics or the world of international agencies. The organisation was rapidly becoming part of the comfortable furniture of society, and respectable' (in Rawcliffe, 1998, p. 106).

The Times (27 September 1995) recorded that Greenpeace strategists were worrying that its confrontational approach and image are increasingly at odds with its core purpose of saving the planet; important strategy changes are taking place within the organisation. *The Times* went on to quote Chris Rose: 'we have to move on from being hunters, hunting out and spotlighting problems, to becoming farmers, nurturing solutions'. He said that increasingly Greenpeace's most important work would mean not high-profile confrontations, but more 'solutions interventions'. Such moves have alienated some traditional supporters who thought that Greenpeace was one organisation that never 'got into bed' with industry, politics or other vested interests.

In this 'solutions' light, the high profile Brent Spar occupation was uncharacteristic of Greenpeace's new approach. Rose acknowledges that the new approach creates intra-organisational problems because, 'while it is possible to communicate an action to stop, for example, the construction of a power plant as a single news photograph, the process of changing a market to increase the use of solar power requires a whole conversation to communicate' (quoted in Warshal, 1996, p. 6).

Melchett observed at the same venue that the environmental struggle was to put solutions into practice. 'Greenpeace's core values remain unchanged. Of course by its very nature, solutions campaigning leads us into more detailed co-operation and alliances with specific sectors of business.' A report in *Environmental Data Services* (29 September 1996) on the Greenpeace Business conference in September 1996, quoted Dr Jeremy Leggett of Greenpeace as saying that 'the time has never been so right for non violent direct action against the "business as usual" corporate polluter. . . . Equally, the time has never been so right for innovative, strategic alliance building around environmental solutions.'

The Second Annual Conference, in October 1997, also had a solutions theme: 'Setting New Trajectories with Business'. When the Chief Executive of BP, John Browne, spoke he noted that he was, in appearing at their conference, in a reversal of normal roles, 'the first BP executive to occupy one of your platforms'. Browne spoke of his company's 'close relationship with Greenpeace' and support for developing the relationship between the environmental movement and business. He, in turn, was complimented by Chris Rose as the oil industry's 'most progressive chief executive'. Solutions campaigning is consistent with the trend to co-operation and dialogue.

Three Examples

Various labels have emerged to capture these developments towards dialogue: critical co-operation, green alliances, collaborative partnerships, win–win partnerships. Stafford *et al.* (2000) list eight examples between 1990 and 2000: Bronx Community Paper Company, Greenfreeze Campaign, McDonald's Sweden Environmental Programme, Nature Conservancy Georgia Roanoke River Project, Paper Task Force, Partnership for Regulatory Innovation and Sustainable Manufacturing, Ricelands Habitat Partnership, and Waste

Reduction Task Force (McDonalds/ Environmental Defense Fund). So the partnership approach does not bring us to a single common path.

However, in the following sections three examples are provided to show that the success of the approach has been variable.

THE BRENT SPAR DIALOGUE PROCESS[3]

A high-profile European example of dialogue was the response by Shell to the occupation of the Brent Spar oil production facility in the North Sea in 1995 by Greenpeace, which led to a consumer boycott, particularly in mainland Europe. As a result Shell decided not to pursue its plan to dispose of the Spar in the deep Atlantic, a course for which it had the permission of the Conservative Government. The Brent Spar is the most cited case both of direct action working, and of a company subsequently involving antagonistic groups in the search for substitute policies.

Annoyed by the political embarrassment caused by Shell's sudden shift from a position the Prime Minister had personally backed, the government signalled that it might not sanction any proposal by Shell for onshore disposal. It indicated that the Shell case for deep-sea disposal had been so convincing that the government would not necessarily change line just to suit a Shell accommodation with protesters.

Within Shell, the search for a new solution was termed the 'Way Forward'. A Shell press release (8 September) confirmed that Shell was to review options and that Greenpeace would be 'one of a number of representative bodies consulted in this connection'. Given that the Conservative Government was bloody mindedly insisting that the dumping option was already approved, at least part of the Shell strategy was to spin matters out until a Labour Government appeared. Labour's opportunistic opposition to the government meant they were likely, in reaction to Conservative policy, to be enthusiastic about rescinding the dumping approval.

The new process began with an invitation for ideas on disposal. Responses were screened to produce 19 potential prime contractors who had generated about 30 schemes between them. The 'long list' of options was then reduced to half a dozen proposals. Shell then gave financial assistance to all short-listed contractors to allow detailed and costed schemes to be produced. The final choice would be made by Shell, which would submit the selected plan to the Department of Trade and Industry (DTI) for approval.

On 22 February 1996 Graham Dunlop, senior project engineer on the Brent Spar Decommissioning project, argued that:

> In many ways the events surrounding Brent Spar illustrated a new climate in which business must operate and of a new way of doing business. Shell

UK had accepted that technocratic compliance with rational, science-based regulation is not in itself enough, and was committed to engaging in a wider political and public domain where the trust, confidence and 'licence to operate' from the public at large had to be won.

The dialogue with groups was at the heart of this new style. The Managing Director of Shell Expro claimed, *'we want to engage, not enrage'*. He went on to say: 'We do not expect participants in the Dialogue Process necessarily to agree. We hope to promote a deeper understanding of the emerging proposals and any issues surrounding them, and of the rationale behind the recommended solution.' (Fourth Environment North Sea Conference, September 1997). On 11 October 1995, Greenpeace welcomed Shell's announcement of 'an open consultation process' and said it would be happy to participate.

Shell then, in effect, had to manage two parallel processes. The first was the process of identifying and developing a new solution. Second, there was a need to ascertain the *public acceptability* (in practice group acceptability) of the new ideas (the Brent Spar Dialogue Process).

The First Brent Spar Dialogue Seminar took place in London on 1 November 1996; the Managing Director of Shell Expro, Heinz Rothermund, started proceedings: 'Brent Spar is Shell's problem and we take responsibility for it. However, we do wish to ensure that when we make decisions these take account of a wide range of opinion.' The first report from the process said that Shell had recognised in the original decision process that there was 'insufficient dialogue and review by interested parties'. About 70 participants were invited to attend (by the Engineering Council not Shell). These ranged from engineers such as Sir Hugh Ford to scientists with a specific interest like Dr Tony Rice to those with a more general interest such as Professor Forrester of Aberdeen University. Groups that were invited included WWF, National Consumer Council, the Green Alliance, the Scottish Fishermens' Federation, Friends of the Earth Europe and Greenpeace Germany.

As recorded in the report, the first seminar sought to 'create a broad understanding of the challenges that need to be resolved. This involves seeking a best balance between the criteria of the environment, safety, technical and economic feasibility, and public acceptability when finding a decision.' The role of the Environment Council was to establish a balance of participants and to facilitate balanced discussion. Shell provided descriptions of options and issues.

In March 1997, around 30 participants took part in a Copenhagen session: this was followed by sessions with 20 participants in Rotterdam in May and 25 participants in Hamburg. There were other Dialogue Seminars after the DNV report assessed the final short list of proposals. A second London seminar with 50 participants looked at the comparative virtues of the 'short list'. (The final 'close out' seminar was on 1 September 1999.)

The decision by Shell to cut up the Spar and use the sections to build a quay in Norway passed with no environmentalist reaction. The dialogue process may then be said to have worked. But there remains the possibility that the process was the sign that Shell was aiming to adopt a policy that was environmentally acceptable, and did not in fact determine the new choice. The dialogue success reflected the underlying identity of purpose between Shell and some in the consulted group who previously might have been opposed: the opponents had their stance undercut by Shell's readiness to move.

The dialogue process may be presented in at least three ways. First there is the idea that it was a trap whose primary objective was to 'muffle' Greenpeace's voice. Greenpeace either became involved in a process that involved a multiplicity of other groups that might be less habitually hostile to Shell, or it could be presented as unwilling to compromise and engage in discussion. If Greenpeace did take part, any objections they might have could be presented as minority concerns. Second, it could be seen as a bit of theatre that let Shell make the retreat it recognised as necessary with a rather superficial justification that this was the result of these politically correct manoeuvres. Third was the official, mutual learning idea that there would be a coming together of values and acceptance of needs on both sides. In fact all these, and other, motivations co-existed, but the second, theatrical or shadow boxing interpretation, was probably dominant.

THE NATIONAL COAL POLICY EXPERIMENT[4]

The date of the National Coal Policy Project (NCPP) (1977–8) in the United States again emphasises that the novelty of dialogue processes can be exaggerated. As described by McFarland (1993, p. 1) the NCPP was an elaborate attempt to mediate political conflicts between the coal industry and environmentalists through conferences that involved both corporate executives and environmental lobbyists. The direct cost was $1.4 million and, in addition, it was estimated that participants put in 15,000 days of work, half of which was paid for by industry in the form of salaries for released time. McFarland says (1993, p. 41) that the founders of the NCPP in the Dow Chemical Company believed that the adversarial process of ordinary lobbying and litigation worked against the discovery of common interests and that a more conciliatory procedure was needed. There were comparable views on the 'other side of the fence' and the Executive Director of the Sierra Club, Michael McCloskey, was quoted as saying:

Both sides have tended to assume that the issues have all been non-nego-
tiable. Industry has tended to assume that environmentalists oppose everything. . . . Environmentalists have tended to assume that industry will never
make any real concessions. With these attitudes many disputes instantly
became ideological. This is unfortunate because many environmental
disputes involve practical differences, which are resolvable.

(McFarland, 1993, p. 41)

In terms of political science, McFarland relates the NCPP experiment to
cooperative pluralism: 'pluralism' in the sense that there were a number of
participants – producer groups and countervailing powers – with conflict-
ing objectives; and 'cooperative' in that the idea was that agreement
directly among the contending forces would produce a policy that government (held at arms-length) would be obliged to accept. McFarland (1993,
p. 7), states the underlying idea was that 'appropriate institutions can help
interest group leaders to find common goals and to learn other aspects of
public policy'.

The project delivered significant agreements on non-trivial topics (Ibid.,
p. 81). The central compromise appeared to be a trade-off on strip mining
between the environmentalists' recognition of the need for flexibility in
administering the Surface Mining and Control Reclamation Act and industrialists' explicit acceptance that many aspects of coal mining required
regulation. Industrialists backed the funding of citizen groups that could
monitor and evaluate the regulatory process (ibid., p. 83). There was a
mutual recognition of legitimacy by participants.

But the widely fêted outcomes were not put into place by Congress. That
perhaps reflected a prior failure by the business and public interest groups
represented on the NCPP to endorse the conclusions. The main problems
were on the environmental side, though McFarland (ibid., p. 112) speculates
that if the environmentalists hadn't sunk the compromise, business would
have done so. McFarland sees some of this opposition as a sort of organisational jealousy: the agreement was entering the 'turf' where other groups
thought they had pre-eminence. For example Louise Dunlap, head of the
Environmental Policy Centre (EPC), thought that the NCPP agreement was
inferior to environmental successes that had been secured in the past. Dunlap
succeeded in getting the Sierra Club Board to order McCloskey not to
participate in the NCPP in January 1978. Dunlap argued that:

- The project was not representative.
- The conclusion was a sell out to the coal companies.
- Existing legislation was better.

- The proposition that the project was a better decision-making forum than Congress was 'arrogance'.
- Environmental groups had scarce resources, and should not waste them by having their leaders work on worthless effort (based on McFarland, 1993, p. 116).

McFarland said that this Sierra Club defection from the NCPP was crucial: why would other groups such as the Environmental Defense Fund or the Audubon Society endorse the conclusions if the EPC and the Sierra Club were opposed? After all, in terms of marketing, there is a constant temptation to outflank a group that appears too moderate: to ask why an environmental group is 'cosying up' to the enemy.

AMNESTY INTERNATIONAL[5]

As far back as the early 1980s Amnesty International (AI) had attempted to involve the private sector in its work, but insufficient resources and (according to a member of its Corporate Approaches Department, Gemma Crijns, speaking at a conference in the United Kingdom in 1999) insufficient knowledge of the private sector prevented any meaningful dialogue. However, by the mid-1990s AI, responding to globalisation pressures, perceived that power had shifted from national governments towards business, and a decision was made to work harder on its approach towards corporations. It concentrated its attention on Northern Hemisphere-based multinational corporations (MNC), Crijns explained, calling on these private companies to contribute to the promotion and protection of human rights in line with the Universal Declaration of Human Rights, and to develop their own company human rights policies in line with international standards. Given that companies are not subject to international law, the basis is more moral obligation than legal requirement. Amnesty International appealed for corporate social responsibility and a recognition of social accountability. Amnesty promised a relationship that would eschew sanctions, boycotts or disinvestment policies, in order to encourage dialogue with business interests committed to non-violation of human rights.

Amnesty holds Roundtable discussions with Dutch MNCs, and in the United Kingdom and the Netherlands has business groups that meet regularly with it. France, Italy and the United States have looked into the possibility of setting up similar groups. The aim of AI is provide education and training for employees of multinational corporations as it considers that mobilising a company's employees can be an effective way of bringing pressure on companies from within, and that public recognition by NGOs of improvements in company practice can be of benefit to business, and is considered a good incentive. Levi-Strauss and Reebok are two high profile multinational companies that have opted to undertake human rights audits within their companies.

Other NGOs have criticised Amnesty International for giving up its right to boycott or use sanctions, but Amnesty argues that if NGOs are to be acknowledged as legitimate entities by the private sector they must listen as well as talk.[6] They see dialogue as a two-way process, with commitment on both sides, according to Crijns.

Problems

There are two particular worries for groups in these exercises. The first is that they are not in a win–win scenario but a 'win/losing the plot' game.

SUSPICION OF INCORPORATION
There is some cynicism from the NGO side that the game is neutralisation of criticism by business, and indeed the more such arrangements are triumphantly presented as a 'solution' by business, the more groups might be suspicious. In a presentation entitled 'The Dangers of Co-optation with Corporations' to a 1998 Oxfam conference, Rowell said, 'dialogue is the most important PR tactic that companies are using to overcome objections to their operations. It is a typical divide and rule tactic.'

Rowell cites Olivier Hoedeman from CEO, a European-based research and campaign group:

> Attempts by business to reach out to some of the NGOs is a response to the challenges thrown up by the grassroot activists. . . . In the last few years we've seen business and governments are using dialogue with NGOs *as a strategy to prevent confrontational campaigning and to split different parts of the environmental movement*, and very often they are successful.
>
> (Quoted in Rowell, 2001, italics added).

Rowell went on to argue that:

> Dialogue is certainly the strategy that PR professionals are getting very rich on. Clients are being offered a number of ways to outwit their 'civil society' opposition. Global PR company Edelman for example advises it clients that 'governments and corporations will only succeed by establish-ing working relationships with NGOs that are not adversarial. . . . To help

assist its 'stakeholder dialogue' efforts Edelman recently employed Jonathan Wootliff, ex-head of Greenpeace International's communications division.

(Ibid.)

He pointed to the Institute of Public Relations' book on *Managing Activism* (Deegan, cited above), which attempts to show 'how companies can "deal" with activists and pressure groups, who "represent a growing threat to organisations around the globe"'. He noted too a very similar approach in Germany and quoted a leaked paper from the Association of German Industries highlighting the benefits of 'dialogue' to evade conflicts without business 'giving up' its 'own points of view'. The availability of such quotes undermine the efforts of those who genuinely want a cooperative approach. Interest groups can read too; manipulative operations will not only fail as one-off examples but will devalue the currency of co-operation. Such operations, as the NCPP example confirms, require trust. Within organisations it is an easier role to sit on the sidelines 'rubbishing' moves that involve some organisational risk. If the currency of partnerships is eroded there will be fewer risk takers in organisations.

In his earlier book (with the subtitle *Global Subversion of the Environmental Movement*) Rowell (1996, p. 111) saw co-option strategies as simply a device to undermine opposition. He cited praise for co-operation from pro-business lobbyists – with no green motivation – as evidence that partnership cannot be a winning strategy for the groups. Rowell says that, 'in order to try to defeat groups like Greenpeace, co-option rather than confrontation is seen as the way forward'.

He quotes O'Dwyer's PR Services in February 1994: 'each side is willing to work with the other'. He also quotes a board member from the oil company ARCO who noted that 'while we are working with them, they don't have time to sue us', and a PR representative who stated that 'the goal is to isolate the radicals, "cultivate" the idealists, and "educate" them into becoming realists, then co-opt the realists into agreeing with the industry'. The same source was also quoted later advocating building alliances with carefully chosen activists for mutual benefit.

WINNING THE ARGUMENT AND LOSING THE MEMBERS?

The second major group concern is in the relationship between recruitment and the style adopted to influence policy. Rowell (1998) argues that the mainstream campaigning groups could find themselves losing grassroots support if they become too close to business. This has perhaps two elements. First is the professionalisation of staff. Murphy and Bendell (1997, p. 58) note that the sort of technical expertise that large groups require means that they need to recruit specialist staff.

> The problem is that in the near future environmental groups may have people in top management with no fundamental ideological commitment to environmental issues. These people may have more in common with company directors than . . . the people whose environments they are meant to be protecting.
>
> (Murphy and Bendell, 1997, p. 58)

There is a view that although an insider strategy may produce a policy payoff it is not what motivates members. The premise in the literature is that groups depending on a membership that receives no selective material rewards must stick close to the protest mode. Wilson (1995, p. xi) offers a powerful simplification: 'ideological incentives, especially if threat oriented, tend to constrain and radicalize the leaders of an association, whereas selective incentives, especially material ones, tend to bestow discretionary authority on such leaders'.

As Phillips (1994, p. 97) notes the 'success' of the environment groups in Canada may have been achieved to the detriment of participation by supporters. 'In part the success of the environmental movement in getting its world-view absorbed into popular political culture has been its own undoing as a movement and has propelled it further into institutional forms.' The argument is that the expertise of the environmental organisations has seen them gain access to decision making, but at a cost.

There is actually an asymmetry for business and groups involved in dialogue. This is demonstrated by Murphy and Bendell's discussion (1997, p. 196) of the Environmental Defense Fund partnership with McDonald's on a waste management strategy. Even to be seen to be sitting down with the EDF made McDonald's seem respectable to a constituency of customers that might have worried about environmental criticism of multi-nationals. But even to sit at the table with McDonald's was a threat to a part of the EDF constituency. Fred Krupp, Executive Director of the EDF, noted that:

> Most of our members are people with deep suspicions about corporations' behaviour toward the environment; they give to environmental groups as a way to have a watchdog over the corporations; so it is very risky to take an organisation like EDF and work with corporations.
>
> (Quoted in Murphy and Bendell, 1997, p. 196)

In the second example discussed earlier in the chapter, the EPC success in derailing the NCPP suggests that in the competition for interest group supporters, there is an attractive strategy of 'purity' in sitting outside the meetings.

Membership pressure within those 'pressure businesses' (Jordan and Maloney, 1997) that rely on mail order for their communication with the wider public is one reason why some oversell the institutionalisation in political and business circles of such groups. Groups cannot afford to lose their membership credibility – something that will happen if they desert the news pages. Moreover, the potential to cause disruption is precisely the sort of characteristic that makes business willing to sit down to bargain. Groups are likely to be more effective at the negotiation table if they are also on the streets.

Conclusion

The three examples selected above sketch in some of the range of results from these practices. The Amnesty case gets a generally 'good press' but there is NGO suspicion that business is 'let off the hook', and a group such as Amnesty can be outflanked in the rhetoric game by other voices that seek popular controversy. The Brent Spar example shows a success that was not so much due to the dynamic of the dialogue as to the strategic needs of the critical groups and Shell when they entered the process. The NCPP case is perhaps the most ambitious recorded, and ultimately it failed because the well-intentioned partners could not 'sell' agreement to the wider political system.

It is debatable whether the partnerships make much sense without an opposition phase. As Murphy and Bendell (1997, p. 216) note it is often the direct action phase that leads to meaningful discussion: the 'good' is predicated on the 'bad' experience. The Brent Spar dialogue was simply not possible without the more famous Brent Spar occupation.

Partnerships are more likely to succeed if the target is recognised to be some attainable and realistic improvement. But this incrementalism is easy to criticise. It can also be criticised as a desertion by the groups of their role of heightening ambitions for progress: instead the process becomes one of closing the gap by reducing expectations. There is also the distraction argument: that groups should not be investing scarce resources in helping companies. Murphy and Bendell (1997, p. 231) note that 'as they focus more on solutions for the problems already defined, their ability – and desire – to identify emerging issues may be lost in the process. Some would argue that society needs problems if it is to continue evolving; before solutions must come problems.' Murphy and Bendell add that 'environmental-ists who advocate the solutions agenda need to ask themselves: Who is going to champion new problems in the future?'

Stafford *et al.* (2000, p. 123), while noting that much of the developing literature on collaboration has emphasised advantages, go on to observe that 'such partnerships are fraught with paradoxes and complexities that cause the relationships to be unstable and strategically precarious'. Collab-oration is not an inevitably successful device as groups and corporations do not always have compatible goals. Failure to cooperate is also a possibility. And there can be problems when it comes to testing whether a partnership has indeed been successful. What indicators do NGOs and corporations use to assess success? Advocacy of the approach needs to be balanced by discussion of evidence of failure, and levels of success.

Church (1999) noted that one of the problems NGOs face with increased 'insider' status is that getting into the boardroom gets them nearer the seat of power but takes them away from the public eye, and he warns that these organisations must also maintain the trust of their supporters. However, he also challenges the hypersceptical view that the changing tactics of corpo-rations are no more than hype or spin. He believes that the change in atti-tude by big business interests is a recognition that public attitudes have changed, and that as a result of education and pressure by NGOs consen-sus has changed. Watching out too closely and suspiciously for the costs of involvement risks losing the benefits.

Murphy and Bendell (1997, p. 195) cite Fred Krupp of the EDF with the best metaphor here. He said that environmental groups would be more successful if they deployed more tools in their toolkit. 'We should continue to aggressively lobby, aggressively litigate, aggressively criticise. . . . We also should be able to problem-solve with corporations.'

Critical co-operation is most likely to be successful, according to Covey and Brown (2001), where the partners share both a high level of conflict-ing interests and a high level of converging interests. But, they add, there must also exist between the parties a symmetry of power, recognised rights, and the necessary negotiating skills. Critical co-operation thus appears to be the most appropriate mechanism when the 'opponents' are most evenly matched.

It would appear then that the partnership approach for both sides can be selectively useful: as a tool in the kit, but not as a magic wand.

Notes

1. Shell's CEO, Chris Fay, speaking to the Institute of Chartered Accountants in the UK.
2. Discussion of solutions campaigning based on Jordan (2001, pp. 325–37)
3. The Dialogue Process suggests reference to 'policy-oriented learning'. Sabatier (1988, following Heclo) said that, 'policy-oriented learning refers to relatively enduring alterations of thought or behavioural intentions which result from experience and which are concerned with the attainment (or revision) of policy objectives'. The discussion in this section is based on Jordan (2001, pp. 236–41)
4. Discussion based on McFarland (1993) as summarised in Jordan (2001, pp. 241–6)
5. This section is summarised from section 3.4 of an INTRAC Workshop report from 1998, 'NGOs and the Private Sector', posted on Business–ngo–relations archive January 1999.
6. Another example of an NGO change in approach away from conflict and direct action can be found in the current relationship between environmental groups and the fishing industry. Hernes and Mikalsen (2002, p. 15) point out that environmental action in fisheries bears little resemblance to past crusades. As the fishing industry and environment groups have grown to accept that there must be a commitment to sustainable and responsible fishing, there has grown a 'stronger emphasis on co-operation and participation – at the expense of direct and disruptive action.'

CHAPTER 3

Trade Associations, Change and the New Activism

Justin Greenwood

It's Like the Alamo Out There!

It is coming from all directions, and it is very, very unpredictable. There is a breakdown of trust and a corresponding rise in corrosive cynicism in both corporate activity and in mainstream politics. Trust is the cement in the relationship between institutions and civil society. When trust breaks down, civil society either withdraws from participation, or expresses protest outside the mainstream channels of participation. Risk-related investment falls. Participation in elections declines, and alternative outlets of political expression arise. The press becomes cynical, hostile or negative, and seeks out bad news. Suspicion sets in, and irresistible pressures grow for openness, transparency and accountability. The information and opportunities so yielded reap a crop of issues upon which cynics make hay, and the Internet spills out more and more information, opening up new fronts as it does so. Even potential good news stories are interpreted and reported negatively, and those with news to tell become defensive and/or incommunicative. The downward spiral continues. Company managers and public affairs leaders lose the ability to predict when and from which direction the next missile will be coming their way.

These factors help to explain the climate in which brand-name and other companies have found themselves to be targets of activism, sometimes in very isolated positions. The corporate world reveals a tendency to shoot itself in the foot by yielding a clutch of household-name companies whose financial practice scandals have resulted in losses for millions and acute misery for thousands, raising wider public interest agendas. Mainstream public interest groups are turned from potential friends into foes, and the everyday citizen becomes a business critic. Politicians respond with agendas with seemingly limitless regulatory frontiers that catch companies on the back foot.

To what extent do, and could, trade associations, as collective representative bodies for constituencies of companies, help? Can they help defend their members in public perception, in politics, and help their members to adapt and respond? Or are they simply left as by-standers in the entire process, becoming less and less relevant to the constituencies they serve? Where there is variation, what are its patterns, and causal factors?

Corporate Responses

'Healthy, profitable, forward-thinking companies . . . have recognised that, in order to operate successfully, they must satisfy the three elements of sustainable development: financial, environmental, and social' (European Round Table of Industrialists, 2001, p. 1).

The European Round Table of Industrialists (ERT) is a forum of industrial leaders (at chief executive officer or chairperson level) of many of the largest firms in Europe (it currently has 42 members). The position adopted by the ERT reveals that large firms have come to accept that they are publicly accountable for their operations, and have developed programmes to communicate their credentials of good corporate citizenry. Annual company reports bulge with details of community programmes and evidence to demonstrate that ethical practices are fully mainstreamed into company activities in terms of environmental, social and human rights, employee relations and procurement operations. They acknowledge the reality that corporate accountability now extends far beyond their shareholders into a much wider stakeholder constituency. These realities mean that the collective public affairs wisdom that engagement in public debate will do more harm than good is a thing of the past for companies whose activities have already become issues of high politics. Companies at the sharp end have entered public debate, with mixed success.

Inevitably, these displays are most evident among companies that have been most subject to criticism and activism. Biotechnology firms such as Monsanto have spent hugely on newspaper advertising campaigns that are now widely regarded as a failure, opening new cans of worms and stirring up hornets' nests. Others have adopted a wider range of tactics, which go beyond communication issues. Among petrochemical companies, Shell has responded extensively and through diffuse outlets to criticisms of its operations following reporting of events to which it has been connected in the Niger Delta, and attempts to dispose the Brent Spar oil platform. BP has positioned itself as part of the solution to problems of climate change, through a deliberate decision to enter public debate and acknowledge the contribution of fossil fuels, by re-engineering itself, and through re-presenting itself to the public as an energy (including renewables) company 'Beyond Petroleum'. In doing so, it has won the acclaim of the media, investors, environmental groups and President Clinton, resulting in an invitation for the BP CEO, John Browne, to the White House to discuss the future of energy policy with him (Bryceson, 2002a). Unilever, as the largest buyer of fish in the world, forewarned of a major Greenpeace campaign to target it about depletion of fish stocks, did likewise by establishing the Marine Stewardship Council partnership with the World Wide Fund for Nature (WWF) for brand differentiation of sustainable fisheries (Bryceson, 2002b). These examples were not corporate gestures, but a way of engaging with change in a way endorsed by public interest groups and consistent with shareholder value. The reputational advantage for the companies concerned was considerable.

What Can Trade Associations Do?

These types of actions are within the remit of individual companies to take. An individual company responsible only for its own actions and facing bottom-line pressures as a result of being targeted by activists will be responsive. Typically, new activists distinguish between leader and laggard firms, and single out a particular high-profile 'name' laggard. A company singled out for its performance relative to others tends to keep the problem to itself, and may become inward looking rather than turn to trade associations for help. McDonald's, for instance, rarely participates in trade associations. The campaign against Huntingdon Life Sciences and any of its corporate associates was deliberately designed to isolate it and to make it difficult for any trade association or other company to come to its rescue. Under these circumstances, collective action becomes almost impossible. Christopher Cliffe, from Huntingdon Life Sciences, is on record as complaining that trade associations melted away in the heat of the conflict and left his company to hang out to dry. And yet, in more 'normal' conditions, trade associations can also be the ideal collective cloaks for firms, perfectly suited to fronting difficult public affairs issues with which companies do not wish to be individually associated with in public profile.

For companies not (yet) in the front line of target activism, some of the normal rules of public affairs have been modified rather than discarded. Traditionally, business public affairs strategies have been modelled on keeping its interests out of the public gaze where they can be contested in open and unpredictable public arenas. These strategies are aimed at confining corporate affairs within private, exclusive arenas with government regulators. Provided business can get what it wanted from these 'behind closed doors' exchanges, it does not need to engage the public, and has only done so at times of desperation when it has lost the case in private arenas, risking in the process the privileged relationship it has enjoyed with government. Thus, the successes of trade associations are private, and their failures public. Collectively, business has used trade associations as the 'head above the parapet public voice' when it has failed to secure its objectives in public policy. One example is the extensive newspaper advertising campaigns by the Association of the British Pharmaceutical Industry (ABPI) against government proposals in the mid-1980s for a limited list of prescribable drugs available under the National Health Service (NHS). As well as being unsuccessful, such campaigns have almost always been counter productive. Thus Kenneth Clarke, as Health Minister, publicly criticised the ABPI advertisements by the industry as deliberately alarmist because they seemed to imply to some that medicines would no longer be available under the NHS.

These lessons were learnt by trade associations, and the errors were rarely repeated thereafter. What has emerged instead is an adaptation involving a more targeted use of newspaper advertising by associations and companies, aimed not at the general public but more at policy makers by locating the specialist media outlets that policy practitioners read. *European Voice* is a Brussels-based newspaper with a circulation of a little over 40,000, whose readers are an elite band of EU policy makers, public affairs practitioners, and observers. Consequently, the paper has frequently been the home for full-page advertisements from both companies and trade associations. Recent examples include those addressed to long-term image building, such as the 'Pfizer Forum' series and the EU biotechnology trade association Europabio's current advertisements on biotechnology and the benefits for developing countries. They also include issue fire-fighters, such as American aviation interests opposed to the introduction of regulation that would force them to use expensive 'hush kits' in European airspace. Engaging public opinion in this way has long been a role performed by American trade associations, where insurance, chemical, brewing and tobacco trade associations have frequently mounted major educational efforts through outlets such as the *New York Times* and the *Wall Street Journal* (Gupta and Brubaker, 1990).

These types of industries have learnt that some limited form of public engagement is unavoidable. The Internet has provided a new outlet to put their case in some detail. The websites of trade associations whose constituents are acutely affected by 'new activism' usually take the opportunity to explain the position of their members. Hence, a visit to the websites of the UK Bioindustry Association (BIA) (www.bioindustry.org) or the European Cosmetic, Toiletries and Perfumery Association (COLIPA) (www.colipa.org) reveals detailed perspectives about the use of animals in scientific research and testing. The first of these contains a number of statements about Huntingdon Life Sciences, comment that is carefully restricted to the general issues about intimidation by protestors rather than getting involved with the detailed case of the individual firm. Thus, the new rule of thumb for those likely to be affected seems to be a qualified, selective use of targeted media devices as a means to influence its external environment.

Companies targeted by a 'common enemy' can develop effective collective solutions through trade associations, although, as is discussed later, only under highly specific conditions. The chlorine industry was targeted by Greenpeace with the slogan 'Chlorine free by '93', stimulating the formation of a highly effective and proactive EU trade association, Euro Chlor, in 1989. While this example will be discussed more fully later, the point to note now is that its embeddedness with policy-making institutions has helped the industry to safely expand world production of chlorine from 35 million tons p.a. in 1993 to 44 million in 2001 (Gilliat, 2002). Some associations emerged as 'issue niche' organisations, developing at a later stage into a permanent and highly effective specialist trade association structure. Thus, the EU business association, Alliance on Beverage Cartons and the Environment (ACE) emerged in the late 1980s in response to regulatory threats emerging from (unfounded) wider public interest concerns about dioxins leaking from drink cartons into their contents. When the 'scare' receded, the organisation transformed itself into a highly effective specialist trade association for carton board converters. Some 'single issue' collective structures have arisen because of the inability of the trade association to tackle the underlying issues effectively, and have remained as separate, parallel structures to trade associations. The decade-old Portman group in the United Kingdom and the Amsterdam group at the EU level are both specialist structures that enable alcoholic drink producers to respond to social concerns about alcohol consumption.

These three examples – chlorine, paper board converters and drinks – are all from relatively concentrated industries populated by firms of similar size at a mature stage in the product cycle, in which overcapacity and competition issues have periodically emerged. It is in these circumstances that collective structures can emerge, and are developed through the identity of grappling with a 'common enemy'.

Business Collective Action and the Social Environment: More Consensus than Conflict

The cases above reveal a number of wider points about business collective action structures and the social environment that they address:

- It is not just a phenomenon of very recent years.
- It has emerged in response not only to public interest activism, but also – and perhaps principally – to government regulatory responses to the wider agenda. While public interest activism intensively consumes the resources of individual companies affected, the wider impact upon business and the agendas of public affairs personnel in companies has been directed more towards addressing the government regulatory agenda than the 'new activists'. One network leader described the latter as a 'minor irritant'.
- Trade associations can be in the forefront of business responses to the new activism, but only under highly specific circumstances.
- Business has sought to address the wider issues raised in specialist collective action structures.

None the less, the wider agenda has crystallised in recent years into a relatively new phrase, that of 'corporate social responsibility', reflecting and resulting from initiatives led by both business, and public authorities to come to terms with the wider agendas. It has become a mainstream political issue, and developing partnership with mainstream public interest groups has become an orthodox public affairs strategy. Set alongside the context of 'new activism', engaging with public interest groups has become a relatively attractive and civilised prospect, and the opportunity to learn in such a way that skirmishes with 'new activists' might best be avoided. Alcohol Concern and the European Public Health Alliance may well be public critics of the drinks industry, but they can at least be engaged in dialogue, learnt from, and possibly even tamed. As Sabatier's model of policy change reminds us, these exchanges become meaningful over time, as policy actors trade perspectives and incorporate aspects of each other's agendas (Sabatier, 1988). 'Light' green organisations such as WWF have become much sought after partners for companies and trade associations, while even 'darker' green organisations such as Friends of the Earth and Greenpeace have become acceptable organisations to listen to and seek to learn from. Greenpeace itself has been subject to criticisms that it has become over institutionalised by this process, de-radicalised, and has lost its independent campaigning capacity (see Chapter 1).

There is now a mature tradition of purposeful alliances among private and public interest groups, and some of these have now developed into formal organisations bridging these ranges of interests. Some have emerged from business-led initiatives, while others have arisen from actions by public authorities seeking 'concertation' between diverse stakeholders. One example of the latter is the European Partners for the Environment (EPE), a European Commission-initiated structure under the EU Environmental Vth Action Programme (Lenschow, 1999), now operating as an independent association. This organisation brings together public interest groups (such as WWF and the European Environmental Bureau) with businesses (such as Unilever and Procter and Gamble) and trade unions (including the European Trade Union Congress – ETUC) and public (mainly local) authorities, to:

> build the ground for consensus on sustainability. . . . Dialogue built through long-term relationships between partners and strengthened by trust leads to common practical action. . . . Partners meet in an informal atmosphere to float ideas, seek common solutions and constructively engage in debate and projects of mutual interest. Each partner takes away this learning and feeds it into the work of his or her own organisation.
>
> (EPE, 2002)

These relationships are more common between private and public interests than are conflict and confrontation. Admittedly, they are more common to Brussels than to member state environments, because Brussels politics is of an almost solely institutional kind in which popular protest activities are all but absent. None the less, dialogue is more common than daggers at the national level. All mainstream public affairs consultancies have developed brokering services for companies with public interest groups, and have developed services for NGOs with the more lucrative corporate brokering role in mind. Many such consultancies now employ former public interest group activists to enhance their capacity to do this and to add to their profile. And a new branch of public affairs consultancy has emerged, geared at advising business how to engage with its critics in civil society, how to talk to them and how to learn from them.

Corporate Social Responsibility and Political Institutions

A recent Green Paper from the European Commission on corporate social responsibility (CSR) defines the concept as one 'whereby companies integrate social and environmental concerns in their business operations and in their interaction with their stakeholders on a voluntary basis' (European Commission, 2001, p. 4).

A successor Commission communication, together with the wider course of European politics, reveals the width and extent of the CSR agenda (European Commission, 2002). CSR has become a window of opportunity for both business and its opponents, and a regulatory bag large enough to include just about anything. For instance, a recent European Parliament debate on the Green Paper saw an attempt to introduce measures to regulate corporate (only) lobbying (*Public Affairs Newsletter*, 2002). The 2002 communication dreams of integrating CSR in all EU policies, ranging from employment and social affairs, to policies concerned with enterprise, the environment, consumer affairs, public procurement, external relations and trade, and public administrations. Indeed, one of the strategic priorities of the European Union, agreed by member states and the Commission at the Lisbon Summit of March 2000, reflects the wider debate of CSR through the Union's goal of becoming, by 2010, 'the most competitive and dynamic knowledge-based economy in the world, capable of sustainable economic growth with more and better jobs and greater social cohesion' (European Commission, 2002, p. 4).

The Commission CSR agenda is being driven by the Directorate General for Employment and Social Affairs, which has become the most expansionist and politically committed of the Commission's services. This Directorate has aggressively sought to expand the frontiers of European integration into 'social Europe' by using a mixture of compelling rhetoric and the initiation and nurturing of public interest groups able to act as a demand constituency upon member states for European integration. In this way, organisations such as the European Women's Lobby have been able to bring forward discourses of equality which member states find hard to resist, and push member states to propose the effective introduction of new competencies into the EU Treaties (Helfferich and Kolb, 2001). In promoting CSR, the Directorate General for Employment and Social Affairs is also seeking to team up with public interest groups to develop an expansionist agenda, and is seeking to free its hand by using classic divide and rule strategies. The 2002 communication reflects that business wants to avoid regulation, while labour, public interest, and to a certain extent also some constituencies of investors, seek regulation. It proposes to establish a 'Multi Stakeholder Forum' bringing together 40 European representative organisations of employers, employees, consumers and civil society as well as professional associations and business networks, and to report by 2004.

Corporate Social Responsibility and Business-Led Initiatives

The EU agenda has succeeded in putting business on the back foot. It could hardly be otherwise at a time when the regulatory window of opportunity includes Enron as well as Swampy. Business interest associations at the EU level have responded predictably, arguing that measures to achieve CSR should be left to the voluntary initiative of companies themselves, and pointing to the progressive record of many. In addition, both the ERT and the Union of Industrial and Employers' Confederations of Europe (UNICE) have argued that EU-level legislation is unnecessary because of the existence of global level initiatives. These include the International Labour Organisation (ILO) Tripartite Declaration, the United Nations (UN) Global Compact and the Organisation for Economic Cooperation and Development (OECD) Guidelines for Multinational Enterprises, favoured by the ERT. Some of these have resulted from input from trade unions and public interest groups as well as business. ERT and UNICE joined forces, along with the business forum corporate social responsibility Europe, to write a joint letter to the President of the European Commission in June 2002, putting the above case.

ERT and UNICE, as well as the EU Committee of the American Chamber of Commerce, the Association for the Monetary Union of Europe and Europabio, have themselves begun to be targeted by activists, and in particular by Corporate Observatory Europe (COE). COE describes itself as a research and campaign group that

> exposes the threats to democracy, equality, social justice and the environment posed by the economic and political power exercised by corporations and their lobby groups . . . (and) endeavours to support progressive groups whose interests are threatened by corporate conduct.
>
> (Balanyá *et al.*, 2000, p. xi)

The ERT has been particularly singled out for the 'malevolent impacts of its influence' (ibid.) by COE, which published a photograph of its members and summary details of any transgressions of their companies. Much of this activity, however, seems to have gone unnoticed by the associations themselves, and appears to be limited to the production of critical literature. The only demonstrations witnessed by the Brussels headquarters of UNICE have come from symbolic publicity stunt events organised by its institutional sparring partner, the European Trade Union Confederation (ETUC), and not by 'new activists'. EU-oriented protest tends to find national rather than EU targets (Imig and Tarrow, 2001), and EU politics takes an institutional form rather than that of social movement. None the less, it is true of most environments that trade associations have rarely been the target for protest.

On the whole, trade associations have not been in the front line of business-led initiatives for corporate social responsibility. Some of the principal EU business associations were not even consulted by the Commission in the formulation of its policy papers. While all the main EU associations have position papers on it, the leading organisations have been best-practice business networks which have emerged in specific response to CSR, such as Corporate Social Responsibility Europe. CSR Europe describes itself as a 'business-to-business network for corporate social responsibility in Europe. . . . Our mission is to help companies achieve profitability by placing Corporate Social Responsibility in the mainstream of business practice' (CSR Europe, 2002).

CSR Europe's 60 company members include brand name companies such as BP, BT, Coca-Cola, Diageo, EdF, Ford, General Motors, Hewlett Packard, IBM, L'Oreal, Levi-Strauss, Microsoft, Motorola, Nestlé, PricewaterhouseCoopers, Proctor and Gamble, Shell and Unilever. CSR Europe comments that the interest of many of its members arises from past mistakes that have damaged their reputation and business operations. In addition to offering the opportunity for good positioning and exchange of best practice, CSR Europe interacts with governments and with public interest groups, inviting Amnesty International and Human Rights Watch to speak at member meetings. It has a network of national partners, and once again it is not horizontal general business associations that dominate, but CSR-specific business networks.

As with the EU context, associations such as the Confederation of British Industry have a position on CSR (opposed to enforcement, concerned about diverting business from the core mission of wealth creation), but leave the mainstay of activities to specialist networks. The website of the CBI's Trade Association Forum shows no evidence of any activities in corporate social responsibility. Instead, CSR as a horizontal business issue is primarily developed by a clutch of specialist networks, such as the UK Business in the Community (BITC) organisation. BITC is a network of over 650 UK-based companies, including 75 of the 100 largest publicly quoted firms, and is a national partner of CSR Europe. BITC members commit themselves to 'continually improving, measuring and reporting the impact their business has on the environment, marketplace, workplace and community, and actively engaging in partnerships to tackle disadvantage and create enterprising communities' (BITC, 2002).

BITC is one of a number of UK business networks concerned with corporate social responsibility, alongside organisations such as Common Purpose, the Institute of Business Ethics, and the Prince of Wales International Business Leaders Forum where multinational companies address concerns with developing economies. Many of these organisations have overlapping membership, revealing the strong identity and positioning that comes with the membership badge. Corporate social responsibility has become high politics – the subject of a recent address to the US nation by President Bush – and so business has needed specialist identity organisations to allow companies to demonstrate their credentials, rather than hiding their bushels through trade associations.

Some of the larger trade associations have historically developed symbolic activities that resemble corporate social responsibility activities, such as community relations schemes or the projection of innovative member practice (such as the 'Eco house') in annual reports for positioning purposes. The largest UK trade association, the Association of British Insurers, has operated a modest staff secondment scheme in conjunction with Business in the Community, seconding up to four staff for limited projects involving around 40 hours work with charities (Boleat, 2001). These limited activities provide a means of staff development for the association, as well as positioning, but rarely involve the mainstreaming of corporate social responsibility activities in the work of the association or in developing mainstreamed CSR practice among its members.

Trade Associations and the New Activism: Opportunities and Limitations

To some, trade associations are simply by-passed by the 'new activism'. One experienced (EU) public affairs practitioner who has worked for a large company public affairs office, an international public interest group and a public affairs consultancy, reflected to the author that:

> [new activism] is precisely one reason why trade associations are in decline. Campaigning organisations focus on brand-name companies, differentiate between leaders and laggards, and certainly try to get past trade associations. Even the NGOs get fed up with trade associations, and frustrated with their lowest common denominator positions (just as politicians do) and seek out the company spokesperson. Look at '*Beyond Philanthropy*' by Oxfam/Voluntary Service Overseas/Save the Children (oxfam.org.uk), for example: no mention of the EU, International, or US

pharmaceutical manufacturers trade associations. They have become irrelevant on the access to medicines issue.

(Personal correspondence, October 2002)

While public affairs consultants need to be sceptical of trade associations because they provide alternative services, this hostile view of trade associations is worth recording because it is not an uncommon one, and for some the 'new politics' of activism is one that makes trade associations irrelevant. But it is a very one-sided view of their capabilities. As has been outlined, their potential to act as collective cloaks for their members on controversial issues where companies would rather not argue the case puts trade associations in the perfect place to bring value to their members by engaging those who directly target their industries.

Certainly, trade associations have structural limitations. They are collective bodies, and any process of aggregating opinion between different entities involves some degree of compromise, as well as delays in responding to issues while common positions are built. But emphasising the diluted nature of opinion and sluggish response times is to make rather cheap points about organisations whose purpose it is to find common positions and act upon them. The flip side is to reflect on the 'miracle', as the former General Secretary of UNICE has put it, of being able to reach common positions to a sufficient level to enable them to act upon them (Tyszkiewicz, 2002). The legitimacy of trade associations arises from the breadth of constituency they encompass. The alternative of multiple dialogues and outright public affairs competition is an unacceptable scenario for political institutions and private interests alike. Membership of trade associations is normal political behaviour, and for anything other than the smallest firms the costs of non-membership, and the inability to influence the positions the associations take, are too high.

The criticism above also ignores the high degree of variation between trade associations, which differ in their capacities as a result of the environment in which they operate and the extent to which there are shared interests among their members. At one extreme lie associations in Germanic Europe, which form part of corporatist governance systems in which they regulate the activities of their members. At the other are associations in highly pluralist political systems where associations compete with each other and their members to influence public policies. Typically, political systems in which decision making is highly fragmented afford a high degree of access to decision making, but low degrees of influence, because the dispersal of authority insulates the system from special interest capture. In these circumstances, decision-making institutions accept all comers, and associations compete for voice with their members. In political systems where power and decision making are concentrated, the reverse is true. That is, access is difficult but, once it is obtained, private interests can be highly influential (Risse-Kappen, 1995). Hence, to observers embedded in the EU political system, the limitations of trade associations may be more striking than their strength. In pre-war Germany, where 50 per cent of regulation directed at industry was exercised by controls exerted by trade associations, such organisations look very significant indeed (Schneiberg and Hollingsworth, 1991). In other comparative settings, associations can act as agents of economic development (Doner and Schneider, 2001). In the right circumstances, trade associations can act as powerful intermediaries between state and civil society, delivering the compliance of their members for governance mechanisms in return for a place at the policy-making table and the award of a near monopoly of governmental recognition. These advanced roles are not possible in fragmented authority structures such as the EU where there is no central authority to grant associations these roles.

As well as operating in a fragmented authority system, EU trade associations also face the disadvantage of being restricted function organisations. They are designed for political representation in EU institutions. They do not undertake the wider range of functions, such as membership services, that can be found among national associations. Consequently, they operate on a more restricted resource base in that they are almost totally reliant on membership subscriptions. This means that they lack autonomy from their members, and become communication media for the short-term demands of their members. To bring value to its members, an association needs autonomy from them so as to lead their perceptions of where their interests lie on issues. As one commentator has observed, it is 'better that my interests are represented than my more-or-less shaky opinions' (Burnheim, in Phillips, 1995). This requires a substantial heritage of trust between members and their association, a product of both structural industry features in which competition is limited, and the usual dynamics of inter-personal relations in which trust is earned over time.

These factors also help explain preferences within political institutions for working with associations or firms. The structural weaknesses transmitted to associations as a result of working within fragmented power systems means that they have limited capacity to bring value to policy makers. When confronted with weak and poorly resourced associations, policy makers turn to companies for information, ideas and assistance with governance. When associations can deliver these things as well as concerted, collective opinion, and simplify the consultative life of policy makers, then policy makers prefer associations. Even in relatively difficult circumstances, however, trade associations can still be important players, and political systems find it difficult to live without them. Thus, in the EU, trade associations help the resource-slim political institutions by providing information and expertise, yield intelligence about national differences and advance warning about political issues in the Council of Ministers, and provide the capacity for implementation. They also act as a bridge that allows remote political institutions to come closer to street level concerns. In addition, they have provided a means for policy implementation, and are the powerhouse in street level European integration through the support they provide to their members to participate in the structures of European standardisation. By doing so, they lower transaction costs for a wide range of stakeholders beyond their own members.

The ability of an association to bring value to its members also depends upon the extent to which its constituency has shared interests. Typically, associations work well where their member companies are of a similar size, where an industry is relatively concentrated, where there is some degree of maturity in the product cycle, where there are commodity products that are difficult to differentiate on factors other than price, and where there are common shared problems such as overcapacity which the association can help manage (Greenwood, 2002; see also Bennett, 1999). These features also make industries prone to cartel-like behaviour. Associations representing industries with a 'common enemy' also tend to have a high degree of unity and cohesion. Hence, associations that work well for their members are those in sectors such as steel, cement and chlorine, while sectors in which associations are marginal players are those such as tourism and retail. Typically, the former set of collective organisations finds high membership densities and a high degree of trust between members of an association, while the latter type of association displays low membership densities and low intra-member trust.

Thus, some associations are very well geared to taking political action on behalf of their members, displaying a high level of shared values and the capacity to act relatively quickly. Because of these attributes, together with stable and appropriate leadership, the European chlorine association, Euro Chlor, has become the normal route for political action by its members rather than one of a number of channels. It has developed a monopoly on the supply of information aggregated at a certain level, and is regarded by its interlocutors in policy-making institutions as a more reliable source of information on chlorine and pollution than national governments. It has been well able to develop self-regulation, thus making itself useful to public authorities by undertaking public protection functions and to its members by deflecting governmental regulation over which it has less control. It has bought its members sufficient time to adapt their production processes from the use of mercury in chlorine production to other processes. It has prevented members who do not use mercury in their production processes from threatening the business of competitors who do, through focusing upon common interests. The association is not only well equipped to respond to threats by 'new activists'; a principal source of its collective action capability is the threat posed by its members 'common enemy', Greenpeace.

Conclusion

Trade associations belong to the world of order and organisation rather than chaos and unpredictability. These paradoxes help explain why the same factors which make them strengths in 'Alamo' climates are also those that make them weaknesses. When order and structure break down, trade associations can be an anchor and a familiar routine against uncertainty. Their routinised and bureaucratised structures can also make them ill equipped to deal with change and unconventional contexts.

Yes, trade associations are slower to act than are single companies who do not have to composite a range of views. Companies will always be best placed to re-engineer themselves so that they can adapt both to new expectations that they be accountable for their social and environmental performance, and to direct targeting from activists. Certainly, business responses to corporate social responsibility have emerged outside trade associations. But the important point is that these responses have arisen in collective structures that resemble interest associations. As single issue organisations, business-led corporate social responsibility organisations are best able to respond to the needs of business. They provide the opportunity for good corporate positioning by enabling firms to demonstrate the badge of good citizenship. They help deflect the threat of governmental regulation. And they help disseminate best practice. As new organisations, business-led corporate social responsibility organisations can be responsive. All organisations become conservative and bureaucratised with age, and trade associations are no exception. Trade associations have wider agendas, and it is not surprising that they are peripheral players in the debate on corporate social responsibility.

Yet trade associations are by no means without value to business in the contexts of new agendas for accountability, and activism. They help their members to engage with politics by providing internal fora for exchange between members, and in political socialisation. They become learning organisations for their members. They provide an outlet for members to engage with regulatory authority, help to prevent hostile agendas from escalating, and deliver alternative self-regulatory governance solutions that policy makers find attractive because of their low transaction costs. They can broker partnerships and dialogue with mainstream public interest groups from which their members learn and adjust. And they help address activist agendas by providing a collective cloak to engage with issues that companies find difficult to take on alone.

Trade associations are extremely sensitive to the political environments in which they operate. Where they are embedded in unfavourable structures of fragmented political decision making and endowed with a narrow range of functions, the prospects for their bringing value to their members are unfavourable. Where they gain access to concentrated political decision-making structures they can be highly influential, quasi-autonomous intermediaries between government and civil society, undertaking public interest governance functions. Where there are shared common interests and similar structural characteristics among their members, trade associations can be cohesive and responsive organisations, developing mechanisms to deflect external threats. Some trade associations owe much of their cohesion to common external threats from new activism, and have proved adept at responding to them in the wider interests of their members.

Trade associations seek to position and reconcile enlightened self-interest with the broader public interests of civil society. This approach is also one that lies at the heart of corporate social responsibility (Gupta and Brubaker, 1990). This chapter has shown that, while trade associations differ greatly in their ability to handle the type of issues presented by 'new activism', they are in concept ideally placed to do so. They can find and broker collective, industry-wide solutions so that no one member faces competitive disadvantage in responding to 'social responsibility' challenges alone. Mechanisms such as self-regulation and environmental standard setting, devised and rigorously policed by trade associations so as to ensure compliance, can raise overall standards and in doing so protect members and meet public interest goals. As such, they can become part of the solution rather than part of the problem. Where there are problems, trade associations are better placed than their members to take flak because they do not risk taking bottom-line losses in so doing. They can lead their members' perceptions of what their interests are on given issues, and engage public audiences on issues that are too sensitive for a single company to tackle alone.

To do all of these things, a trade association needs strength and sufficient independence from its members, together with safeguards to prevent it from being over-dominated by any one constituency of members. In turn, these factors enhance public confidence and trust as the association delivers on common goods by impartially enforcing standards. These properties of trade associations are common where governments make them 'must belong' organisations for their members by endowing trade associations with recognition as policy and governance partners. Such arrangements are more common to the Germanic than the Anglo-American models of capitalism.

CHAPTER 4

Lobbying in a World of Tensions

Svein S. Andersen and Kjell A. Eliassen

The Changing Nature of EU Lobbying

Brussels is becoming increasingly important as the central decision-making arena in Europe. More and more it is taking on the functions as the capital of the Union. This has implications with regard to both the number and the types of interests attempting to exert influence there. Brussels is also becoming a key arena for establishing networks, developing European projects and cross-European business activities and so on. Such related activities reinforce the importance of being present, because the opportunities of this complex system cannot be handled from a distance. A key challenge is to develop the strategic competence to deal effectively with the opportunities of the expanded EU lobbying system.

The key questions raised in this chapter are: To what extent and in what ways are we witnessing an institutionalisation of lobbying in Brussels? What are the effects of the emerging EU governance system and the coming enlargement? We pursue these issues through, first, developing a conceptual framework for lobbying in the EU and, second, discussing stages and trends in EU lobbying in relation to the numerous empirical studies available on specific issues and lobbying activities in different areas. In addition we raise some concerns about democratic accountability in EU decision making.

During the past two decades all the key political actors in Europe, such as companies, interest groups, governments and local authorities, have increasingly directed their attention towards the EU. This increased attention is closely linked to the revitalisation of the EU through the successful launch of the internal market and the general expansion of EU legislation and other programmes. One of the most striking aspects of this is the explosive growth of direct interest representation; in other words, lobbying.

Today's EU decision-making system is characterised by a number of tensions arising from fragmented processes and the need for order and rationality. Tensions arise between traditional functional interests and a wide variety of new interests, between special interests and the common good, and between direct representation and representative democracy. The enlargements to the East will increase these tensions, but at the same time increase the need to develop the potential for handling complex patterns of inconsistency, competition and conflict. Lobbying may add to the complexity of the EU policy-making system, but it may be the only way to make this system work.

In the next section we will briefly describe characteristics of EU lobbying.

What is EU Lobbying?

Lobbying is as old as the EEC. Immediately after 1957, Europe-wide pressure groups were established within the various areas of Community policy. By 1970, more than 300 Euro-groups could be identified (Philip, 1987, p. 75). The Community institutions have always been the object of lobbying. However, both the volume and style of lobbying have since changed dramatically, particularly during the 1980s.

In 1980, Community officials registered all of the formally recognised Euro-groups, which at that stage numbered 439 (Economic and Social Committee, 1980). In addition there were unrecognised Euro-groups and other lobbies active in Brussels (Philip, 1987, p. 76). The limited number reflects the fact that the EC was in a period of stagnation and that EC decision making was organised around inputs through national channels. By the end of the 1980s the number of lobbyists had increased ten times since the early 1970s, and it had increased four times since 1985. This explosive growth was due to the invasion of professional lobbyists, accounting firms, legal advisors and representatives of individual companies, regions and cities.

Lobbying is an informal mechanism for exerting influence. A key question is what distinguishes lobbying from all other forms of informal influence in political-administrative decision-making processes. A major distinction is made between liberal interest group competition and neo-corporatist integrated participation in elite networks. Lobbying is usually associated with the former, but lobbyists are not necessarily representatives of interest groups. In principle anyone can engage in lobbying. Theories of liberal interest group competition often simply assume some mechanism of competition and selection to explain outcomes. In such cases processes are not assumed to have independent effects on outcomes. However, in systems characterised by a relatively fragmented policy-making process, the lobbying process itself often has a genuine impact on results. This is a key lesson from EU lobbying.

EU lobbying stands in contrast to the integrated corporatist participation of various interest groups in public decision making. Representative associations may of course engage in lobbying, but in principle any one at all can engage in the lobbying of one or more of the EU institutions. In contrast to the situation in Washington, where lobbying is well established, the lobbying system in Brussels is still at its formative stage. For this reason, lobbying in Brussels also includes activities aimed at simply acquiring information about how the system works and establishing the participant as an important actor, which are matters that are seen as preconditions for influencing decision making.

The new pattern of lobbying is different from traditional national systems of interest articulation in Europe, where elements of corporatism have played an important part. In some ways it may seem closer to what we associate with traditional US lobbying, focusing on competition between interests and specialised politics. Van Schendelen argues that EU lobbying is characterised by extreme complexity and openness: 'There are many routes by which to approach any authoritative player and always there is an indirect route. In addition to all these formal linkages there are the infinite informal ones [that] every actor is free to develop' (van Schendelen, 1993, p. 11).

The EU is characterised by multiple tensions. On the one hand, between many actors, issues, arenas and levels. On the other hand, between efficiency and the limited scope and legitimacy of special interests. Some structuring elements have emerged over the last ten years. The lobbying process can be divided into four major stages

1. Establishing actors at the European scene.
2. Developing strategies.
3. Gaining access.
4. Acquiring opportunities for influence.

Since the early 1980s, studies have shown that interest associations and companies need to *establish themselves as actors on the European scene*: for example, to present and position themselves as legitimate, competent, well-informed and interesting contacts and partners for key actors in various EU institutions. This stage may sometimes be time consuming and not everyone succeeds. It is useful, although not strictly necessary, to be permanently present in Brussels. Criteria for being acknowledged may be claims for representativity, degree of affectedness and ability to make a substantial contribution to policy formulation. In some cases, actors, or groups of actors, may gain recognition because they control strategic resources that can affect the success of policy making and implementation.

Lobbying strategies have several aspects, including gaining access to important information, establishing visibility and confidence among key actors, gaining access to policy-making processes and being able to influence the progress, likelihood of success and the actual content of an outcome. Some actors build strategies around specific competences. These actors cover everything from attending scientific conferences, visiting key universities and research centres, collecting and preparing background materials and presenting written inputs to central actors in an ongoing process. Other actors are more reactive, responding to agenda setting or initiatives from partners and competitors. Some actors, through their experience, resources and legitimacy, may serve as catalysts and coalition builders.

Gaining access is linked both to actors' reputation and strategic competence. In other words, the likelihood of gaining access may partly depend upon a long-term commitment to the policy-making system in Brussels. Generally, access to top-level decision makers is quite restricted, but is more open at lower levels. However, this does not necessarily imply that higher-level contacts are always more important. Key elements of proposals are developed and formulated by key personnel in different units of the Commission. Still, access is not the same as influence: the number of actors with access is much larger than those with impact.

Influence is difficult to measure as it is often hard to identify input measures relating to the influence of particular interests in final decisions. In principle, however, types of influence vary with the stages of the decision-making processes. At the earliest stage of Commission preparations, before a proposal becomes official, lobbying is often highly technical (legal or scientific) or, in some cases, related to high-level political interests in the member states. When lobbying is dominated by technical aspects, specialised competence may outweigh representativity. In the middle stage, when the proposal is processed in the Council and the parliament, technical lobbying is often still the key to influence, but the importance of representativity (and nationality) increases. In the final stages, as decisions are made within the Council, or in deliberations between the Council, Commission and parliament, the political aspects will be more important.

So far we have discussed the four major aspects of EU lobbying, which has characterised the process from the early 1980s. In the next sections we use this typology to evaluate the development of the EU lobbying system after the Single European Act and the Treaty of Maastricht in the late 1980s and early 1990s, after the expansion to the North, the treaties of Amsterdam and Nice in the late 1990s and, finally, in relation to the challenges of the enlargement to the East.

The Late 1980s and Early 1990s: The Mobilising Effect of the Single Act

From the mid-1980s it was clear that something was going to happen to the EC. This was reflected in the growth in the number of associations and lobbyists taking an interest in Brussels. A survey conducted in 1985–6 registered 659 federations at the European level represented in Brussels, and about 6000 lobbyists and national interest associations in member countries deemed to be of relevance for the policy-making process in Brussels (Morris *et al.*, 1986).

The Single European Act represented a revitalisation of the decision-making system in Brussels. The 279 Directives to be implemented before 1992 suddenly turned the EC into an important political arena. The growth of direct lobbying of the EC's institutions also contributed towards developing a European political system independent of the Member States. All the important actors in European politics, such as businesses, trade unions and other interests groups, and local and national authorities, focused on the EC system. This increased interest for the EC's central institutions was closely linked to the internal market and the general expansion of the EC's spheres of competence.

There are no exact figures for the total number of lobbyists in 1990, but all estimates indicated that lobbying exploded in the period between 1987 and 1990. Attempts made in 1990 to estimate the total number of interest groups or lobbyists generally varied between 3000 and 10,000, depending on how lobbyists were defined. The highest number includes all who tried to get access to key actors in EC decision making, including those who came to Brussels to pursue particular issues, as well as those who were more permanently positioned in the European capital. There seemed to be a general consensus, however, about the explosive nature of this phenomenon in the late 1980s. Economically, it became a growth business, worth about £100 million a year in 1990 and increasing at the rate of 100 per cent a year (Bartholomew and Brooks, 1989; Zagorin, 1989; Newman, 1990).

Mazey and Richardson (1993) discuss the Community-level activity of national and European interest groups but not with a focus on the emerging EU-level institutional system. They emphasise the newness of the system, describing the system of interest representation at the EU level as in a state of flux. In this situation groups seek to develop new strategies for EU lobbying while EU policy makers struggle to cope with these new forms of influence (Mazey and Richardson, 1993, p. 4). An interesting observation is that interest groups tend to shift their lobbying to Brussels in the early stages of national policy disputes.

Van Schendelen (1994, p. 275–88) made the first attempt to provide a systematic description of national differences in efforts to influence EU policies. Although he discusses theories of lobbying and the development of EU lobbying, his focus is on the articulation of national interests in Brussels. His study covers most EU countries and a couple of the EFTA countries, where the interest groups try to operate from outside. One of his conclusions is that attempts to influence the EU are increasingly based on spontaneous lobbying rather than going through national power systems.

Another group of studies makes the EU level the focal concern. A few studies addressed the systemic aspects of the European Union as a new political system and EU lobbying as part of it (Andersen and Eliassen, 1991, 1993). However, several articles and books focused on practical challenges to EU lobbying in the 1990s (Mack, 1989; Gardner, 1991; Andersen, 1992; Collins, 1993; Stern, 1992; Sassen, 1992; Club de Bruxelles, 1994). These guides were often based on anecdotes and presented within the framework of strategic interaction and persuasion (Andersen, 1992).

In the late 1980s, all stages were characterised by unclear requirements and a relatively high degree of openness. The key to success was to be present and know where and how to lobby. There were important variations across sectors. Some sectors, like agriculture, but also labour market policy, had elements of corporatist structure and *modus operandi*. Other sectors, like finance and shipping, were characterised by few actors but a low level of institutionalisation of the lobbying process. Most sectors where characterised by many actors, many access points and unclear rules and procedures governing the lobbying process.

At that time, several factors pointed towards the need for a higher degree of institutionalisation. There were at least two important reasons behind this tendency. The first was the limited capacity of the EU decision-making system to handle the great number and variety of inputs. The number of interest representatives in Brussels increased dramatically in the decade after 1985. Meanwhile, the number of states in the EU and the EEA increased. Also, the possible symbolic impact of Brussels as the capital of Europe and the need to be present there cannot be ignored.

Another reason was the changing authority and decision-making logic of the EU system. Again, there were several factors at play. One was the breakthrough of supranational authority, introducing qualified majority voting in the Council and co-operation and co-decision with the parliament. Another factor was the increased institutionalisation of policy and law making at the EU level. One indicator is the increased importance of the so-called 'first pillar,' as in the Maastrict Treaty, with supranational decision making and all EU institutions involved in the decision-making process. This procedure is called the Community method.

The Maastricht Treaty further enhanced this development in two dimensions. The first was the increased use of qualified majority voting, and the inclusion of new policy areas in the first pillar where the majority procedure is applied. In addition, the Maastricht Treaty created the social protocol and strengthened the social dialogue, thus introducing one of the few examples of a deliberate corporatist arrangement in the European Union. After Maastrich, the social partners were even granted legislative powers without the consent of the parliament (Dølvik, 1999). However, by strengthening the co-decision procedure, the parliament's authority and attraction as a target of lobbying was increased.

The Maastricht Treaty did not have the same dramatic effects on the EU lobbying system as the Single Act. Still, it reinforced arrangements that stimulated existing lobbying patterns. The Commission was still the key target for lobbyists. The Council of Ministers continued to be important in the final decision stage although the parliament became more important. The introduction of formal corporatist arrangements was not an attempt to restructure the general pattern of lobbying, but rather complementary to it.

In the years leading up to the Amsterdam Treaty there was a tendency towards increased institutionalisation of some elements of the lobbying process, such as the search for representativity and the need to balance different opinions. However, such tendencies did not lead to an increased corporatisation of interest representation in Brussels. Institutionalisation reflected some overarching concerns and capacity problems in central EU institutions. The question still remained, however, to what extent and how the treaty reforms would affect the future institutionalisation process.

The Middle and Late 1990s: Treaty Reforms and the Institutionalisation of a European Political Space

The development of EU lobbying is consistent with fundamental insights about institutionalisation processes (Olson, 2001). One general hypothesis is that the higher the level of institutionalisation of a political system (in terms of polity, key institutions etc.), the easier it is to institutionalise a new area. Established concepts, rules and practices will then shape new areas. Another general hypothesis is that institutionalisation will be harder the more complex and open-ended it appears. In the case of EU lobbying we find that there is a lack of a clear and specific institutional framework, and that even the simpler and sector-specific issues may have wider system implications. This is an important reason why EU lobbying appears so complex, fragmented and fluid in many studies.

Institutionalisation can imply at least two things. First is the establishment of an authoritative political space, the relative importance of institutions, the representativity of actors and legitimacy of outcomes. The second relates to more specific rules and regulations about the legitimacy and rights of actors, and rules governing how and where to achieve influence.

The degree of institutionalisation of EU lobbying has been more limited than some expected a decade ago. The possibility of direct influence is linked to the general changes in the institutional set-up and decision-making system of the EU. Thus, one could assume that the changes resulting from the Amsterdam and Nice treaties would affect lobbying. There are some such effects, especially due to the changing roles and importance of the EU institutions, and the increased importance of Brussels as key arena for policy making. On the other hand, a clear and specific framework for lobbying is still lacking.

One important implication of institutional reform is the increased importance of the EU Parliament and the increased use of majority voting in the Council. Some had expected this to reduce the importance of the Commission as a key target for lobbyists, but it has remained the key focus for them (Pedler, 2002). Another important change is that Brussels has become more central, both in terms of formal decision-making authority and as a location for informal networking and decision-shaping activities. In other words, Brussels can increasingly be regarded as the capital of Europe, with traditional capital functions.

When we look at the processes of lobbying, the degree of institutionalisation is limited at all stages. Nevertheless, elements of institutionalisation can be found. One such is an increased screening and vetting of the actors trying to become involved. This is mainly due to the sheer number of potentially interested parties attempting to gain influence compared to the bureaucratic capacity of the EU system. Representatives of the EU system seem to put increased emphasis on the relevance and importance of the lobbyists that are given access. Such structuring and limiting processes seem most important in the access phase.

Another element of institutionalisation is of a corporatist type. While agriculture has developed furthest in this direction, labour market policy has acquired elements of it through the establishing and strengthening of the social dialogue at Maastrich and Amsterdam. Still, the Commission is the key target for lobbyists. Elements of corporatist coordination can also be found in other areas, such as industrial policy, but they are limited and do not constitute a substantial trend of a corporatist development.

To the extent that we find corporatist elements, they mainly represent an institutionalisation of stages two, three and four in the lobbying process: the stages of developing strategies, gaining access and acquiring opportunities for influence.

These tendencies are also well illustrated in the development of the analytical focus and arguments in the literature on lobbying (Greenwood and Aspinwall, 1998; Andersen and Eliassen, 1998). The general conclusion is that there is no clear pattern emerging with respect to the organisation of lobbying and the strategies for gaining influence. On the contrary, there are great variations with respect to what kind of actors are mobilised and how they pursue their interests.

Although specialised expertise in policy making is more important in the EU than in the Member States, the result is not institutionalisation of clear patterns of participation. The role of expertise limits the ways one can express political arguments. However, it can also be seen as an extension of a political discourse that allows actors without a shared language, values or the like to be accepted as legitimate participants. Thus, experts tend to discipline the discourse without establishing boundaries of political participation. In principle, anyone holding the relevant expertise, or able to buy it, has access.

A counter-tendency to that of increased institutionalisation, and thus more order and predictability, is found in the growing skills and strategic capacities of many established lobbying interests, which create more complex alliances and paths leading to access and influence. In the last few years, since Lisbon, the European Union has changed its strong emphasis on law making to include the new 'open method of coordination'. This changes the opportunity space and strategies for lobbying interests. The strong emphasis on technical expertise is complemented by a stronger political dimension, which also has to be exercised at the national and regional levels. This tendency may reflect the changing emphasis in the EU, away from law making to implementation and the struggle over distribution of funds. In this process, the importance of the Council increases relative to the Commission. A third factor pulling towards increased complexity is the growing number of issue areas exhibiting a global dimension (Pedler, 2002).

So far we have pointed to the dual tendency of institutionalisation and increased complexity of EU lobbying processes. Rather than getting one or the other, we seem to experience both. Pedler (2002) and Tenbücken (2002) both emphasise the importance of ad hoc and issue-specific strategies and alliances as a key element in successful lobbying processes. This picture is confirmed by a number of studies (Andersen and Eliassen, 2000; van Schendelen, 2002; Pedler, 2002). Another observation is that EU-level lobbying in many cases has become as important, or even more important, than national-level lobbying. Tenbücken (2002) argues that this is the case for multinational companies.

Presently, a key question is how the EU lobbying system is going to be affected by EU enlargement to the East.

Enlargement: New Lobbying Patterns?

The EU political system is developing along several dimensions, reflecting the continuous process of integration among existing Member States. However, in relation to the lobbying system, two elements of the changing context seems to be of particular importance in the years to come: the enlargement, in terms of new actors, issues, alliances and ways of understanding system and stratagems on the one hand, and on the other hand the institutional reforms that will alter formal mandates and procedures, and create new ways of dealing with classical tensions between national and supranational interests, and between small and big countries.

In the next few years the number of member countries in the European Union will expand dramatically, from 15 to at least 25 and maybe even 30. Even the 1995 expansion (Austria, Finland, Sweden) increased the complexity of the lobbying process. It led to an increased need for focus on the representativity of interest groups and a balance between different interests involved. For instance, alcohol retail distribution became a hot issue (Pedler and Rautvuori, 2002), and other issues like gender, employment and social welfare became more important. In relation to all these issues, strong and influential interest associations were mobilised. These associations had long and deep traditions of involvement in the political decision-making process at the national level. However, in Brussels they had to adapt their strategies and alliances in accordance with the established rules of the game.

It is likely that the accession of the next ten new member countries will present numerous other important issues with strong national political links. This is already demonstrated in the negotiations over the accession treaties (Pedler, 2002; Drapl et al., 2002). These new countries not only add substantially to the variety of interests active in Brussels, they also represent considerable variations with respect to democratic traditions, administrative structure and the relative importance of different societal and economic interests. We discuss the challenges of enlargement in relation to the four major stages of the lobbying process described previously: establishing actors at the European scene, developing strategies, gaining access and acquiring opportunities for influence.

With regard to the first stage, establishing presence, we already see a tendency towards a new wave of actors from new members. They need to make themselves known in the Brussels establishment. Some are already there, but many more will follow. Some will go through their European-level associations, such as ETUC and UNICE. Others will use national government channels or their nationals in the central EU institutions. The third option, to establish themselves as independent players, is more demanding. In any case, the competition for attention will increase in the years to come.

Developing strategies and strategic competences is the next step. In this respect it seems likely that the main lobbying strategies of new Member States will be linked to aspects of the particular challenges these new member countries face. Strategies will be based on arguments about repre-sentativity in the individual countries and in the new countries as a group, the need for legitimacy of EU policies in new countries and their particu-lar competence on national local affairs. The established and experienced actors may find that their strategic competence and capacity becomes more valuable.

Gaining access as individual interests is likely to be more difficult because of the complexity and capacity problems facing central EU insti-tutions. Some sort of more aggregated interest representation is more likely to provide access. This is particularly true if the new interest groups are able to gain access to already existing European-level associations with a long history of involvement in EU decision making. However, highly competent and very resourceful specialised interests may still be able to acquire access on an individual basis. This is more likely if they have either special resources, like needed expertise, or powerful backing from national political establishments.

Influence based on particular concerns and interests is likely to become more difficult for everyone, both incumbents and entrants. It is important to remember that there may be a great difference between being accepted as a participant and really exercising influence. An implication is that selective benefits of active EU lobbying may benefit the few clever or lucky ones, or those able to organise broad coalitions. It may be that influ-ence comes to reflect a certain asymmetry between old and new members. For old members the problem is to achieve legitimacy in Brussels. For the new members an equal challenge may be to build legitimacy for central EU decisions within their home constituencies.

It is important to remember that enlargement and the resulting expansion of the lobbying system run parallel with a growing attention from non-European interest groups as a consequence of growing internationalisation and globalisation. For instance, both Japanese and US companies have become increasingly active and effective in the EU decision-making process over the last years (Kewly, 2002; Van der Storm, 2002). This adds to the complexity, and within the present institutional system it is hard to see how all this can be handled efficiently and democratically. This points to the importance of institutional reform, simplifying both the overall system and the decision-making procedures.

Even if EU lobbying is problematic in relation to democratic theory, it is widely recognised as a key factor contributing to the efficiency of EU policy making. In this pragmatic sense, lobbying has contributed positively to the legitimacy of the system, and it has been an important precondition for the implementation of the 1992 programme. The EU bureaucracy is small compared with Member State bureaucracies, and it has limited expertise and capacity. The paradox, however, is that because direct parliamentary influence is weak in the EU, there is a pressing political need for consultation with affected interests. Thus, the independent legitimising aspect of lobbying is perceived as stronger rather than weaker in many quarters. However, the basic problem remains. The role of lobbying will be a recurring theme in both public and academic debate in relation to further institutional reforms and the debate about EU democracy.

Implications for an Emerging Democratic Polity

Lobbying is a form of direct interest representation, which in democratic theory cannot be legitimised in its own right. The acceptance of such input in a democratic process rests on its relationship to, and oversight by, democratically elected representatives. Thus, the debate on lobbying is closely related to overall attempts to improve democratic transparency and accountability in the European Union.

The democratic deficit relating to EU lobbying has been addressed in all treaty reforms. A major part of the efforts to solve this problem has been to strengthen the role and influence of the European Parliament over the last 15 years. At the same time the role of specialised interest representation has also gained weight. However, a tension between these two kinds of logic of political representation remains. In consequence, the gap between normative ideas of parliamentary democracy and the role of specialised policy networks in everyday decision making has grown for some time.

Still, a striking characteristic of EU lobbying is that it takes place in a context where the European Parliament has limited powers and the European-level party system is weak. The acceptance of widespread EU-level lobbying seems to reflect the belief that it increases efficiency and sectional rationality. Thus, it may be the case that the democratic deficit and the complexity of the decision-making process in the European Union is also a major reason for the Union's success so far. However, for a long time, the Union has placed more emphasis on efficiency and the participation of elites and specialised interest representatives than that of wider social concerns and the broad involvement of EU citizens.

In the Amsterdam Treaty the imbalance between democracy and efficiency was, once more, partly addressed in an institutional way. But it left the underlying problems unaddressed. After the conference in Amsterdam, May 1997, the Comité des Régions stated that:

> European integration has brought immense benefits for people over the last 40 years. These achievements are enormous, but they bring with them new problems and new challenges. One such challenge is to simplify and clarify the decision-making process. This is essential both for the function of the Union and for the purpose of ensuring its legitimacy and credibility. The Union must develop its capacity for action and be closer to the people. Another necessary change has to do with strengthening the politics of consensus building. It is imperative that the EU open up for a significant consensual and participatory democracy in Europe.
>
> (Therborn, 1997)

That statement is much broader than the question of the democratic deficit regarding the decision-making processes.

The European Union needs to strengthen not only democracy but also the welfare state and civil society. However, achieving an effective link at the EU level appears to be difficult. The difficulty of achieving such broad and complex objectives may well be greater when they are pursued at that level than at the national one. The common civic identity is weak. Moreover, with a view to increasing its legitimacy, the European Union has assumed many obligations that conform with or lead to a welfare state's provisions. Unfortunately, inability to meet those obligations jeopardises both the Union's legitimacy and the implementation of other obligations. This illustrates the fact that the Union has neither the governance structure nor the budgetary means to take on some key roles of the nation-states.

Some have argued that the present decision-making system is based on the successful de-politicisation, and, therefore, de-contextualisation, of issues. A part of this is the emphasis on output legitimacy rather than the transparency and democratic legitimacy of participants in the process (Beyer and Kerremans, 2002). The present lobbying process may be considered chaotic, but it is accepted because of the relative importance of the knowledge and rationality attributed to it. The essence of the lobbying system in the European Union can in be summarised, in a single sentence, as follows: The European Union trades competence and legitimacy for influence. The EU system controls access to influence, but at the same time it needs support and input from affected parties. In the future, too many may be offering their competence and support compared to the system's ability to process such inputs. An important part of the solution to this challenge is institutional reform, which simplifies the decision-making process. To the extent that the European Union introduces majority decision making and a clearer demarcation of roles between central institutions, it will become more like a 'normal' political system.

However, the EU system represents a degree of complexity, with tensions and paradoxes, which may threaten a traditional liberal-democratic model. There are simply too many different actors and interests to deal with through normal party systems of interest representation and aggregation, which play a more important role at the national level. If this is correct, it means that the lobbying system is not a symptom of the newness of the EU systems, that is, the relatively low degree of institutionalisation of a new polity. It may also reflect the inherent complexity of governing a very heterogeneous Europe.

Note

The title of this chapter is inspired by the UNESCO report, edited by the philosopher Arne Næss, discussing challenges to various concepts of democracy in a world characterised by tensions between rich and poor, North and South, communism and capitalism, and so on.

CHAPTER 5

The Politics of the Fuel Protests
Towards a New Form of Disruptive Action?

Nick Robinson

Introduction

The fuel protests of September 2000 were an extremely dramatic event, causing huge disruption across Western Europe as hauliers and farmers combined to blockade oil refineries and depots, closing off the supply of fuel. The protests precipitated widespread panic buying by the public across Europe, so that within a week almost all of petrol stations across Europe were totally dry. The protests were particularly striking in that the action seemed to sweep across Europe, with the hauliers and farmers apparently performing copycat action that led to the rapid capitulation of national governments across the European Union.

In the United Kingdom the protests had a similarly dramatic effect. Within five days almost all of petrol stations on the British mainland were totally dry; the government appeared to be in turmoil, having been totally unprepared for the protests; and the public's overwhelming support for the action of the protesters resulted in the Conservative party enjoying an unprecedented (albeit brief) lead in the opinion polls.

The fuel protests seem, on the surface, to demonstrate something quite new, with hitherto 'conservative' groups becoming increasingly radicalised and forcing the capitulation of government. This chapter focuses on events in the United Kingdom to reflect on whether this is indeed the case. To this end the protests themselves can be used as a vehicle for reflecting on a number of questions concerning the changing nature of lobbying activity in general.[1]

First, there are a number of questions in relation to the groups themselves, such as whether or not the protests were unprecedented, and whether they were exceptionally radical. Is it the case that the protesters had a transformative (i.e. party political) agenda that was focused on bringing down the Labour Government or were they just pragmatically trying to regain their status as policy insiders?

Second, what was the legacy of the protests? Did they have any lasting effect? How important have they been in forcing changes to the broad thrust of policy in the transport area? Have the groups who felt marginalised during the protests been able to force themselves back into the formal policy process as policy insiders as a result of their action?

Third, what lessons can be drawn from the protests for the future of direct action? Is it likely to become increasingly prevalent as a form of political participation? What (if any) are the potential costs for hitherto insider groups from embarking on such action? How, if at all, is the policy process attuned to responding to the demands of direct action?

A Brief History of the Fuel Protests

The UK fuel protests began at the Stanlow refinery in Cheshire on the night of 7 September 2000 when approximately 150 protesters blockaded the exit of the refinery for several hours. Although the police cleared the exits the following morning, only one of the 60 Shell petrol tankers scheduled to leave did so, with company officials claiming that it was unsafe for tankers to drive past the remnants of the blockade. The protests then rapidly spread to other fuel depots and refineries; by 11 September most of the country's oil refineries and depots were effectively closed. Widespread panic buying of petrol hugely exacerbated the impact of the blockades, so that 90 per cent of petrol stations had run out of fuel by 13 September.

The government reaction to the fuel protests over the week which the protests lasted was volatile. It made an initial attempt to ignore them and continue with its pre-arranged programme of business in order to deflate the protests and prevent panic buying of petrol. Subsequently it instigated instruments of crisis management with plans put in place to 'guarantee' the supply of fuel to essential services, with the army put on stand-by to deliver fuel if required.[2]

The government was also involved in direct dialogue with the key actors, holding discussions with both the oil companies and the police with a view to re-opening the immediate supply of fuel and to securing future supplies. Yet perhaps more decisively than the government's talks, the unions increasingly became involved in direct negotiations with the drivers at the fuel depots. In particular, on 13 September a delegation of union officials negotiated a vital breakthrough at the Grangemouth refinery in Scotland when they secured the agreement of the tanker drivers to drive once more.

The political discourse surrounding the fuel protests became increasingly bitter, with both the government and the trade unions publicly accusing the protesters of threatening the functioning of the NHS, undermining the operation of the economy, and being violent and anti-democratic, and claiming the oil companies were in collusion with them, thus justifying the use of the full force of the instruments of the state in response.

While government discourse was generally confrontational, an important conciliatory tone was also struck, in particular by Chancellor Gordon Brown, who emphasised that he would 'look and listen' as part of a process of drawing up his 2001 budget providing the protesters engaged in 'conventional dialogue'. This kept open a mechanism by which the protesters could end their action while keeping their integrity intact, but also further undermined the more direct means they had adopted by suggesting that they could secure their ends through conventional dialogue.

The protests ended almost as suddenly as they had begun: at Stanlow the protesters called off their action at 5 a.m. on 14 September, setting the government a 60-day deadline for concessions on the cost of fuel. (The explanation offered by the protesters for ending the action when they did was that the high level of public support that they had built up was likely to erode if the public was subjected to significant, long-term inconvenience.) In the short term, the fallout from the protests was considerable: the government was widely perceived as both incompetent and wrong, while the protesters retained considerable public support for their actions, despite the disruption they had caused.

The events surrounding the politics of the fuel protests were remarkable in many ways and they raise a number of fascinating questions. It is the aim of this chapter to address these questions, reflecting on matters relating to the protesters, the legacy of the protests and the lessons that can be drawn from them.

The Actions of the Protesters

The politics of the fuel protests raise a number of questions with regards to whether or not the protests were unprecedented. Were they a 'new' phenomenon? Were they more radical than what had passed before? Did the movement signify a rejection of 'traditional' groups? How innovative was the use of new technologies such as the Internet, e-mail and mobile telephones?

One possible view is these protests were indeed quite new because prior to them it had seemed almost inconceivable that the actors involved would undertake any form of direct action. A leading member of the British Roads Federation articulated such a view in 1996:

> It would be great if you could get 50 truckers, or 100 truckers, to drive into central London and block off all the roads and say, 'we want better facilities'. Realistically, that is not going to happen because the people who, if you like, are in charge of those sorts of organisations are traditionally conservative (and that is with a small 'c').
>
> (Interview with author, 21 August 1996)

Academic studies of the agricultural and haulage sectors have also emphasised that producer groups have historically enjoyed good access to government via their peak organisations, thus forming an integral part of the 'policy community' (Dudley, 1983, p. 109. See Finer, 1958; Hamer, 1987; Plowden, 1971; and Robinson, 2000, pp. 55–62 for coverage of the road lobby; and Dowding, 1991, pp. 154–7; Grant, 2000, p. 170; and Marsh and Smith, 2000, pp. 12; 16–17 for coverage of the agricultural sector). Thus historically the activity of these groups has been centred on using the tactics of insider groups to influence policy makers rather than disruption.

> Our organisation [the Road Haulage Association], which has a very long history, we are not an extremist organisation. We don't resort to sensational, publicity type things. We lobby quietly, we can get in and to put it bluntly, if we want a question asked in parliament – it will be asked, and we won't pay for it.
>
> (Interview with author, 21 August, 1996)

However, since the mid-1990s both the farming groups and the road hauliers have seen their historically close ties to their respective client departments come under increasing pressure, pushing the representative bodies for these groups towards outsider status. (See Dudley and Richardson, 1996, pp. 76–80, and Dudley and Richardson, 2000, Ch. 8 for coverage of the changes in the transport case; Grant, 2001, for changes within the agricultural sector; and Robinson, 2002, pp. 61–3 for coverage of both sectors.) Furthermore, marginal groups (typically small-scale hauliers and farmers) who have been particularly hard-hit by political and economic changes have increasingly broken away from their representative organisations, becoming policy outsiders; as a result they have begun to adopt the tactics of direct action and extra-legal activity which are increasingly 'forced on' outsider groups (see Cobb and Elder, 1972, pp. 21–2 for this model).

Thus the fuel protests marked a sharp change of strategy towards direct action, with a campaign of blockading oil refineries and go-slows on the motorways centred on capturing the attention of the media in a highly photogenic manner –a classic tactic of an outsider group (see Anderson, 1997 on the media and direct action; and Maloney *et al.*, 1994, and Grant, 2000, Ch. 2 for a typology of groups).

The fuel protests also appear to be 'new' because the action that was undertaken was done so by economically motivated producer groups. Historically, in the United Kingdom, the only economically motivated groups to have been frequently involved in disruptive action have been trade unions representing organised labour (Evans, 1997, p. 111). Thus, a campaign of highly visible and disruptive direct action by a network of producer groups is indeed new.

Finally, the protests also appear to be 'new' because the scale of the disruption was unprecedented. Not since the oil crises of the 1970s (and the associated strike action by public sector workers in the energy sectors) has Britain faced such developments, with the actions of the protesters effectively closing off all transport contingent activity within the entire economy for the duration of the fuel protests (Ingle, 2001, p. 185).

However, an alternative reading of the fuel protests is that in fact they were neither radical nor unprecedented. From this perspective, the protesters merely adopted the same disruptive tactics that had been used for a number of years by other groups both within the United Kingdom and across Western Europe.

First, the actions of the fuel protesters drew inspiration from the campaigns of the direct action movement in general, and the anti-roads groups and anti-capitalist demonstrators in particular, who had been making use of tactics centred on physical obstruction in order to gain widespread media attention since the mid-1990s (Dudley and Richardson, 1996, pp. 78–9; Bryant, 1996, pp. 187–216).[3] In the case of the UK protests against road building, for example, such tactics focused on the occupation of road construction sites, with the use of increasing elaborate forms of technical innovation in the form of walkways between the trees, tunnels, tripods and lock-ons (Doherty, 2000, pp. 65–72).

Second, the use which the fuel protesters made of 'new' technologies such as mobile phones and the Internet also reflects the tactics of historical outsider groups such as the anti-capitalist demonstrators. As McKay makes clear such modern technologies have been crucial for the exchange of information and coordination of activity to help the development of a coordinated global protest movement (McKay, 1998, pp. 10–11). Thus while the use of these forms of communication may be new to the particular groups involved in the fuel protests, their use does not itself demonstrate genuine innovation as they have in the past been used extensively by groups historically opposed to the fuel protesters.

Third, a persuasive argument can also be made that such action was not new as it built on a strong tradition of active protest by economically motivated producer groups within continental Europe, where producer groups have found representation within the electoral arena of politics. At one level, the petit bourgeoisie has a strong history of political activism, being the basis of the post-war right-wing Poujadist movement in France for example. At another level, producer groups such as the farmers have a history of making use of direct action across continental Europe in order to oppose national and EU policy (Imig and Tarrow, 2001).

In particular, it is important to remember that in late August and early September protests in France in which fishermen, hauliers and farmers blockaded the ports, fuel terminals and depots preceded the fuel protests in the United Kingdom. By the end of August the French Government had offered significant concessions to the fishermen and within four days of the action by the farmers and hauliers (9 September) the government had also offered significant concessions to these groups (*Observer*, 10 September 2000, p. 3). The protests in France were therefore both quick and apparently powerful, seeming to achieve the results that the protesters wanted. The apparent success of the protests in France is very important in explaining the subsequent protests on the British mainland.

Thus a persuasive argument could be made that the actions of the fuel protesters were not in fact unique or new in any real sense, and that these groups were simply drawing lessons from the direct action movement and other producer groups in continental Europe. From this point of view, therefore, the protests were only unique in so far as it was the UK producer groups that were making use of direct action for the first time.

In summary, the evidence does tend towards the view that the nature of the protests was not really new, but their significance should nevertheless not be downplayed. While it is true that they did adopt their tactics from elsewhere, they were clearly very important as they demonstrate the radicalisation of hitherto small 'c' conservative groups, the extraordinary lengths that hitherto insider groups will go to regain their status as policy insiders, and the remarkable capacity of direct action to totally destabilise the economic and political system.

The Motives of the Protesters

The fuel protests also raise a number of important questions concerning the motives of the protesters, with the key question being: did the protesters have a party political agenda focused on destabilising the Labour Government and promoting the Conservative Party, or was their motivation less radical, centred on securing a return to a more favourable economic position and to their status as policy insiders?

One possible view is that the protestors had a highly radical, transformative party political agenda focused on destabilising the Labour Government. This view is most closely associated with commentators on the left, who have tended to view the hauliers and farmers as examples of a frustrated right-wing petit bourgeoisie mounting a politically motivated campaign against the Labour Government. TUC General Secretary John Monks clearly articulated such a view to the TUC Annual Congress, which happened to be running at the same time as the fuel protests:

> Let me remind you of another occasion that trucks and lorries were used by the self-employed and the far right to attack democracy. That was in 1973 in Chile – and it started a chain of events which brought down the Allende Government. That is why today we call upon Britain's trade unionists to work normally and to play no part in this bosses' blockade.
>
> (TUC congress, Glasgow, 13 September 2000, reported in *Guardian*,
> 14 September 2000)

Similar comments were made by Margaret Beckett, then Leader of the House of Commons (*Guardian*, 16 September 2000, p. 1).

From this perspective the hauliers, frustrated by the electoral failures of the Conservative party, attempted to mount an extra-electoral campaign designed to influence the democratic process. Thus the primary motive of the hauliers was widespread disruption leading to regime change, ushering in a new political elite supportive of their overall aims, namely to promote the broad interests of farmers and small businesses.

However the evidence for such a view is limited. While it is true that there were a number of Internet statements that pointed to broader political objectives, and while it may also be true that in general the participating individuals did support the Conservative Party, it seems that to place such a strong instrumental emphasis on the motives of the protesters is to overstate their objectives (See Boycott the Pumps, 2000, for an example of politically motivated communication on the Internet and the *Guardian*, 26 October 2000, p. 4, for an examination of the party political sympathies of some of the key activists).

In fact, as I will show, the protestors were motivated by political and economic changes that in combination had reduced both their political influence and their economic security, rather than any broader transformative aims. Thus an alternative, and much less radical reading of the motives of the protesters, is to view them as essentially reactionary and pragmatic. The protesters were a collection of individuals driven to action by a combination of the long-term shift in the orientation of government policy away from their interests and short-term factors (such as the rising price of oil). Reading the protests in this way also eliminates the danger of confusing any enthusiasm for widespread change that may have developed after the protests had begun with the motives of the protesters for launching the protests in the first place. Thus, while it is true that some of the protesters did indeed gain a thirst for broader political objectives with the apparent 'success' of their action, this is not the same as saying that such broad objectives motivated their action in the first place.

The key political factor that explains the motivation of the hauliers and the farmers to protest is a growing frustration that stemmed from their increasing marginalisation within the policy process (Grant, 2001, p. 343–5; Robinson, 2002, pp. 61–3).

In the case of the hauliers, marginalisation developed from the mid-1990s as first the Major Government and then the Blair Government progressively reduced the scale of the road programme. The Blair Government also introduced a number of important (albeit gradual) changes in government orthodoxy as policies were introduced to increasingly manipulate the transport market to encourage the use of public transport and rail freight at the expense of private transport and road haulage: for example by continuing the fuel duty escalator and considering the introduction of road pricing.

This shift in policy was accompanied by the relative marginalisation of the peak organisations that represent the interests of the hauliers (the FTA and RHA) as the government created a number of institutional structures with quite different priorities to the hauliers. The most important of these changes was the merger of the Department of Transport into the Department of the Environment, Transport and the Regions, demonstrating an increasing focus on environmental priorities and further weakening the hauliers' links with their historical client department. In addition, the government created a number of important advisory bodies (such as the Commission for Integrated Transport), which gave a prominent role to groups such as CPRE and Transport 2000 with very different views.

The cumulative effect of these changes was to make the hauliers 'on the ground' increasingly vulnerable, as they felt that their peak organisations were failing to represent their interests and that they were becoming increasingly marginalised as policy outsiders.

The agricultural sector has also been similarly marginalised, although here the motor for change has principally been changes at the EU rather than the national level, with considerable pressure throughout the 1990s for a reform of the CAP at the EU level making farmers increasingly vulnerable. The reform process has been prompted by a combination of persistent agricultural overproduction, the impending enlargement of the European Union and international pressure through global free trade agreements to reduce protection within the agricultural field, which led to pressure to reduce spending on the CAP. Farm incomes have thus reduced as the close link between the EU farming groups and their client DG has declined. (See Grant, 1997a, Ch. 7 for an overview. See also Rieger, 2000, pp. 193–207 for a critical discussion of the role of international trade. See Daugberg, 1999, for an emphasis on the limited extent of change thus far.) This is a significant change, as agriculture has derived much of its stability in the United Kingdom from the existence of a stable CAP at the EU level.

In the period prior to the fuel protests, the agricultural sector had been further marginalised due to an increasing perception that modern forms of agriculture are damaging to the environment and are responsible for a growing number of food scares. Outbreaks of salmonella in eggs and BSE in cattle, and concerns over the safety of genetically modified foods had led to real concerns being expressed by consumer groups and the media about the way in which food is produced (see for example Grant, 1997b, for discussion of the BSE crisis).

> With more and more groups mobilised to question the very nature of the processes at the heart of modern farming, the agricultural lobby's influence has diminished so that it can no longer exert as much control over food policy. The practical implication of these changes has been to push the agricultural sector towards the status of an outsider group.
>
> (Robinson, 2002, p. 63)

The cumulative effect of such changes has been to increasingly marginalise the agricultural peak organisations, leading farmers 'on the ground' to express similar concerns as the hauliers, namely that their interests were being inadequately protected by their representative bodies.

Accompanying these long-term political changes were a number of apparently unpredictable short-term factors occurring in the period immediately preceding the fuel protests, which served to increase the economic vulnerability of the hauliers in particular.

The first of these was the rise in the price of crude oil, which in September 2000 rose to a ten-year high of $33 per barrel, up from under $10 per barrel in December 1998. Prices of petrol rose similarly, up 40 per cent between January 1999 and June 2000 (OPEC, 2000). These changes had a very profound impact on the hauliers, most of whom ran small businesses operating at the margins with low levels of profitability.

The rise in the price of oil must also be understood against a general climate in which the government enjoyed a significant fiscal surplus for 1999/2000 of £18.9 billion, and in which fuel prices in the United Kingdom were the highest in the European Union, with government taxes responsible for over 70 per cent of the price on the forecourt (HM Treasury, 2000). The protesters thus had a clear sense that the government could afford to offset the rising price in global oil prices by reducing duty in order to compensate the hauliers.

Overall therefore, the motives of the protesters must be seen as reactionary and pragmatic. It would be wrong to suggest that they had any transformative agenda beyond regaining the influence over the policy process that they had historically enjoyed and reducing the cost of fuel in order to secure their economic position.

The Legacy of the Protests: Did They Make a Difference?

The third substantive section of this chapter focuses on the legacy of the protests, attending to the following key questions: Did the actions of the protesters enable them to secure their objectives, namely regaining their former status as policy insiders and changing policy towards their interests? What was the lasting effect of the protests on the government? What effect did the protests have on the public perception of the transport issue?

Such questions are important, as not only do they enable further reflection on the principal questions raised in this chapter (i.e. whether the protests were 'new' and the motives of the protesters), but they also enable us to consider broader questions such as the extent to which these protests have made direct action by producer groups more likely in the future. Is direct action now seen as an increasingly powerful way of securing the aims of a wide variety of groups? And, if so, what is the implication of this for representative democracy?

One possible view is that the protests had an extremely important legacy. At one level, they appeared to erode public support for the Labour Government in the short-term, with widespread public perception that the government was in crisis: administrative competence seemed low and the government was portrayed as arrogant and 'out of touch' with public concerns (Ingle, 2001, pp. 184–6). This feeling was clearly demonstrated by a number of surveys of public opinion conducted during the protests, which revealed that the public overwhelmingly supported the actions of the protesters. Indeed, in the immediate aftermath of the protests, the Conservative Party enjoyed their only period of leadership in the opinion polls over Labour since 1992 (Ingle, 2001, p. 185).[4]

However, the legacy of this decline in support for the Labour Government was short-lived: they rapidly returned (by the beginning of October) to a significant lead in the opinion polls, and the Labour Government won the subsequent election in 2001 with another considerable majority. Thus no lasting damage seems to have been done to the support for the Labour Party *vis-à-vis* the Conservatives, but this may in fact reflect the inability of the Conservative party to exploit the political opportunities provided by the fuel protests rather than the fact that no political damage was done to the Labour party (Rallings and Thrasher, 2001, p. 325).

The legacy of this event for electoral politics could also be considered at a much deeper level, however, being part of a broad trend of political action that demonstrates increasing antipathy with conventional forms of representative electoral democracy. From this point of view, the fuel protests must be viewed alongside phenomena such as declining voter turnout, declining public trust in elected politicians and forms of direct action as part of a broader movement away from these traditional forms of democracy (Blaug, 2002). There is a considerable irony here, as the legacy of these protests has thus been to further erode the perceived legitimacy of electoral forms of democracy and increase the legitimacy of extra-legal non-parliamentary activity, which has historically been a strategy used by a number of the groups whom the hauliers and farmers most violently oppose.

In addition, the protests could be seen as having an important legacy because they helped the protesters to secure a number of their demands. At one level, the protests seem to have had an effect in changing the nature of the policy process, with both the peak organisations representing the farmers and hauliers becoming increasingly reincorporated within the policy process and the leaders of the protests themselves becoming incorporated within the formal policy process through meetings with ministers (Grant, 2001, p. 342). At another level, the protesters also seem to have been able to secure some concessions in terms of their broad policy objectives: the November 2000 budget reduced road tax for lorries by an average of £715 per year (over 50 per cent), reduced road tax on cars of up to 1,500 cc by £55 per year, reduced fuel duty on ultra-low sulphur petrol by 3p a litre, and froze all other fuel duty (*Guardian*, 9

November 2000, p. 1). The farmers, in contrast, did not gain directly from any targeted benefits in the budget, but they were already the beneficiaries of subsidised 'red' diesel, which only attracts a quarter of the levy of regular diesel. In fact, as Grant points out, rather than trying to secure further concessions there was major concern within the NFU leadership that any overly aggressive campaigning by the farmers might in fact draw attention to the benefits they were already receiving, leading to their withdrawal (Grant, 2001, p. 344). Thus the protests seemed to have an important impact on the nature of the policy process and of the outputs of that process.

Finally, the protests could be seen as having an important legacy across the whole transport sector, as they seem to have placed considerable pressure for a shift of policy ethos away from anti-car measures towards a pro-car focus. For example, following the protests there has been an increase in the scale of the road programme, the DETR was increasingly acknowledged to be unwieldy and was split up into separate departments and, crucially, the government seemed to back off from delivering many of the more contentious proposals within the White Paper, such as road pricing.

However, there is an important alternative reading of the legacy of the protests that fundamentally questions their importance in bringing about these changes. As I have argued elsewhere, in the initial period following the election of the Labour Government, the government tried to change policy to reflect the fact that transport had increasingly come to be seen as a policy problem in terms of congestion, air pollution and so forth. At a practical level, this change in ethos was accompanied by proposals to reduce the scale of the road programme, undertake significant expansions of public transport investment and implement restrictions on road transport, such as workplace parking charges and road pricing, which were explicitly designed to reduce road traffic (Robinson, 2000, pp. 258–62).

Even as early as 1999, however, it became increasingly clear to members of the government that the delivery of such a programme was fraught with enormous difficulties. At one level, certain sections of the media and the public reacted violently to the government's proposals to restrict car use, with widespread opposition to the proposed introduction of workplace parking charges and urban road pricing in particular. The public's reaction was important as it symbolised an important transformation of public attitudes towards the car: whereas in the mid-1990s the public was increasingly concerned with the environmental effects of the car, by the late 1990s they had shifted towards concern that government restrictions would impose unreasonable burdens on people's 'right' to use a car (Robinson, 2000, pp. 262–9). Thus the apparent success of the fuel protests in mobilising public opinion must be understood in the context of a shift in public opinion that predated the fuel protests by several years.

At the same time, the government was also backing away from implementing proposals to restrict road transport as it became increasingly clear that any widespread restrictions on people's right to travel would meet considerable problems, as they interfered with the operation of the market place. Measures such as road pricing are fundamentally designed to restrict the operation of the market, pricing marginal motorists off the road. They challenge the rights of certain (marginal) motorists to own a car, forcing them onto public transport. Such a change of policy focus has the effect of restricting the personal mobility of those affected. For the Labour Government, however, there were real difficulties here: personal mobility is closely associated with many of the fundamental rationales of the capitalist state, predicated as it is on values such as freedom, liberty and access. The crucial point, therefore, is that the government had already backed away from any serious intentions to undermine the status of the road transport sector. The climate of thinking surrounding transport policy was already undergoing considerable change in the period leading up to the fuel protests.

From this point of view, the apparent legacy of the protests must thus be seen alongside these broad changes to the trajectory of policy already in train prior to the protests: the public had already moved away from environmental concerns to mobility concerns, and the government had already down-scaled its plans to restrict car use significantly and was moving back towards projects to accommodate projected traffic growth and encourage mode switching.

The concessions made by the government to the hauliers therefore need to be understood as reflecting this more pragmatic way of thinking. Even if the fuel protests had not happened, we would have expected considerable changes in the policy process: the hauliers would have been increasingly reincorporated within the process and the outcomes of government policy gradually changed to reflect their preferences, even if they had done nothing.

However, that is not to say that these protests did not matter at all. At the very least they publicised the nature of the shift which was occurring in government policy, they probably accelerated the changes that were afoot, and the government probably made slightly more concessions than it otherwise would have done. While the protests were important, what is crucial to understand is that they owe their success to the fact that they were pushing in the same direction as already occurring broad changes in the trajectory of government policy. Their importance thus needs to be accurately qualified.

Learning from the Fuel Protests: Some Lessons for Future Direct Action

In the final section of this chapter I offer some brief thoughts on the lessons that can be drawn from the events surrounding the fuel protests of September 2000. Given that the focus of this piece is primarily on the actions and motives of the protesters, the comments offered here are principally concerned to evaluate the lessons which can be gained from the fuel protests for the groups directly involved. (See Robinson, 2002, for coverage of the lessons which can be drawn for the government from the protests.)

The first observation is that direct action clearly does work, providing that the conditions are conducive. As I have shown throughout this chapter, direct action has the capacity to communicate the interests of groups forcefully by causing widespread disruption to the political system.

However, a cautionary note should also be struck for any erstwhile insider groups considering direct action for three key reasons. First, direct action is clearly a sign of weakness: groups do not engage in direct action unless they are marginalized, and it is a desperate tactic with unpredictable results.

Second, direct action clearly poses significant dangers for democracy. If the type of action undertaken during the fuel protests occurred more regularly, it is difficult to comprehend how traditional representative democracy, relying as it does on consultation and compromise within the policy process, could continue to function, since direct action is not built around such strategies and values.

Third, a proliferation of direct action would demonstrate a widespread fragmentation of peak insider organisations and the radicalisation of those groups. Ultimately if national peak organisations such as the NFU, RHA or FTA are unable to control their memberships, this will weaken their legitimacy in the eyes of the government in the long term.

Overall, governments continue to prefer dealing with insider groups, with the government and the civil service organised on these terms. Thus groups that cannot control their members and that do not have an insider strategy will never be able to have any serious dealings with government. This is important as studies of policy making emphasise that only insider groups can secure influence over policy because they are uniquely placed to influence its the detail. The policy process is predicated on dialogue, compromise and consultation, and consequently the government cannot interact in any sustained way with groups that rely on direct action. Thus direct action will generally fail to influence the detail of policy, with serious implications for its capacity to influence the policy process.

Thus, cumulatively many lessons can be drawn from a consideration of the fuel protests for democracy, the policy process and the strategy of erstwhile insider groups for the future. The crucial point, however, is that while direct action can achieve some results if the conditions are right, erstwhile insider groups cannot see it as a replacement for traditional forms of activity. While it is true that it may help them in the short term to regain their insider status, direct action cannot be expected to achieve the desired results for such groups in the long term as it will lower their legitimacy in the eyes of the government, which is organised to interact with groups on the basis of dialogue, consultation and compromise and not popular protest.

Conclusion

This chapter has looked at the politics of the fuel protests. In particular, it has reflected on a number of questions connected with the protests, namely the extent to which the protests were unprecedented or exceptionally radical, the extent to which they had any important lasting legacy, and the extent to which lessons could be drawn from them for future forms of direct action.

Overall, I have argued that the protests were extremely important, leading to a level of disruption of a degree unprecedented since the 1970s. With the government seeming totally unprepared for the fuel protests, they led over a period of seven days to almost total paralysis of the UK economy as the transport system was totally disrupted by the complete blockage of the fuel supply chain.

In addition, the fuel protests witnessed the unprecedented mobilisation of hitherto small 'c' conservative groups. This marked a significant change, as traditionally these groups had enjoyed close links to their respective 'client department' via their peak organisations, with the 'rank and file' happy to acquiesce in this relationship. The fuel protests showed a very real change from this historical pattern, demonstrating that if groups are pushed from a status of insider to outsider they are likely to react violently to this change. There are thus a number of real reasons to emphasise the importance and uniqueness of the protests.

This chapter has also emphasised, however, that we should be careful not to exaggerate the uniqueness, in academic terms, of these protests. At one level, while it is true that the tactics of the hauliers and farmers were unprecedented in UK producer groups, they were tactics that had been employed both by other direct action groups in the United Kingdom and elsewhere, and also by other producer groups within continental Europe. In addition, the motivation of the groups was neither new nor particularly radical. Their agenda did not centre on party political transformation, their motives for action indeed being essentially pragmatic and reactionary, focused on regaining access to the political system and a return to their previously held economic status. Finally, we should be careful not to place too much emphasis on the unique capacity of these protests to change the nature of government policy in the transport field. The chapter has emphasised that while they may have accelerated policy change, their apparent success was due to the fact that the protests worked alongside existing changes of policy emanating from central government. They did not create a paradigm shift, but just brought into focus one that was already there.

Thus, while these protests are certainly very important, demonstrating both a very considerable capacity for disruption and also the spread of direct action from traditional outsider groups to economically motivated producer groups, their tactics, motives and impact are not new. Instead they can be seen as a continuation of a lengthy tradition of policy learning in terms of tactics, pragmatism in terms of motives, and conditionality in terms of impact for their effectiveness, inherited from other direct action groups in the United Kingdom and elsewhere.

Notes

1. Questions addressing why the protests happened are not considered in this article as they fall outside its scope. I have examined this issue elsewhere (see Robinson, 2002).
2. See Robinson (2003) for fuller coverage of the government's response in terms of both varying discourses employed and action taken.
3. Attempts by anti-roads groups to use the media actually date back to the 1970s, with protests at that time centred on disrupting the highway inquiry process (Tyme, 1978). However, the protests during the 1970s attracted comparatively limited media exposure in contrast to those in the 1990s. Thus the later protests can be seen as a genuine innovation due to the scale of the disruption that they caused and the level of media attention they commanded.
4. The overwhelming level of public support for the actions of the protesters was reflected in a number of surveys. For example a telephone poll conducted by BBC Radio 2 on the Jimmy Young show received over 150,000 phone calls, with 91 per cent of respondents supporting the protests (*Guardian*, 15 September 2000, p. 4).

CHAPTER 6

Public Affairs Challenges for Multinational Corporations

Mark Hatcher

Introduction

Increasingly extensive forms of political networks, greater interaction between public institutions and private groups (enormously facilitated by the Internet) and increased collaboration between national regulators to tackle cross-border issues (such as global financial regulation and world trade) are creating a new contested space for activists, whether regulatory, business or other non-government actors. Against this background public affairs practitioners in multinational corporations need to be able to engage with the new networks, to identify critical dependencies and to manage interactions between government and non-governmental actors in the development of public policy solutions that impact on business and the wider community. This new environment presents four main challenges for multinationals:

- to engage visibly with public policy issues under debate
- to run with the grain of the new political and regulatory dynamic
- to invest in shaping the new regulatory environment in which to do business
- to organise themselves to optimise desired policy outcomes.

Context

The 'Battle of Seattle' opened a new chapter in relations between government and business. After a day of demonstrations and rioting that shut down the opening of the World Trade Organisation (WTO) Ministerial Conference in Seattle on 30 November 1999, the Mayor of this normally laid-back city declared a civil emergency, called in the US National Guard and imposed an all-night curfew. More than 60,000 people had converged on the city, bent on disruption. Organised by about 700 different groups, ranging from staid associations like the Sierra Club and the AFL–CIO to fringe groups like the Raging Grannies and Dyke Action, the protestors staged a 'Seattle Tea Party', dumping Chinese steel and hormone-treated beef into the bay. They smashed windows and daubed the walls of multinational chains like Starbucks and McDonald's. They claimed the WTO to be a secretive, undemocratic, unaccountable body that was intent on trampling over the interests of poor countries, ignoring workers' rights and encouraging the destruction of natural resources in the pursuit of free markets. While President Clinton wanted to launch a new round of global trade talks to burnish his post-impeachment record, what happened in Seattle was a tear gas round, with unprecedented media coverage.

The aims of the Seattle protestors varied but they all agreed on one thing: a new trade round had to be stopped, before it had started. They succeeded, up to a point. Many of the non-governmental organisations (NGOs) and others involved proved exceptionally good at organising themselves and using their influence through aggressive marketing, lobbying and the Internet. Protesting against globalisation had become a global venture. Unlike the protestors on the streets, governments and the business lobby looked less sure footed. Their media responses appeared to be defensive. Global capitalism looked vulnerable. At the time Seattle demonstrated the apparent effectiveness of global civil society, gathered together at a parallel summit, deploying a mixed bag of arguments against corporate-driven, state-promoted globalisation. No one would deny that globalisation or free trade can bring painful upheaval but no one in the business community or among governments seemed to be able to articulate persuasively the benefits and prosperity that free trade can bring. Part of the reason may have been that international organisations like the International Monetary Fund (IMF) and the World Bank appeared to have lost their moral authority. The cold war had given the United States and Europe a natural leadership role over countries outside the Communist bloc. When the Berlin Wall fell, this role fell with it. Yet the governments of the world's leading economies and the international institutions they supported remained, in the public eye, western institutions.

For a time, a run of anti-capitalist demonstrations at parallel summits seemed to provide evidence of a trend of global disconnection developing between government and business. Angry protests greeted ministers and officials gathering in September 2000 at the autumn meeting of the IMF–World Bank in Prague. In January 2001 protestors behind barricades made their presence felt to the political and business elite who lumbered up the Swiss mountains to the World Economic Forum at Davos. At the same time the first World Social Forum was held in Porto Allegre, led by Brazilian progressive organisations and Attac, a French-based network demanding a Tobin tax on currency transactions and challenging globalisation. The 20,000 activists attracted from around the world called for democracy in the management of globalisation and a stronger role for national governments. Porto Allegre inspired the Genoa Social Forum, attracting more than 100,000 people from all over Europe to an alternative summit on the margins of the meeting of G8 Ministers in Genoa in July 2001.

The heterogeneous and largely fragmented groups that organised these manifestations of popular discontent, coupled with the widespread media coverage they engendered, provided a vocal and sometimes articulate challenge to governments and official institutions with whose international gatherings they had been timed to coincide. Their messages, although not always directly related to the agendas under discussion, represented apparently widespread discontent about the failings of neoliberal market economics, the conduct of corporations, the nature and impact of the lending policies of international financial institutions, the regulation of financial markets and the absence of effective global governance. Previously, international and economic diplomacy had been conducted by states acting largely on their own, in private session away from the public gaze. Nowadays, meetings of IMF Ministers, the UN, WTO and other multilateral institutions provide opportunities for a wider array of interests to be seen and up to a point heard, if not in the conference halls at least on the periphery. Pressure from citizens, communities and associations as well as business lobby groups that claim seats in these arenas is intensifying as international summitry has grown. In the middle of the nineteenth century there were probably no more than two or three inter-state conferences or congresses each year. Nowadays the scale and diversity of these events, attracting cohorts of officials and media commentators as well as hordes of security staff, provide a vivid demonstration of the complex interdependence of states and other actors, operating through an increasing number of political, economic, social and cultural channels.

The tragic events of September 11 muted anti-capitalist groups. Their generalised discontent and disparate messages were overtaken by uncertainty and fear created by terrorists prepared to strike at any moment deep within the citadels of capitalism. Anxiety about a clash of civilisations looked set to reinforce the politics of national identity and security. Shifts in public discourse about where the new world order appeared to be heading were accompanied by a marked softening of the US economy. Dotcom entrepreneurs fell to earth and, following a string of company collapses of which Enron and WorldCom were the most egregious examples, there was a crisis of confidence in corporate America. The need to re-build public trust in financial markets led to a raft of understandable, but rushed, regulatory responses designed to shore up investor confidence. Communism might have been a dying creed but confidence in capitalism was fragile.

A survey by Gallup suggests that democratic institutions as well as global and large national corporations have suffered a dramatic loss of trust in the opinion of people around the world.[1] Respondents were asked to rate their level of trust in 17 different institutions 'to operate in the best interest of society'. Global and large domestic companies were equally distrusted, ranking next to national legislative bodies at the bottom of the trust ratings. With low trust levels in traditional institutions, NGOs including environmental and social advocacy groups appeared to fare rather better, enjoying the second highest trust ratings in the survey (next to the armed forces).[2] NGOs were particularly trusted by citizens in the European Union and North America.

These high levels of public distrust in traditional institutions might appear to provide further evidence of societal disintegration yet global capital markets, global brands, global supply chains and powerful communications technology to feed a 24/7 news appetite are powerful drivers of economic and business interdependence. Despite the recent synchronous global economic slowdown, the volume of cross-border flows of goods, services and capital, increasing labour market specialisation between countries, and changing patterns of international trade and finance are continuing to forge closer economic ties. That said, however, globalists should reflect on the fact that national frameworks for public policy making remain, to a large extent, separate in the global arena. In some areas (pre-eminently in the financial services sector) it is possible to talk about global markets and global regulatory initiatives (or layered regulatory regimes that transcend regions or states). But most multinational corporations, and the regulatory frameworks within which they operate, remain focused on national or regional markets. The politics with which these businesses have to deal remains firmly rooted in the sovereignty of the state (Soros, 2002, p. 9). National governments remain important. They continue to be the focus of political power, as well as decision making, and it is to these governments that businesses have to relate on a day-to-day basis, often in relation to very long-term investments.[3] They alone have formal political authority to regulate economic and other activity, to levy taxes and to set the rules, sometimes imperfect but none the less the rules, that regulate competition. For example, Microsoft was nearly broken apart by regulators as a result of the extensive anti-trust litigation with which they have been engaged in the United States, which has also attracted the attention of regulatory counterparts in the European Union.

In global public affairs it is the international interdependence of national political and regulatory activity that has become the prevailing theme, particularly in the financial and capital markets, rather than global integration. Indeed the world's capital markets are probably as integrated today as they were in 1913 (following a significant period of disintegration between 1914 and 1945). The regulatory and other contested spaces in which businesses now operate have been shaped powerfully by the events of the past 50 years. Since the end of the Second World War, many governments have followed the principles of macroeconomic liberalism, reducing their external economic sovereignty on a reciprocal basis, lowering tariff barriers and easing capital controls and currency restrictions. The cooperative competition between governments in the 1960s and 1970s, followed by increased liberalisation and cross-border deregulation in the 1980s, provided a fertile seed bed for multinational corporations to develop regional (and occasionally global) strategies for foreign direct investment, intra-firm trade and international sourcing. Restructuring and de-industrialisation of OECD economies has led to outsourcing of manufacturing production in the transition economies of Eastern Europe, Latin America and Asia. The developing countries' share of world exports and foreign investment has also been growing, and services markets are changing for the benefit of the developed world as well as a number of developing countries with their growing populations of more highly-skilled workers and comparative cost advantages. For example, for some years Indian outsourcing firms have been handling routine customer service calls from developed country companies and this work is now evolving to include processing transactions, life sciences research and software development. Indians are now offering investment banks in London and New York chartered accountants and MBA students for a fraction of the cost and as a possible solution to the pressures they face from regulators to separate research from banking.

Globalisation, or regionalisation depending on your standpoint (Rugman, 2000), has been essentially a corporate phenomenon. Governments have not really been engaged in the dynamics of globalisation themselves, although they can have a profound effect on the conditions in which globalisation takes place. Although it is true to say that markets are no longer defined by (nor do they depend on) territories for their operation, they do depend initially on political power and economic networks for their creation. The world's most powerful governments can, and do, retain considerable bargaining power with multinationals because these businesses require access to markets and resources, and sovereign states can grant or withhold permission.

The growing internationalisation of business has encouraged firms to try to weld formerly segmented national markets into a single whole that spans national boundaries and to develop 'global' (or regional) business models. At the same time national governments have been gradually losing exclusive power to regulate their territories, in which the corporations do business. As a result we are witnessing a mismatch between economic and political geography. Multinationals, as well as global and regional organisations (including NGOs), are challenging the *operational* sovereignty of states. Governments, which are bounded by territoriality, can no longer project their public policy making and regulatory capacity over the territory within which global business and markets operate, in the absence of reciprocal arrangements or mutual recognition agreements. So although globalisation integrates along one dimension (the economic or private), it fragments along another (the political or public) (Reinicke, 1998, pp. 7, 62–5). Globalisation of business activity is leading to increased levels of international regulation, in which private and public sector participants act in a continuous contest, one asserting economic the other jurisdictional competence, in the process of rule making, code drafting and standard setting. A good example of the interplay of these forces is the recent efforts in the United States to strengthen corporate governance. Congressional legislation (the Sarbanes–Oxley Act of 2002) and related rule making by the US Securities and Exchange Commission, designed to deal with failings in the US model of corporate governance, sought to extend the reach of domestic regulators beyond the United States to bind markets and a variety of participants in the US capital markets. It prompted intense lobbying by foreign governments and regulators, as well as by multinational firms operating outside the United States, in order to minimise the extraterritorial effects of the new rules, and with some success.

Even the most powerful nation-states are becoming more fragmented policy-making arenas that are permeated by trans-national networks (both governmental and intergovernmental), as well as by locally based agencies and forces. The new world order is not predicated on the death of the nation-state, anymore than it represents a shift to supra-state, sub-state or non-state actors. Rather it envisages a state that is becoming disaggregated into functional parts (see Slaughter, 1997) that are networking with their counterparts abroad, dialoguing with affected interests and consulting with civil society. Together they are weaving thickening webs of global inter-connectedness. This is not to say that borders have lost their business. Indeed in some respects borders (or rather the cultural identities partly defined by borders) have become more significant. Instead, state boundaries have become increasingly permeable, with greater mobility of capital, the growth of more integrated capital markets in the European Union and the United States, the development of internationally competitive tax regimes and more flexible labour markets. Even at a time of heightened sensitivity to international terrorism and the need for increased vigilance by immigration and nationality authorities, the permeability of borders can still apply as many governments (mindful of the effects of changing demographic profiles and national skills shortages) recognise the need for further liberalisation of rules governing the movement of people in order better to manage economic migration, and some are actually relaxing border controls.

All politics remain local ultimately because they are embedded in some discrete national formation accountable to people on the ground. Nevertheless the increasingly extensive forms of political networks, the greater level of interaction among public institutions and private groups (enormously facilitated by the Internet and the 'globalisation of information'), and the growing collaboration among national regulators to tackle such cross-border issues of economic and financial regulation and world trade for example, is creating a new contested space for activists, whether regulatory, business or non-governmental. The striking features of this landscape are greater co-operation and coordination between state and non-state actors. There is a blurring of definitions of 'public' and 'private' sector domains and practices; and in some cases public regulatory bodies (like the International Accounting Standards Board) are privately funded. Increasingly there is a blending of 'domestic' and 'foreign'. The old command and control hierarchical systems of government within and between states are in transition. A new, complex, pluralistic, multilayered system of global and regional governance is being created.

Against the background described above, the ability to identify and manage critical dependencies, to build and manage multi-country coalitions of interest, and exercise skills in cross-border negotiation will be key to fashioning effective public policy outcomes that recognise the new political and regulatory dynamics. For public affairs practitioners in multinational corporations, engaging with increasingly extensive forms of networks and managing interactions between governmental and non-governmental actors in the development of public policy solutions that impact on business and the wider community presents four main challenges.

First Challenge: Engage in Debate

The first challenge is to encourage CEOs and other senior board members of leading companies (or those that aspire to leadership positions) to engage visibly with public policy issues under debate, perhaps to 'own an issue' and lead the debate. The issues will vary in detail by sector and according to how heavily those sectors are regulated. Examples are the biotechnology sector (managing public concern in the European Union about the safety of GM food imports), pharmaceutical companies (lobbying developing country governments about the import of cheap copies of patented medicines to combat AIDS), the high-tech sector (arguing for light-touch regulation of e-commerce), professional services firms (avoiding unnecessarily restrictive limitations that could lower the quality of audits for example) or financial services players (calling for a closer and more integrated EU capital market). Market leaders in these sectors can be expected to, and do, have positions on these kinds of sectoral issues. Indeed being *the* market leader may carry with it the heavy responsibility of leading the public debate on a particular issue above and beyond what a representative body may be able to do. But business leaders are often less clear about communicating with external stakeholders on broader, 'horizontal issues': the benefits of free trade against protectionism, for example, or issues of corporate social responsibility, the development of early warning systems to prevent EU–US trade disputes, the creation of trans-Atlantic anti-trust procedures or the need for closer co-operation between US and EU financial market regulators, to take some examples that, as we have seen, are becoming the subject of much more public debate.

The commercial success, not to say survival, of leading businesses may well depend upon their visible engagement in public policy development. Companies are now far more vulnerable to international public opinion because people have learnt how to harness their potential power as consumers (or, to use Noreena Hertz's (2001) description, 'political shoppers'). Nevertheless many business leaders underestimate the political, economic and social changes they face, attributing the low public trust in which they are held to the effects of a particular stage in the economic cycle, or the excesses of a few (recently dethroned) celebrity CEOs and quick fix responses by regulators. With few exceptions, most business leaders remain shrouded in anonymity or are simply invisible to those who do not read the business pages. Yet they are popularly seen as the main beneficiaries of globalisation, at the expense of the vulnerable or less well organised. The motivations of business leaders are thus capable of misinterpretation by anti-capitalists playing to different agendas. It is no longer enough for a CEO to be able to say that he (or, less commonly, she) is 'dining at the top table' and having useful private conversations, important though that may be. Engagement needs to be authentic and visible. When Seattle's best-known entrepreneur, Bill Gates (at the time chairman of Microsoft) was asked in 1999 what he thought about the bedlam being created by protestors in the city, he was reported (through a spokesman) as saying it was 'not appropriate' to comment (*Wall Street Journal*, 3 December 1999).

The absence of any business counter-argument to the anti-capitalists was depressing. For example, it could have been argued that for every low-skilled job that is exported from an industrialised country like the United States to the developing world through liberalisation of barriers to market entry, several new ones are created in India and China, for example, giving workers in those countries an opportunity to participate in the modern world. Properly managed, globalisation can release impoverished peasants who are eager to acquire industrial skills to escape from poverty or from dependence on employers in inefficient local companies locked into a web of cronyism and corruption.

The problem is that business leaders have done too little to put the case for responsible globalisation. The multilateral trading system, for all its imperfections, has an indispensable role to play in managing global economic interdependence. The rules-based system administered by the WTO gives even the smallest and poorest countries greater leverage and security than they would have outside the system. It is a system that replaces 'power' in international trade relations with the rule of 'law'. The thickening web of global institutions and accords of which the WTO is a part reflect the emergence of a new, but still fragile international order (see Panitchpakdi, 2002).

Another more recent example of a matter of legitimate public interest on which business leaders are expected to have points of view – and to artic-ulate their positions to a wide array of stakeholders – concerns corporate governance. The market economy depends on the twin pillars of efficient capital markets and good corporate governance, but as we have seen global capitalism needs to regain public trust. The collapse of Enron acted as a lens to sharpen the focus of what creates public trust in markets, namely transparency, accountability and integrity.

Transparency in this context is a requirement that corporations provide shareholders with information they need to make informed decisions. For a variety of reasons (and recent corporate collapses in the United States have provided examples), management and boards may have been reluctant to make information available that investors needed and wanted. Yet stakehold-ers – investors, auditors, analysts, media commentators, regulators, suppliers, employees – have become increasingly aware of the importance of transparency. They are unwilling to be left in the dark.

Besides transparency of information, there needs to be a commitment to accountability. Managements need to be accountable for using shareholders' money to make decisions that will create shareholder value; accountancy firms need to be accountable to the public and shareholders; and investment analysts need to be responsible for providing objective research that is free from conflicts of interest.

Transparency and accountability do not by themselves earn public trust. In the end both depend on people of integrity who 'do the right thing'. Embracing and demonstrating these three elements is key to building an environment of public trust – a message that should resonate with concerned CEOs and boards around the world.[4]

Second Challenge: Run with the Grain of the New Political and Regulatory Dynamic

The second challenge for multinational companies is to engage with government and non-government actors in a way that demonstrates an understanding of the new political and regulatory dynamics described above. A recent survey of over 1100 CEOs drawn from 33 countries showed that while 45 per cent of those polled thought that the anti-globalisation movement did not represent a genuine threat to doing business in years to come, 33 per cent did think so.[5] Against the background of increased international interdependency, the need for public policy engagement will involve formal as well as more informal actors. It will involve identifying the critical dependencies between regulators and trans-national networks (for example, in the context of securities and financial regulation, the International Organization of Securities Commissions (IOSCO), the Committee of European Securities' Regulators (CESR), and the Financial Action Task Force), sometimes operating in the shadow of global or supra-national public authorities. Such involvement may include contributing to the discussions of these networks and fora, helping them to set agendas, providing information about the operation of markets, framing issues for discussion, developing proposals and recommendations, crafting rules and implementing programmes.

Businesses may well also need to connect with more informal groups and networks that increasingly owe their existence and effectiveness to the Internet. As the world is moving towards the articulation of rules and principles rather than powerplay, towards persuasion rather than coercion, NGOs and other civil society groups will gain a greater share of voice in public policy development in areas such as trade policy. Business lobbies need to acknowledge the potential of these groups for shaping debate, and where appropriate they should engage with them. Involving these groups in public policy development and advocacy can help to frame issues and create momentum for change. In this connection it is important to avoid the common pitfall of making assumptions about what NGOs and other stake-holders may be saying; understanding and responding to one's critics are parts of the art of developing a public policy case. The European Union's trade commissioner, Pascal Lamy recognised this in his opening remarks to the WTO Ministerial Conference at Seattle:

> Of course life would be easier for some of us if they were not there. We could carry on in our usual way concocting lengthy texts in incomprehensible jargon among ourselves. I sometimes hear trade negotiators refer to the interest shown by the NGOs as an invasion. . . . At the same time they hope the locusts will go away and devour some other field. The fact is these rallies have a legitimate right to demonstrate and we should listen to them. We should discuss the issues with them.

There is much that multinational enterprises can learn from the World Bank's experience of constructive engagement with NGOs and civil society, which emphasises the importance of early involvement in project design and engagement with these groups on a country by country basis, as well as more extensive disclosure of corporate policy and information. Greater emphasis will be placed on establishing and maintaining regular, open dialogue on 'big picture' policy issues such as environmental performance, labour rights and business ethics, in preference to more informal, private conversations with selected audiences. As NGOs build their legitimacy in global governance, and (in the case of some organisations) address their critics' concerns about such matters as lack of transparency and accountability, reliability of research, disconnection from local communities and short-termism (campaign slogans do not build constituencies for change), NGOs will come to play a much more significant role in public affairs generally, and in advancing the ideals of sustainable development in particular. Multinationals that ignore them or downplay their contribution will do so at their peril (Edwards, 2000).

Third Challenge: Invest in Shaping the New Regulatory Environment in Which to Do Business

Leading businesses want to invest in the environment in which they aim to do business. They can do this in several ways. They can help to fashion the regulatory architecture that makes international trade possible and encourages business competitiveness. They can pioneer voluntary, corporate-led initiatives in the public interest and they can work for accords that tackle trans-national issues that elude national state solutions.

As an example of proactively developing regulation, a number of multi-nationals became concerned to help policy makers balance the benefits of the Internet and e-business against fears that global market places will undermine national standards and regulations. Cross-border transmission of ideas and know-how, the movement of capital and the interoperability of technology and communications solutions call for innovation and creativity in a fast-paced environment. While governments can and should set objectives, private innovation and initiative should be engaged to satisfy public demand in a cost-efficient and technologically effective way. Considerations such as these led a group of 20 cross-sector, European-based businesses, including a number from the high-tech sector, to come together (with the help of PricewaterhouseCoopers) to form the European e-business Tax Group. It might be thought surprising that these businesses should want to suspend their competitive instincts and collaborate with the European Commission to help design an indirect tax regime for the Internet. Conventional wisdom would suggest that the increasing disconnection between the space in which national governments can project their regulatory capacity and the spaces in which markets are growing and developing is a matter to be exploited. However these businesses recognised that it was better to be proactive and help inform the EU policy-making process at a very early stage of policy development, and to make some of their commercial experience available to officials, rather than have an imperfectly developed 'solution' imposed upon them. It was a challenging experience to recognise the need for interoperability of policy design for the EU tax treatment of e-business transactions while respecting the right of Member States to reach decisions about their own tax base, but the group gained the attention of policy makers – in the European Commission, the OECD and the revenue authorities of Member State administrations – by engaging in a series of dialogues with a broad range of stakeholders in ways that reflect the multilayered, interdependent nature of policy making operating across borders. A website, a series of position papers, regular meetings with officials, targeted media relations activity and regular information exchange among the group members face-to-face and electronically contributed to the group's success.

Regulation may be a blunt instrument. Legislation is often reactive, and is time-consuming to develop and amend. In a recent survey, 51 per cent of European CEOs cited over-regulation as a 'significant' or 'one of the biggest' threats to business.[6] A similar proportion of the total number of 992 participating CEOs considered that governments were 'out of touch with business needs'. A more systemic and holistic approach, one that recognises today's interdependent stakeholder society and the power of consumer activists, may be called for, as the following example demonstrates. In response to growing public concern about global warming and the contribution of the motor industry, a group of European automotive manufacturers offered a voluntary 'collective' agreement to the European Commission to reduce CO_2 emissions from new cars. After some hesitation, the Commission reached an agreement with the manufacturers. Reduction of emissions will happen earlier than would have been possible through EU legislation, unforeseen and possibly unintended consequences of rushed regulation have been avoided, and the threat of legislation being imposed if this approach does not work satisfactorily remains. A byproduct of this approach has been to improve competition between vehicle manufacturers in order to bring home the benefits of improved fuel consumption to consumers more quickly.[7]

Farsighted businesses may want to push for better quality regulation of markets than government actors operating on their own can provide. Critics of economic liberalisation often focus on deregulation and self-regulation as an attack on standards, but many of the world's best companies recognise that mere compliance with the national legal minimum or entering the lowest-cost race to the bottom does not always resonate positively with consumers. PricewaterhouseCoopers' *Millennium Poll* of 22,000 consumers around the world showed that a majority of citizens in 18 out of 21 countries believed that companies should go beyond the minimum legal definition of their role in society. The finding was particularly strong in North America and Australia, and weakest in Russia, Turkey and Kazakhstan. However national regulatory regimes by themselves, while establishing the *legal* bottom line for corporate social responsibility, cannot satisfy the new consumer activism that transcends traditional political and regulatory frameworks. Businesses may therefore want to support initiatives that in effect bypass the legal mechanisms of the state by creating frameworks based on shared understandings between a wide array of stakeholders. The OECD's Guidelines for Multinational Enterprises, for example, create an international code providing rules on such matters as corruption (don't engage in it), technology (transfer it) and taxation (pay what you owe). Another example is the UN's Global Compact, launched at the World Economic Forum July meeting in 2000, calling upon the world's largest businesses to sign up to core principles based on the Universal Declaration of Human Rights, the ILO's Fundamental Principles on Rights at Work and the Rio principles on the environment. Another is the Global Reporting Initiative, which aims to develop globally applicable guidelines for businesses to report on their economic, environmental and social performance.

These frameworks or codes are not regulatory instruments in the strict sense, but rather a value base to promote learning and provide an informed guide to corporate behaviour. They use the power of transparency and dialogue to identify and spread good practice. The principles they espouse can be internalised by businesses, as an integral part of their strategies and day-to-day operations. They are creating *de facto* non-statutory regulatory environments. Critics will say that these codes have no binding force on multinationals, but they represent attempts, based on considered and impartial evaluations of possible public policy solutions, to provide guidance on trans-national issues that national authorities are wrestling with and NGOs are unable to address. Their effectiveness depends on the power of public opinion and consumers, for in today's interdependent world corporate reputation is a critical element of business survival – and no amount of regulation will safeguard (or restore) reputation.[8]

Fourth Challenge: Organise to Optimise Outcomes

To address these challenges effectively, multinational firms need to organise themselves so that they are able at an early stage to identify changes in their external environments, to understand and interpret the effects of those changes on their business operations, and to respond appropriately.

A large number of organisational permutations can be envisaged but one thing is clear: a team of public affairs practitioners or external consultants dedicated to 'messaging' to stakeholders is unlikely to achieve desired outcomes. Rather, senior market-facing executives and service line leaders, who can speak with authority and credibility on behalf of the business, need to be organised and incentivised (perhaps as part of a statement of agreed business objectives) to give governments, regulators and third parties the same degree of attention that they would give to their key accounts and customers. A group of such participants, drawn from a business' major territories or regions and supported by public policy analysts and other functional experts, may meet from time to time to agree strategies, exchange views and develop positions. The group may be encouraged to agree global position statements – top-line views, perhaps indicating where global convergence on a public policy issue relevant to business is necessary or desirable – from which territory positions can be crafted to address local cultures, issues and concerns. The group may need to agree how to persuade stakeholders (within as well as outside the organisation) to be the firm's advocates, recognising that these stakeholders are operating in different national markets and regulatory regimes (which may overlap at supra-national level). In many cases these stakeholders (especially regulators) are operating increasingly in co-operation with one another across national boundaries – and in the case of grassroots campaigners, they will often be feeding off one another's messages and claims.

The group may wish to consider commissioning research by an independent source (such as a respected research foundation like the Brookings Institution or a think tank) to lend weight to its cause or to counter ill-informed or misleading comment by consumer activists. It may undertake polling or carry out focus group research to gauge the popular mood on an issue. It may organise interactive webcasts, bringing together speakers to debate an issue from different perspectives and to facilitate public engagement, in addition to placing op eds with quality print media.

In between meetings of the group, individual members will need to be encouraged to share by intranet and conference calls their intelligence of national policy developments as well as their insights, for this will be the lifeblood of the group's collective endeavour.

Turning a business' stakeholders into its advocates depends on having shared interests, which implies having a dialogue or at least creating the potential for one. A number of business lobby groups have helped to facilitate such a dialogue on trans-national issues. The Trans-Atlantic Business Dialogue (TABD), founded in 1995 with the backing of the Clinton Administration and the European Commission, is a good example of a 'public–private partnership' in trans-Atlantic public policy development whereby shared interests between policy makers and business leaders can be surfaced. There is nothing secretive about the TABD's agenda, which can be accessed at its website, together with its reports, recommendations and details of its activities. The European Roundtable of Industrialists has brought together the leaders of Europe's largest manufacturing companies and, through a series of influential reports, played an important part in informing policy development by the European Commission, not least on the Single Market. The European Services Forum (ESF), to take another example, has provided pan-European, cross-sectoral advice on services trade liberalisation to the European Commission, which acts on behalf of the EU Member States in international trade negotiations. The ESF provides a business perspective, on 'horizontal' rather than sectoral issues, which is informed by the views of its members (businesses and European federations), various civil society groups and NGOs with whom it is in regular contact on a range of issues such as principles of domestic regulation, trade and investment, trade facilitation, government procurement, e-commerce and the movement of people.

Through business lobby groups like these, and networking events like meetings of the World Economic Forum, multinational firms can provide valuable input to policy makers and those who influence them, in more or less structured ways. The effectiveness of these groups varies over time and according to the membership, and it is no doubt tempting for some of the participants to claim a degree of influence over public policy outcomes that overstates the case. However the rise of 'global civil society' and increasing focus on corporate social responsibility is compelling business leaders, especially those running multinational firms, to use their own resources as well as external platforms provided by business lobby groups to engage with the wide range of actors that now occupies the contested spaces in which political decisions and regulatory responses are made. Many business leaders have an important story to tell about the prosperity they create, the benefits of innovation, the transfer of technology and the development of people.

Conclusion

Globalisation of business has been accompanied by globalisation of activism. Failure to manage a key stakeholder relationship in one territory can undermine the trust and integrity of a multinational business around the world. Businesses that want to stay in business need to cultivate their stakeholders by listening to them, engaging with them, and demonstrating transparency, accountability and integrity. The battle of Seattle and subsequent manifestations of public discontent about globalisation showed that anti-capitalist opinions are strongly held by some and tacitly supported by many. They revealed weaknesses in the ability of national authorities to project their political authority and regulatory capacity over the territory in which multinational businesses and global markets increasingly operate. As part of the process of rebuilding public trust in business, the new corporate activism will show responsible business leaders actively engaged in a new dialogue with government and non-government actors. These business leaders will be helping to create regulatory environments that enable business to meet the rising expectations of shareholders, regulators, employees, NGOs and activist groups. They will be organising themselves to speak with all their stakeholders about the benefits that business can bring to help create a more prosperous and stable world for all.

Notes

This paper is based on a presentation to the DLA Lobbying in the Twenty-First Century Conference (see *Journal of Public Affairs* (2003), Vol. 3). The views expressed in this paper are those of the author alone.

1. *Voice of the People* survey by Gallup International, presented to the World Economic Forum, in January 2003, surveying the opinions of more than 36,000 people drawn from 47 countries. The survey was conducted between July and September 2002.
2. Very high ratings for armed forces occurred in states of heightened alert (including India, Israel, Pakistan and the United States).
3. See also the House of Lords Select Committee on Economic Affairs on *Globalisation* (Session 2002-03) HL 5–1, para. 162, acknowledging the concern that while some multinationals have the capacity to become 'footloose', in practice their mobility is constrained. The committee noted that once undertaken, FDI is locked in to national markets to a considerable extent which, in the opinion of George Soros who gave evidence to the committee, could make it a 'hostage to the government of [a] country': *ibid*, para.160.
4. See the remarks of Sam DiPiazza, Global CEO of PricewaterhouseCoopers, on 'Building Public Trust: The Future of Corporate Reporting', made to the National Press Club, Washington, D.C., on 17 June 2002.
5. *5th Annual Global CEO Survey* (2002), by PricewaterhouseCoopers in conjunction with the World Economic Forum.
6. *6th Global CEO Survey* (2003) by PricewaterhouseCoopers in conjunction with the World Economic Forum.
7. See Wolfgang Schneider in the European Business Forum Special Report on *Sustainable Development* (2003), pp. 12–13.
8. One of the main messages from PricewaterhouseCoopers' *6th Annual Global CEO Survey* (2003) is that CEOs consider corporate reputation to be the key driver of business' approach to sustainability; and an increasing proportion of those polled (79 per cent compared with 69 per cent in 2002) agreed that sustainability was vital to profitability.

CHAPTER 7

Cyberactivism and Corporations
New Strategies for New Media

Chris Thomas

Overview

Activists have a demonstrable advantage – in terms of skill and experience – in the effective use of online media as a tool for protest and dissent. This chapter outlines both the challenge that corporations face and some possible, practical solutions. It presents a view on the key trends driving increased use of the Web by activists, their impact on corporate communications, a typology of the ways in which the Web has been used by anti-corporate activists, and concrete advice on response.

Changing Media Landscape

The boom and subsequent burst of the dotcom bubble was the big business story of recent years. It would be wrong however to take this to mean that the relevance of the Internet for business is in decline. Beyond the hype, as a source of news, entertainment and information, and as a facilitator of new community groups, use of the Internet – particularly e-mail and newsgroups – continues to grow steadily. The Internet becomes an active tool for more people, of broader socio-demographic origin and in more countries – developed and developing – each year.

Clearly, it was to be expected that the rise of a completely new media would have a knock-on effect on the corporate communications landscape. This effect has been driven by three distinct trends:

- Democratisation of publishing rights: barriers to entry for those wishing to publish are now virtually non-existent. The drivers of success have also changed: the ability to innovate, to leverage technical know-how and media savvy are worth more than the established brands and logistical capabilities of old-media heavy-hitters.

- Polarisation of media opinion: as the barriers to entry for publication have lowered, the professional journalistic prerequisite of objectivity has been largely eliminated, other than in 'official' media sources.
- Globalisation: by hosting sites in international free-speech havens such as the United States, publication of material that in old media terms could have fallen foul of many nations' regulatory barriers – censorship or libel laws – is almost impossible to stop.

News stories are increasingly broken locally by small, independent publishers, and spread among community groups by e-mail or the Web. Reaction online to the destruction of the World Trade Center is a case in point: online news media could not cope with the numbers of people seeking to use them for updates, and generally resorted to restricting access: a frustrating situation for their audience. Similarly, despite allocating round-the-clock coverage and the best efforts of on-the-scene journalists, most broadcast news channels struggled to identify and break developments in the story in a timely fashion. In contrast, community interest/discussion groups such as Metafilter – the membership of which included local residents, workers and 'experts' on relevant issues – were a hive of activity, bringing eye-witness accounts of developments and filtering the members' finds in other news sources into an informative, quickly updated and accessible thread.[1] This deftly illustrates two key characteristics of the Web: that it facilitates the filtering and viral spread of information; and that online community groups have become perfectly capable of stepping into the breach in the face of a breakdown of traditional information sources.

At the same time as alternative and community-based models for breaking news have been in the ascendant, decades-long accusations of bias levelled at the mass media – justified or not – have taken their toll on its credibility. There is declining confidence in the integrity and accuracy of traditional media, and increasingly audiences find trust in the judgement of online community peers to be a good substitute for institutional credibility.[2]

The implications are clear: the influence of mass media – the established vehicle for corporate communications – is becoming diluted by the proliferation of alternative media sources. The mass media's nature and behaviour is well-understood by corporations, who are practiced at mobilising a combination of superior resources and the well-regulated nature of traditional publishing in order to ensure that their point of view is widely heard. Rising acceptance and use of alternative media channels online has forced companies out of their complacency. They can no longer rely on dominance of communication channels, and must be prepared for a level of public scrutiny and discussion of their methods, motives and messages by stakeholders to which they are thus far unaccustomed.

Increased CSR Activity is Driven by the Internet

Pre-Internet, the resource advantage held by businesses strongly supported their communication activities, giving them an enhanced ability to make their opinions heard. While this is still true online, the line has blurred somewhat as barriers to communication have reduced: there is a much greater opportunity now for stakeholders to hear alternative views from independently published media. The online savvy of NGOs and campaign groups has, to an extent, been forced upon them. At a clear disadvantage when communicating through traditional media, they had to make the best of the opportunities available to them, and were quick to seize on the potential of the Internet, long before corporations had come to terms with a change in the old order. This is a crucial advantage, and one that NGOs have successfully leveraged in a number of cases, for example McSpotlight.[3]

At the same time, the development of the Web has coincided with an age in which corporations' motives are treated with more and more suspicion. Numerous examples illustrate the breakdown of trust between corporations and consumers: animal testing, Thalidomide and the *Exxon Valdez* are just a few. A clear credibility gap has developed between corporate messages and public perceptions. There is a frequently held assumption that the Web hosts an 'anti-corporate culture'. But the Internet does not, in itself, change people's beliefs or values: it is the people themselves who hold those beliefs, and the Internet that enables their free expression.

So what are the implications for corporations? If anything, the Web has increased the importance of effective corporate communications. In the old order, companies relied on a strategy of 'command and control', only communicating when there were problems, and resorting to litigation in the face of dissent. The experiences of corporations such as eToys (examined later in this chapter) suggest that companies must rethink their approach to corporate communications. They should have a light touch, avoiding litigation and actions that could be perceived as 'corporate bullying'. They must be open to alternative points of view, and ready to enter a dialogue in order to make their points: engaging with their critics is key. Companies that do not react to this new imperative risk fatal long-term reputational decline.

A key point is that CSR is not simply about altruism: the concurrent rise of socially responsible investment products and initiatives and the increasing capacity of consumers to educate themselves about the ethical impacts of their purchasing decisions can be attributed to the

Internet. Both trends can have a direct effect on the financial health of a corporation (in the former case by limiting its potential financial backers, in the latter by limiting its potential customers). CSR is a prudent adaptation to changing circumstances: countering the increased ability of stakeholders to scrutinise corporate activities and motives with openness and complementary action.

Online Activism

Activists have had a head-start over corporations in terms of using the Web, and many groups have developed an impressive command of the medium. Supported by the three principles of democratisation, polarisation and globalisation, the Web in many ways is a tailor-made solution to activist needs. It has provided a cheap and accessible platform from which to share information and experience, argue compelling but relatively unknown principles, coordinate with like-minded people, and attack the methods and messages of their corporate opponents.

It is worth remembering that activism isn't only anti-corporate. In fact, although there is clearly a grey area between the two, political activism is probably more common. Nevertheless, the ways in which the Web has tended to be used as a tool to further activist objectives are fairly similar, whether corporate or political in nature. Here we present a typology of online activism tactics, and some suggestions on how online threat can be turned to competitive advantage.

Electronic Attack

Sometimes known as hacktivism or cyberterrorism (largely depending on whether or not one approves, it seems), a bewildering array of tactics and methods are available for activists to attack corporations. Legally, many of the forms of attack fall within grey areas: generally untested in court, or subject in some countries to laws for which there are not always international equivalents. To date, there has been a tremendous amount of attention paid to the risk of electronic attack: an acknowledgement of corporate vulnerability to hacktivists with better technical skills.

Disruptive tactics such as the denial-of-service attack – an attempt to make websites inaccessible by bombarding them with requests for information, using specially designed software to automate the process – are the most common tool for activists. Starbucks and the World Trade Organisation (WTO) are among the organisations to have suffered from this attention-grabbing and disruptive tactic.[4] The legal situation relating to denial-of-service attacks is unclear: theoretically it is illegal in the United States to maliciously take down a website, but hacktivists argue that denial-of-service attacks do not qualify under this law. While threats of prosecution have been made from time to time, none has been followed up in court, so the waters remain untested. Irrespective of the legal situation, legal action is generally only a hypothetical solution, as attacks tend to be coordinated anonymously.

A step more serious, unauthorised access to and use of corporate mail services is potentially hugely damaging, and – more to the point – facilitates direct communication with two of an organisation's most crucial stakeholder groups: customers and employees. In the US case of Intel v Hamidi, the chip manufacturer sued an ex-employee for accessing the company mail server in order to send e-mail to former colleagues.[5] The mail leaked news of layoffs and made derogatory comments about management. Samsung was the victim of a similar sting: one of the earliest (and largest) such attacks.[6] The culprit was never located, but seems likely to have been a disgruntled customer, who first sent apparent spam e-mail, and then legal threats purporting to come from Samsung and its representatives. The recipients were outraged: Samsung received up to 10,000 complaining e-mails a day at peak, and estimates that the episode cost it millions of dollars.

It might be expected that a high-profile hack of a company's web presence would be their largest fear. However, hacks are a fairly blunt instrument. Short of the obvious (but short-term) disruption caused by restricting commercial traffic to their website, the tactic does little more than raise awareness of the hackers' cause: an end that can be reached by alternative means. Similarly, activists with a social or political agenda tend to work within at least the letter (if not the spirit of the law), as otherwise they risk loss of sympathy for their own cause. Consequently, purely cause-motivated hacks of corporate sites are rare.

Subversion is a potentially more damaging approach: creating the opportunity to confuse stakeholders by, for example, making them believe parody sites are authentic. For example, the RTMark collective's parody of the WTO/GATT site resulted in it receiving a misdirected invitation to send a speaker to the Conference on International Services in Salzburg, Austria – the heavy-handed satire of the site content clearly having passed entirely over the conference organisers' heads.[7] The resulting speech was, predictably, a farce: it included a succession of pointedly derogative, racist or politically objectionable remarks, presented as a 'plain-speaking' explanation of actual WTO policy. As expected, a triumphant stunt of this magnitude was a magnet for media coverage and interest among online audiences.

The most ambitious hacktivism project is also the best known, involving a clash between online toy retailer eToys.com, and the coincidentally named European art collective Etoy. When a US court ruled in favour of a corporate claim of brand confusion, and stripped the etoy.com domain name from its artist owners (who had operated the domain for two years before eToys.com had registered theirs), there was outrage among online communities. Their resulting campaign was ruthless: the so-called 'Toywar' aimed to damage the retailer financially as much as possible.[8] Toywar exploited the busy pre-Christmas period, encouraging and soliciting e-mailed complaints to eToys' management, and launching denial-of-service attacks tailored to exploit vulnerabilities provided by the sites' e-commerce mechanisms.[9] The *coup de grâce* came from the participation of activists posing as investors in discussion forums, well-armed with financial facts and figures and a remit to talk down the prospects for eToys as much as possible. The company's opponents note that the campaign coincided with a drop in the share price of eToys from \$67 to \$15 over the course of two months, the point at which eToys eventually capitulated: it dropped the case and returned the domain. The Toywar campaign was an unqualified success for hacktivism.

THE CORPORATE RESPONSE TO ELECTRONIC ATTACK

It is worth reiterating that electronic attacks are not always motivated by traditional ethical or social causes. Disgruntled customers increasingly have the technical nous to make their feelings known in this way, and organised groups of hackers have gone on record to describe the poor standards of IT security at many firms as either an affront or a challenge, responding accordingly.[10] All corporations should then consider such attacks a threat. While morally speaking there is little question that most activities covered here are 'attacks', the law currently offers little protection to victims. Attempted legal action has tended to be based on a convoluted use of principles established for other purposes. For example, in the Intel v Hamidi case mentioned earlier, Intel was unable to sue for actual trespass, eventually suing on the basis of 'trespass to chattels': a principle of law that predates the Internet by several hundred years.

Options for combating such tactics are straightforward, but somewhat limited in scope. The first and most obvious thing that companies can do is to tighten up on their security. The Information Security Breaches Survey 2002, managed by PWC on behalf of the UK Department of Trade and Industry, notes that while information security is an acknowledged priority at board level, concrete action is very limited: only 27 per cent of companies in its survey have any sort of policy on information security, which it identifies as 'the most basic discipline' of all.[11] A similar number of companies – slightly over a quarter – carry out background checks on employees, the group identified by the report as the single weakest link in the security chain. Finally, it argues that there is widespread under-investment: a recommended level of 3–5 per cent of IT budget spent on information security (rising to 10 per cent in high risk industries, such as financial services) is compared against its survey, which shows that only a quarter of firms spend more than 1 per cent.

However, better security will not defuse all electronic attacks. Those exploiting infrastructural vulnerabilities (such as denial-of-service attacks) or inevitable skill gaps between hackers and corporate IT staff will in all likelihood continue to be a threat, however effective a company's security is. Similarly, it is fair to say that such approaches are unlikely to be widely employed by mainstream or 'respectable' activist groups; consequently their negative effects are likely to be limited. Contingency planning is the only real solution to these attacks, particularly the design of mechanisms that can reduce the financial hit taken by e-commerce downtime. This could be done by, for example, preparing a mirror of the site on an alternative domain.

Finally, the more extreme or subversive tactics are of most concern, particularly those that involve participation in investor discussion boards or unauthorised use of e-mail facilities. All reach critical customer, investor and employee stakeholder groups, and present a substantial threat, both in bottom-line terms (as with Samsung and eToys) or, perhaps more critically, in terms of reputation loss. For companies at risk of such attack – particularly those involved in traditionally threatened business areas such as lifesciences or biotechnology – there are no quick fixes. Monitoring and enhanced security are valuable for the management and reduction of risk and potential impact, but ultimate solutions are all focused around long-term efforts to alter the environment in which such attacks occur: governmental lobbying for better legislative protection, active engagement with the grievances of critics or attempts to argue against the substance or integrity of issues and activists.

Organise for Direct Action

Although publishing activities command the bulk of interest (and indeed activity) online, the Internet was designed first and foremost to facilitate two-way communication. It is wholly unsurprising that some of the most interesting developments in the Web have been towards the creation of new ways of communicating and interacting, for individuals as well as community groups. Offline, means of building communities have tended to focus on affinities: finding like-minded groups of people through activities of mutual interest. The onset of the Internet – both as a medium for the publication of news, manifestos and opinions, and as a tool for building community groups – follows essentially the same offline paradigm, but with a couple of key differences.

A significant difference has been the ability of activist groups with disparate focuses and geographical locations, but shared opponents – corporate or governmental – to coordinate their activities via the Web, acting globally and in concert with each other. For the typical protestor, the objective is not disruption or destruction, but publicity: a mass-media platform for the activists' message, facilitated by anticipated news interest in the strength and commitment of their support. In recent years, the objectivity of mainstream media sources has been called into question, with accusations that they tend to deliberately underplay the level of support for anti-corporate or capitalist protests, or fail to report on protests at all. Concerted, globally coordinated action, such as the WTO protests of recent years, is most usually an attempt to force wider publicity by the sheer scale of participation.

Publicity is not always the objective of direct action. More extreme groups have had limited success using the Web to organise for different, more direct goals. For example, SHAC (Stop Huntingdon Animal Cruelty) was set up in 1999 with a single purpose: to shut down Huntingdon Life Sciences, Europe's biggest contract animal research centre. Its tactics are simple but effective: to target all of Huntingdon Life Sciences' key stakeholders – employees, suppliers, management, customers and investors – through direct protest and action. SHAC's campaign of persistent direct action and protest has been a qualified success, made possible by a grassroots network of websites and a mailing list that boasts more than 12,000 members. The success is qualified as HLS is still in business. However it has had an extremely close shave: since 2000 SHAC has 'persuaded' a large number of Huntingdon Life Sciences' investors to divest their holdings, and its banker – Royal Bank of Scotland – to cancel its overdraft facility. HLS was prepared to file for bankruptcy in the early part of 2001, until US financier Stephens Inc. stepped in to provide eleventh-hour funding.

Corporate Response to Organisation of Protests Online

Confrontational and aggressive protests are a traumatic prospect for any corporation, not least because they can be extremely difficult to counter. However, web-coordinated action has vulnerabilities as well as strengths, and these can be exploited by companies. The main weakness derives from the intrinsically public and hence insecure nature of the medium. The implication is that, unless the activists achieve an extremely high level of security through close vetting of participants and use of sophisticated, secure communication channels, it is possible for companies to make themselves as aware of proposed direct action as the activists themselves, and act appropriately. The typical online activist group does not have these sorts of levels of security (although there are exceptions, such as the notorious Wombles).[12] Newsletters are generally open to subscription with little or no vetting, and websites are generally publicly accessible.

Monitoring is a useful tool that corporations can use to keep up on threats of direct action. There is an established group of companies in Europe and the United States, expert in the Web and practised at locating threatening or otherwise relevant content from websites and mailing lists, ensuring that clients can act to engage with activists, or – if direct action is inevitable – attempt damage limitation.

The online savvy of activists has already been noted, and as they have become more aware of corporate monitoring of their channels of communication, they have increasingly tended to use more secure channels. This would include the use of vetted mailing lists, password-protected websites for organisation or dissemination of information, and even reversion to traditional, offline methods. As a result, to a certain extent the value of monitoring as a tool for early identification of direct action is declining. The silver lining of that, however, is that activist abstinence from mainstream web channels means that it is harder for them to inform and mobilise high numbers of protestors to the same extent as before, and tends to limit their numbers to existing and active protesters, rather than 'passing trade'. Monitoring is still a valuable activity, but it is less useful as an aggressive, counter-activist tactic: supporting pre-emption or legal challenges to protest. Rather, with an increasing focus on CSR, the emphasis is on threatened companies fully understanding the nature and likely manifestation of their stakeholders' grievances. Monitoring continues to form an important part of this continual process of planning, assessment and response.

The current business environment puts a heavy obligation on corporations to value and protect their reputations. In view of this, generally speaking, a much softer approach should be taken towards online activism than has been seen at points in the past. Companies should steer clear of tactics involving the use of legal threats as a scare tactic, entrapment, misrepresentation of identity or motive or deliberate disruption of activity or infrastructure, irrespective of their strict adherence to the letter of the law. This advice is driven by ethical considerations, but the practicalities carry equal weight: the potential reputational damage to companies found perpetrating 'dirty tricks' (including McDonald's among others), or taking actions that facilitate their portrayal as 'corporate bullies' is serious indeed.[13]

Globalisation of Local Campaigns

The last quarter of the twentieth century taught us that globalisation is not only a matter of changing business practice. General public interest in campaigns such as Live Aid and watershed events such as Tiananman Square show that notions of justice, human rights and poverty are applied globally. The increase in availability of a broader range of media, particularly alternative viewpoints or those from other countries, can be seen as both a cause and manifestation of this interest. The globalisation of local campaigns has created a new quandary for global corporations, who must fear a 'lowest common denominator effect': a tendency, if they apply different standards of behaviour or performance in different global markets, to be judged on their worst attributes.

To corporations, this globalisation of local campaigns means an increased ability for activists to scrutinise corporate activities globally, and widely publicise those that most significantly support their arguments. As noted, human or animal rights and the environment are the most typical drivers of issue globalisation. An example at one end of the scale is the mobilisation of global opinion to lobby the South Korean Government for increased regulation of the traditional dog meat trade, leveraged through attempts to organise boycotts of Korean companies such as Samsung or Daewoo, or to exploit opportunities presented by sporting events such as the 2002 soccer World Cup. At the other end of the scale are protests against engineering or infrastructural projects in the developing world, perceived to treat either the local population or environment with less consideration than they would receive in Western, developed countries.

A recent example of the latter concerns BP, which is involved in the construction of an oil pipeline in Central Asia. While antipathy towards the construction is probably partly driven by geopolitical concerns about the energy interests of Western countries in Asia and the Middle East, the substance of activists' arguments relates to a perceived tendency in the region for governments and corporations to collude to abuse the rights of local communities affected by proposed development work. The pipeline campaign against BP is at an early stage, although momentum is clearly building. In early December 2002, an NGO called Rising Tide launched a concerted action: occupying the London offices of ERM – the environmental impact consultancy retained by BP – posting photographs and an account of the action on various online independent media sites, and setting up an issue-driven microsite (http://www.erm-concerns.com) to put its case to the public. The protest follows the model seen for previous, similar issues such as the development of the Ilisu dam in Turkey. This issue offers a clear potential to focus public scrutiny in core markets on BP's actions in the region. More importantly, it creates a strong possibility of reputational damage should that scrutiny suggest that BP's behaviour does not meet the standards that its customers, employees and investors expect.

Global publicising of local issues has tended to be carried out through well-established channels, particularly online. The main forums have tended to be cyberactivist communities (discussed elsewhere in this chapter), often set up through established NGOs such as Greenpeace and operated through discussion boards, groups or mailing lists.[14] By organising in this way, activists have been able to make a show of strength: protesting collectively in the most valuable developed markets, in a concerted and coordinated fashion. A key example of this is the StopEsso campaign, which has shown the benefits of organising globally in the face of an opponent prepared to resort to litigation to protect its reputation.[15]

Subversive humour is another common theme in globalised issue activism. Participants have demonstrated their superlative online savvy: on the one hand turning the high public recognition and innovative e-commerce mechanisms of global brands against them, while simultaneously exploiting the mimetic culture of the Web: a tendency for content, comments or web links to be quickly spread among friends and colleagues by e-mail. A good example of this related to Nike, who had launched an innovative online product: trainers that could be custom-stitched with words or phrases of the purchaser's choice. It wasn't long before a customer, Jonah Peretti, requested a pair with 'sweatshop' stitched on them. As the widely published e-mail correspondence shows, Nike's response was humourless and defensive, refusing the order.[16] From an activist perspective, the exchange was a textbook stunt: clearly encapsulating the activists' issue, having a black and white hero and villain, a high interest factor (mainly via *schadenfreude*) for the global mass media, and a suitable, textual format for spreading via e-mail.

While developing world issues tend to capture the attention, but often have variable or uncertain significance for corporate reputation, there are many examples of potentially very damaging issues – often environmental – taking place in key stakeholders' own backyards. One such issue affected Shell in Norco, Louisiana, where a national campaign (culminating in a very negative TV documentary on the subject) was launched concerning the environmental and social implications of their activities in the town. Their response – outlined shortly – was interesting and effective.

CORPORATE RESPONSE TO GLOBALISATION OF LOCAL CAMPAIGNS

The fundamental weapon that activists have here is transparency. They aim to place increased scrutiny on corporate activity, contrasting it with the way in which corporations conduct their affairs in the West. In view of this the main corporate focus should be on ensuring that, given increased transparency, their activities will not reflect badly. Once again, the best solution would be an effective CSR strategy.

Of course, it is rare for activists to publicise causes without their own spin. Given this, it is important that corporations make themselves aware of activists' stance, monitoring and tracking grassroots protests at early stages and ensuring that they have an opportunity to put their own point of view across. This will allow them to address inaccuracies quickly, or argue debatable points. There are several ways to communicate rebuttals and counter-points, most obviously during the general process of publishing corporate social responsibility reports. Similarly, mass media or online communications activities should be deployed to put their case. Companies that have been historically vulnerable to these types of activities have demonstrated a high level of innovation in their responses. For example, in the case of Norco, Shell subverted a typical activist tactic – creation of an issue-specific microsite – in order to present an array of hard fact, opinion and argument in defence of their position.[17]

More aggressive tactics have, occasionally, been used. There have been several recent examples of attempts to turn the difficulty that audiences can have in discerning the credibility and objectivity of online sources against activists. This is typically manifest in the creation of purportedly 'independent' microsites aimed at questioning the moral authority of activist groups. For example, www.activistcash.com was established with a mission to 'root out the funding sources of the most notorious anti-consumer groups'. However, such sites are rarely successful. In order to gain the necessary level of credibility, they inevitably carry a misleading impression of independent motive and funding. These claims are generally quite easy to expose, and the resulting discovery presents a reputational threat to the sites' corporate backers, as well as a greatly reduced impact for the site content.[18] In view of this, the best that can be hoped for from such projects is 'preaching to the converted': reinforcing the message to those that are already hostile to activist groups.

NGO Campaigning

The viral nature of web communication has engendered new ways for activists to educate and leverage protest among grassroots. Online petitions, such as those hosted at thepetitionsite.com are an obvious example. Of more significance, though, are e-mail petitions. Typically, such petitions ask for those in agreement to add their names to the bottom of a list, and forward the mail to all of their friends, family and colleagues. The power of such communications – combining an 'oven-ready' sentiment, the increased credibility that comes from a friend's endorsement and the ability to reach audiences that are generally politically inactive – should not be underestimated. Of course, usually the main objective of activists is to engineer change in corporate policy, but gathering grassroots support by education and politicisation of inactive stakeholder groups, such as potential customers and employees, is an important tool to progress this goal.

As noted, web-savvy activist groups have been quick to grasp and exploit the potential of the medium. Tools to facilitate activism are commonly available and widely used. In many ways, Internet-based tools are extensions of techniques used for earlier forms of electronic communication: fax-protests, an extension of fax-back marketing methods, were common in the 1990s for example. The Internet equivalents – pre-written protests over corporate policy, e-mailed to CEOs and politicians – are ubiquitous, and have proved a handy solution to the inertia that has proven such a barrier to transforming sentiment into action.

The benchmark for cyberactivism has been set by Greenpeace, whose Cyberactivist community network is widely and effectively used.[19] A detailed site review in *Reputation Impact* outlines the features: bulletin boards, interactive chats and downloads of tools and supporting material for use in campaigning such as banners that can be downloaded and used, and pre-written e-mails of protest.[20] The site provides content and news in a number of languages, and encourages the formation of 'Action Groups' designed to encourage people to coordinate mini-campaigns at national or community levels. Greenpeace claims that over 1000 new cyberactivists are joining each month, and emphasises two key principles: elimination of the natural restrictions posed by geographical boundaries and empowerment of the micro-communities of activists. There are important repercussions for international businesses: news stories, rumours or new campaign initiatives can quickly escalate into an international movement.

The advantage of a global spread of support for protest is not merely an increased activist head count. Activists are able to exploit the unregulated gap between the global location of online host and online viewer to sidestep legal action. In July 2002 Greenpeace France was successfully challenged in court by ExxonMobil for trademark infringement: the offending item was a parody of the Esso logo.[21] The campaign's response was to set up a French language StopEsso campaign site in Texas – home state of ExxonMobil.[22] The new site is, of course, protected under the First Amendment to the US Constitution. The episode has had a clearly damaging outcome for ExxonMobil: the site still exists (with a higher profile than before), the issue has been widely publicised in mass and alternative media, and the corporation has opened itself to accusations of corporate bullying, a charge mercilessly and continuously exploited on the StopEsso campaign site.

CORPORATE RESPONSE TO ONLINE NGO CAMPAIGNING

The key to effective response is, as with so many other areas of activism, full use of the potential of the Internet as an online communications channel. While the principles of communication remain similar, whether on or offline, the medium itself differs greatly from the perspective of both publishers and audiences. In consideration of this, best-practice advice should be sought from parties experienced in communicating online who understand the potential contributions of specific tools and approaches.

The first and most obvious step is to have a website that engages with the questions and issues arising from NGO campaigning. Most typically, this means a commitment to online CSR reporting. Web publication must be handled sensitively however. Simply placing a soft-copy document on the site with no mechanism for feedback has two disadvantages: it doesn't use the medium to its full potential and it leaves corporations open to accusations of treating CSR as a publicity exercise.

The Web has great potential for online publishing. In practical terms, it opens two fundamental possibilities: first, the potential to personalise the end-user experience, and second, the ability to directly engage with stakeholders. In terms of the former, presentation of online content in a tailored, non-linear format is strongly recommended. By structuring a report in this way, the needs of those wanting a simple overview of the corporate stance can be catered for alongside the needs of those that would like to examine data and attributions exhaustively. Similarly, by creating versions or 'paths' suitable for different types of stakeholder, the user experience can be effectively personalised. This is particularly relevant when considering groups at either end of a scale of needs. For example, CSR would typically be communicated to employees with a particular corporate citizenship angle or emphasis, while global NGOs would more likely be concerned with absolutes: concrete actions or achievements compared to objectives or expectations.

Taking this principle further, the key dynamic of the Web as a forum for peer-to-peer discussion is as another area in which an effective response can be made. Shell is perceived as one of the first companies to have absorbed this lesson, hosting the Tell Shell forums on its site: an unmoderated place for stakeholders to ask questions, seek information and express their grievances with the company, and for Shell to respond. This has been broadly perceived as a success, and clearly circumvents the traditional accusation that large corporations do not listen to their critics. There are obvious fringe benefits: allowing Shell a good insight into the attitudes and issues that shape its reputation and relationships.

The same type of dynamic can be extended in a more practical sense: the recruitment of 'ambassadors'. This entails convincing influential individuals of the corporate argument, and working with them to disseminate and argue the case online. Such individuals should have a high degree of credibility, be active in online discussion and debate and of course ultimately, once convinced, be sympathetic to the corporate point of view. There is an increasing recognition of the value of these types of programmes, leading to the creation of ambassador identification concepts such as Burson-Marstellar's 'e-fluentials'.[23]

Finally, advertising is another possibility. The Internet offers a good potential to closely target relevant demographics, and there is clear precedent – BASF and Ford among others – for companies to buy advertising space on relevant activist sites or discussion forums in order to highlight their policies or activities in specific areas of concern.

Gripe Sites and Corporate Subversion

Activism essentially entails an attempt to change the behaviour of another party through the application of concerted pressure. While high-profile campaigns tend to be focused on manipulating or leveraging the power of consumers or other large stakeholder groups (such as voters) in order to force policy changes, consumer or employee gripe-based activism has been known to treat reputational damage as an end in itself. So-called gripe sites, set up to publicise individual (and often trivial) complaints, or channel negative feedback from disgruntled consumers or employees, have proven themselves to be an embarrassing and highly effective thorn in the side of a huge range of corporations including, via the Sucks500 site, the entire Fortune 500.[24]

Electrolux has its notorious 'Nothing Sucks Like Electrolux' campaign of the late 1960s to thank for being spared from similar treatment to AOL, Chase Manhattan Bank and other victims of the Web's tendency to amplify complaints, manifest in '…sucks.com' domain names. As well as being an embarrassingly public forum for trivial customer or employee complaints, there is a more serious side to gripe sites, which are an established tool for serious, issue-led activism. The most famous example of this is McSpotlight. Initially set up to publicise the libel trial brought by McDonald's in the United Kingdom against members of London Greenpeace (an activist group unrelated to Greenpeace International), the site is still in existence today as a focal point for criticism of McDonald's and multinationals in general. It documents the lengthy and gruelling trial from the activists' perspective, including full details of the ethically dubious methods used by McDonald's to gather evidence. The trial focused attention on the site, and the site was to focus attention on the claims of the activists. The episode has been hugely damaging for McDonald's, as Eveline Lubbers notes in her book *Battling Big Business*: 'In the courtroom the defendants found a new stage on which to criticise McDonald's in a more detailed way than they ever could have dreamed of' (Lubbers, 2002, p 97). McDonald's isn't the only victim of cause-driven parodies of corporate sites: People for the Ethical Treatment of Animals (PETA) has also used the tactic to great success with its Murder King campaign, and other groups have exploited the potential of registering misspelled corporate domain names, using the forum to publicise damaging content, aimed at accidental visitors.[25]

CORPORATE RESPONSE TO GRIPE SITES

What can be done to combat the threats that these sites pose? In many cases very little, short of direct engagement with complainants. Gripe sites set up by individual consumers are generally protected by the First Amendment in the United States, so unless the site falls into an obvious trap – publishing clearly libellous content, engaging in commercial activity or contravening local copyright or trademark law – pursuing the case through the courts is usually not an option. Companies set on taking the legal route could try to apply cyber-squatting laws, which have proved to be effective under particular circumstances. However, the experience of eToys is a powerful argument against this approach. Recourse to the courts could also be at least a practical option in other cases, although raising the stakes by actual or threatened litigation is a high-risk strategy. It has doubtless proved a successful scare tactic before, and likely will again, but the potential portrayal of the company as a corporate bully, or the possibility that action could be a catalyst for the involvement of other parties (such as free-speech activists) poses a distinct threat.

Corporations are able to limit their reputational liability to gripe sites by applying a thorough planning process to domain registration. They should take care to register all likely permutations and easy misspellings of their corporate and product brands, as well as sites appending or prefixing their brands with common derogatory descriptors (e.g. 'sucks'). This seems an obvious point to make, but in some cases the organisational responsibility for tackling this issue is unclear, and high-profile companies continue to fall victim from time to time. Shell and PricewaterhouseCoopers have learnt this to their cost: in Shell's case the name of the stakeholder discussion forums hosted on its corporate site – Tell Shell – was registered as a domain in its own right (styled 'Tells Hell') by activists.[26] The site now hosts a broadly anti-corporate web log and discussion board. PWC on the other hand was embarrassed by failing to register all permutations of the 'introducingmonday' domain, through which it planned to launch the new brand for its consulting arm. It lost the .co.uk domain to cyber-pranksters, who host a 'we've got your name' joke site at the domain.[27] Obviously registration planning is a preventative: often, short of recourse to cyber-squatting law (for which there is some successful precedent), there is little that can be done once a domain name registration has been made or a site is in existence.

A final option, under the right circumstances, is the subversion or adoption of gripe sites. Companies have been successful in the past in exploiting a sometimes shaky attachment between site operators and their causes. This is most obviously applicable to consumer activism; for example Dunkin' Donuts bought the domain of its main gripe site operator, and subsumed it – initially including the facility to post messages – into its main corporate site. A little less obviously, NTL bought the 'NTHell' gripe/discussion site, leading to speculation as to what it intended to do with it. As it stands, the answer is very little: the site is still in operation. Under the right conditions though, companies have been successful in turning this technique to cause-related gripes: the Tell Shell forums are a good example. The idea is clearly to act as a surrogate for unofficial gripe sites – hopefully focusing criticism in a single location and ensuring that corporations are both aware of it, and able at least to attempt to engage with it. This tactic should certainly be considered, although corporations should be aware that it could be counterproductive if implemented without a corresponding commitment to listening to and engaging with critics.

Strategies for Response

This chapter has outlined the context and tactics of online activism, as well as possible corporate responses. Here in summary is an outline of the tools and tactics available to businesses.

Recommended

It cannot be stressed strongly enough that prevention is better than a cure: McKinsey make a sound case for the serious adoption of CSR as a driver of improved corporate reputation. Reputation is much more than a reflection of like or dislike. It can have numerous concrete implications for business, and open many doors: softer stakeholder behaviours are increasingly recognised as valuable. Typically speaking, such behaviours relate to permissions, or the tendency of stakeholders to give the benefit of the doubt in contentious situations. Such behaviours facilitate numerous commercial benefits; one example offered by McKinsey is the necessary consumer and governmental 'consent' to enter sensitive new markets, such as private pension provision or healthcare in the developing world.[28] I have made my case for a new approach to corporate communications already, but here is an outline of some concrete ways in which this new approach could be implemented.

- *Being in the debate is crucial:* new-media directories, communities and other information resources must be identified, and the corporate perspective represented within them.
- *It is important to develop web-savvy:* clear lessons can be learnt from companies such as Shell, for the use of their website for stakeholder dialogue, or BT for the user-interface created for their online CSR reporting.
- *Corporations should give more in their communications:* they must be prepared to adopt and communicate a stance on issues of mutual relevance to themselves and stakeholder groups, and ensure that they can demonstrate action as well as rhetoric.
- Leaving behind the static, low-function corporate homepages of the past, their resources should be used to *develop information-rich web presences*, contributing to the vast educational potential of the Internet.
- A new approach to *identifying and targeting audiences* is vital: communicating effectively towards discussion groups, communities and alternative media sources should be as much a priority as communicating to traditional media contacts.
- The peer-to-peer nature of web communications creates an opportunity for corporations to bridge the current credibility gap with stakeholders by *developing ambassador programmes:* credible online opinion-leaders that can be counted on to contribute broadly and accurately to discussions.
- *Monitoring the web* should be a core part of corporate communications practice, it is an approach that can support an engagement strategy, identify relevant threats, audiences or ambassadors, and contribute to strategic market research. Various web research companies and approaches are available but in a fundamental sense monitoring the Internet is quite different from monitoring offline media. Due to the vast range of online content, compared to the relatively limited scope of broadcast and print media, an increased human involvement is essential to identify and contextualise truly relevant

Types of activism \\ Tools for Response	Monitoring	Ensure point of view is represented in debates	Expertise in online communications	Adopt and communicate stance	Information-rich website	Identify and target audiences	Ambassador programmes
Electronic attack	□						
Organise for direct action	*		□	□			
Globalisation of local campaigns	*	□	*	*	□	*	□
NGO campaigning	*	□	*	*	□	*	*
Gripe-sites	*	□	□	□	□	*	

Figure 7.1 Recommendations for corporate response

□ = useful mechanism for response
*   = key mechanism for response

material. Web monitoring in some form is ubiquitous in all of the response strategies outlined in this chapter.

Not Recommended

I believe that the increased scrutiny that corporations should expect renders many 'hardball' communications tactics obsolete. The main example is the use of litigation as a counter-activist strategy, certainly if it is used as a scare tactic and in many circumstances when legitimately applied (of course, litigation continues to be a wholly appropriate tactic for addressing significant intellectual property infringements). Companies should think long and hard before resorting to the courts: as the example of eToys shows, even when they win, they can still lose. The disadvantage of long-term damage to corporate reputation should be considered alongside the benefit of potentially eliminating short-term nuisances when considering legal action.

Similarly, use of 'dirty tricks' is less acceptable than ever before. Pre-web, perpetrators could have a reasonable expectation that, even if caught 'spying' or 'agitating', the resulting bad publicity would be fairly limited in scope and short lived. The tendency of the Web to create a focus on a corporation's least-proud moments mean that the risks of undertaking such activities are rarely justified by their potential gains. For instance, the McSpotlight case still haunts McDonald's online, and despite a huge effort to clean up its image, Shell still faces reputational fallout in connection with its dealings in Nigeria.[29] While it is difficult to say whether underhand tactics – leveraging impressive skills in online communication to attack the credibility of opponents, as well as or instead of the substance of their arguments – will be successful in the long term, we advise caution. Perhaps such methods will succeed in 'winning the war' over time, by forcing a credibility gap between activists' messages and actions, but individual battles in the meantime are likely to prove damaging to the combatants' reputations. An individual corporation's interests are, I feel, better served by adopting the new model for corporate communication, treating it as an opportunity, and ultimately turning it to competitive advantage.

Notes

1. Metafilter's website is http://www.metafilter.com
    For details, see also: http://www.metafilter.com/mefi/10034
2. 'According to a poll by the Center for Survey Research and Analysis at the University of Connecticut, Americans trust journalists much less than they do clergymen, judges, doctors and policeman, and slightly less than they do lawyers.'
    http://www.foxnews.com/story/0,2933,52466,00.html
3. http://www.mcspotlight.org is an activist site set up to highlight supposedly unethical policies at McDonald's.
4. http://www.alternet.org/story.html?StoryID=9223
5. California Super.Ct., No. 98AS05067, 27-Apr-99
6. 'Samsung Stung for Millions by Internet Fraud', CNN Interactive, Newsbytes 11-Aug-97
7. http://www.theyesmen.org/wto/
8. http://www.toywar.co.uk/
9. In particular, scripts designed to 'fill' cookie-driven online shopping carts to potentially infinite levels, forcing the site to recalculate the entire contents of the cart every few seconds: http://www.heise.de/tp/english/inhalt/te/5843/1.html

10. 'Friendly hackers' the Con Clave Crew have undertaken mass-hacks in the past to expose security holes in, particularly, what they call 'big server hosting'. Their hack simply exposed weaknesses, without any other disruptive or destructive activity on the victim sites: http://neworder.box.sk/defaced/www.2ams.fr/

11. For Information Security Breaches Survey, see 2002 http://www.pwcglobal.com/Extweb/service.nsf/docid/B2ECC9B0E9EFA3D785256C33005247D3
    For the survey, see http://www.pwcglobal.com/Extweb/ncsurvres.nsf/0cc1191c627d157d8525650600609c03/845a49566045759e80256b9d003a4773/$FILE/ExecSumm_Final_220302.pdf

12. http://www.wombles.org.uk/frameset.htm

13. For McDonald's, see the previously mentioned http://www.mcspotlight.org

14. For example, http://act.greenpeace.org/

15. http://www.stopesso.com/

16. The correspondence was published on http://www.getethical.com/matters/email.html

17. Shell's microsite was http:ww.fenceline.com

18. See http://www.guardian.co.uk/comment/story/0,3604,723899,00.html

19. http://act.greenpeace.org/

20. See *Reputation Impact* issue 7, June 2002.

21. http://www.stopesso.com/press/00000032.php

22. http://www.stopesso.com/press/00000033.php

23. http://www.e-fluentials.com

24. At one end of the scale of seriousness, David Felton set up the gripe-site dunkindonuts.org to complain about the company's failure to sell his preferred type of coffee whitener: http://www.usatoday.com/life/cyber/tech/ctf976.htm
    At the other end is, for example, http://www.sucks500.com

25. See, for example, http://www.murderking.com/ and United Airlines gripe site http://www.untied.com

26. http://www.tellshell.com

27. http://www.introducingmonday.co.uk

28. 'Controversy Incorporated', *The McKinsey Quarterly*, 2002 Number 4. http://www.mckinseyquarterly.com

29. For McDonald's, see http://www.google.com/search?hl=en&ie=UTF-8&oe=UTF-8&q=mcspotlight
    For Shell, see http://www.google.com/search?hl=en&lr=&ie=UTF-8&oe=UTF-8&q=shell+nigeria+ogoni

CHAPTER 8

Stopping the Activist Attackers

Nick Nichols

An appeaser is one who feeds a crocodile, hoping it will eat him last.
Winston Churchill

Introduction

Businesses are being attacked by activists with increasing vehemence and with increasing frequency. But reactions vary: appeasement or attack? It is important to heed George Santayana's sage observation of a century ago: 'Those who cannot remember the past are condemned to repeat it'. This chapter contends that if appeasement is chosen, then retreat and defeat will be the outcomes for businesses. Instead, they should choose to fight back.

The sad reality of today's global political environment is that we now face a new generation of activists, who could come to dominate – not through force of arms, but through pressure, intimidation and even terror to serve their radical agenda. Many lead small, roving guerrilla bands of increasingly vocal, rapacious, confident militants, preying on weak businesses and communities, ganging up on large companies, taking to the streets, demanding tribute, and threatening to unleash actions that (they hope) will overwhelm industries, life styles and social, economic, legal and political institutions. Activists have to be taken seriously by businesses.

Environmental and animal rights activist groups began with legitimate grievances. They became more powerful over time, and as they did, became more demanding, bolder in their assaults, intolerant in their views and, it is contended in this chapter, disingenuous in their claims and indifferent to the havoc and misery they have left in their wake.

Journalist Andrew Goldstein hit the nail on the head when he wrote in *Time Magazine* (26 August 2002) that:

> part of the problem is that it's easier to protest, to hurl venom at practices you don't like, than to find new ways to do business and create change. The dogma of traditional green activism – that business (and economic

growth) is the enemy, that financial markets can't be trusted, that compromise means failure – has done little to save the planet. Which means it's fair to ask the question: Have some of the greens' tactics actually made things worse?

In the face of this activist assault on Western institutions and values, all too many business leaders, middle managers, public relations counsellors and politicians have somehow concluded that the wisest course of action is appeasement: give in to the activists' demands, address even their most illegitimate grievances, present them with victories and honour.

Corporate and social responsibility programmes and stakeholder outreach initiatives are important, but the result of giving in to the whims of new activists is that the attacks continue and the activist groups have become more powerful, wealthy and less accountable than ever before. This is why businesses should fight back.

To encourage business to fight back may be uncomfortable for some in the corporate world. It may require a change in culture, but if constant retreat is to be avoided then this has to be the chosen course of action. This chapter suggests that there are a number of actions that businesses can undertake in order to fight back. This is an unashamed guide to how businesses should behave, developed through personal experience of working with those who have been attacked.

The Myth of the Activists

Many activist groups claim to be representative of the public at large or to stand up against big business. However, in many ways, this is far from the truth and activism could even be termed a business in itself. In the July 2002 edition of *Foundation Watch*, published by the Washington, D.C.-based Capital Research Center, the Center reported that in the United States alone, the assets of environmental groups increased from $3.3 billion in 1990 to $7.9 billion in 1998. Moreover, the number of tax-exempt eco-NGOs in the United States exploded during the same timeframe, from 1802 in 1990 to 4018 in 1998.

Many activists like to portray themselves as Davids battling Goliaths, as protectors of the 'public interest', as advocates for consumers, the poor, indigenous peoples, little animals, the rainforest, the planet. Looking at *Foundation Watch*'s figures, it appears that David has become Goliath.

Also consider the social characteristics of activists. One of the barbs that have been hurled at environmentalists, and one which has caused considerable consternation within the movement, is that they are dominated by white, middle-class men.

Just prior to the 2000 Democratic Party Convention, *Los Angeles Times* reporter Nicholas Riccardi wrote a lengthy story about a 'boot camp' organised by the Ruckus Society to prepare the protesters for their assault on the Democrats. The organisers sought media coverage of their preparations, perhaps for the purpose of communicating their intentions (see *power play 6*, below). However, when it came time for the protest trainees to discuss diversity, the media was barred from the discussion.

According to Riccardi:

> the activists regularly retreat from the news media to discuss race, class and power – overlapping topics that touch a raw nerve in some of the participants. Ruckus and many groups that make up the new, roving protest movement are overwhelmingly white, a jarring sameness in a cause that aspires to global significance.
>
> (Riccardi, 2000)

Businesses should remember these differences between activists and society and take them and use them to their advantage.

Turning the Tide Against Activist Attackers

There is a fundamental difference between business executives and their activist group 'adversaries'. Business people tend to focus their time, energy and resources on developing detailed goals and objectives to shape their response to marketplace attacks. This is what directors and shareholders demand. Companies have to be properly prepared in case of attack. In contrast, the activists are able to concentrate on the strategies and tactics required to launch their attacks.

Many businesses, however, are making a fundamental mistake. Experience shows that corporate crisis management teams often consume scores of hours debating goals and objectives that describe *where they want to be* when the battle is over, rather than *how they are going to get there* (strategies and tactics). For instance, one firm's crisis team spent its entire first meeting debating the criteria for disbanding the team.

- The *goal* for business has to be to anticipate, prepare for and survive the attack.
- The *objective* is to undermine the enemy, or at least their ability and desire to wage war.

- The *strategy* is to fight back, and create real risk for the attackers in their actions.

Now, what tactics, or 'power plays' to fans of American football, should business executives be using to get where they want to be? That is where the focus ought to be and where this chapter concentrates.

As far as business goes, power plays and tactics are about one thing and one thing only: winning. The activists know that; they also aim to win. The organisation with the most effective power plays and tactics will defeat those who fall short on the tactical front when the battle is joined.

To understand the activist attackers, it must be realized that they rarely have any interest in compromise or moderation. As a result, efforts to appease the attackers with anything short of corporate surrender are useless. In fact, the attackers see any concessions made by their targets as signs of weakness that merely invite further demands, and the corporate sector is littered with examples that show this trend at work, especially in the environmental area. A cursory review of how activists have responded to concessions by British Petroleum, the Ford Motor Company and Novartis underscores my contention that the words 'compromise' and 'moderation' are not in the activists' playbook. Activist groups do not disband when a company concedes to what they ask: they simply move on to new demands.

Corporate executives who understand the threat posed by attackers like the Animal Liberation Front (ALF) and Earth Liberation Front (ELF) must also recognise that efforts to launch a counter-attack will require a dramatic shift in how they conduct operations and how they prepare for attacks. In essence, businesses must:

- Reject appeasement and spin as an option.
- Accept the reality that the activists are playing by a different set of rules, which concentrate on outcomes, varying the tactics accordingly.
- Recognise the activists' strengths and weaknesses.
- Be prepared to hold the activists to the law and embrace and exploit the attackers' own rules and tactics to achieve an advantage. In other words, businesses should learn from the activists.

The power plays that follow are powerful weapons that companies, industry groups and determined citizens are using to beat the activists and survive in the twenty-first century. These are the tactics that will help the business fight back.

Power play 1: Flash your brass knuckles. Let the activist attackers worry about how you will use them – and whether they are real or illusory.

When new activists want to drive a consumer products company into retreat, what is their approach? They tell the firm's executives that thousands of members will put skull-and-crossbones stickers on the company's products at retail stores, worldwide. Then, just to make the point, they select a single retail store near the company's headquarters; send in a couple of paid organisers and slap stickers on a few products within camera range of local reporters.

What options does the company have? Often it makes a deal, because the corporate leaders assume that the group will use its members around the planet to continue the campaign. Is there any real evidence that the group is capable of carrying out such a threat?

The companies can use *power play 1* as a powerful weapon if it is prepared to defend its product.

What should the company do in this instance? Inform the group that its threatened attack on a perfectly safe product is nothing short of extortion, and that the company intends to:

- notify law enforcement authorities and retailers of the threat
- continue its *ongoing* investigation in preparation for litigation
- make the company's financial and legal resources available to any retailer who elects to prosecute the group and its members for destroying private property
- alert pro-business activist groups that can effectively pillory the group for its hypocrisy and misdeeds.

The retail stores affected will appreciate the show of force far more than a surrender to the threat. The activist group may well rethink its tactic, especially if its lawyers are informed that the company does not take kindly to extortion.

If this appears an uncomfortable course of action then ask Novartis whether they achieved any benefits from giving in to the activists on genetically engineered foods. Novartis is one of the world's leading agricultural biotechnology companies and the parent company of Gerber. It may appear strange, but Novartis Consumer Health sent a letter to activists in June 2000 informing them that it would stop producing food containing genetically engineered ingredients (Greenpeace, 2000). The letter was leaked to the *New York Times*. (Who could have done that?) *Times* reporter Andrew

Pollack succeeded in getting Novartis to confirm the decision and then wrote,

> The move could put Novartis in a delicate spot, because its agricultural division continues to sell genetically modified seeds. . . . Novartis is a member of a coalition of agricultural biotechnology companies that is spending $50 million to defend the safety of such crops.
>
> (Pollack, 2000)

To add insult, Greenpeace issued a news release taking credit for the Novartis policy change, attacking the company's genetically engineered Bt corn variety, and highlighting the fact that Novartis was caught speaking out of both sides of its corporate mouth. The company's good press lasted for a very short period of time.

This is a clear example of a company, in this case Novartis, failing to think through the implications of a retreat in the face of activist pressure. Novartis' reputation came under fire and activists received support from citizens, agenda-driven foundations and profit-seeking producers of 'organic foods'.

What is the lesson? What happens to companies that cave in to the demands of activist attackers is entirely predictable: more demands, public misrepresentations of the 'deal', critical news coverage, further attacks.

Power play 2: Execute the unexpected

Power play 2 is central to a robust defence and will cause confusion and retreat within the activist's ranks.

What do activists expect a corporate target to do when an attack is launched? They expect company executives to stop acting like a team and focus on self-preservation. This has been the behaviour of business in the past, so it is rational of them to expect this to continue.

If the company reacts at all, the activists expect the target to respond slowly and defensively, and to communicate convoluted messages laced with scientific terms, messages devoid of emotion. They assume the company will refuse media requests for a spokesperson and issue a bland statement instead.

What will the activists not expect? They will not expect rapid action from the business and delivery of a message with power through aggressive media relations and an effective, credible spokesperson. In short, they will not expect a serious counter-attack, a serious downside risk to their behaviour.

Stopping the activists is all about *creating risk*. Creating risk usually requires tactics that violate the activists' expectations. Tactics that stop activists in their tracks can range from high jinks to legal prosecution, and everything in between. It does not matter on which end of the continuum tactics fall. If they are legal and will achieve the mission, they are worth executing. Businesses can make activists think again.

There was a prime example of an activists' outdoor news conference that was completely neutralised by a mime and a simulated minor car accident. It happened in a public park across the street from the target's Washington, D.C. offices. The camera crews showed up to record an activist lambasting industry for environmental and waste management failures. The mime, hired from a local talent agency, jumped in front of the cameras with mime-like weirdness when the speaker started her harangue. And just as she was about to deliver her main message, two cars on an adjacent street appeared to collide, setting off a cacophony of horn blowing and obscenities. The resulting circus proved to be well outside what the media-hound activists expected or were prepared to cope with.

Could the mime tactic be characterised as immature and juvenile? Certainly, but no more so than some of the stunts activists have pulled in the past. How often has the public been treated to the spectacle of Greenpeace activists abseiling down the side of a corporate high-rise with banners unfurled? How about the pie-in-the-face tactic executed by activists against government officials and business executives? It's all about theatre, and it works.

The result of this stunt was no news coverage and very frustrated activists. The organiser of the stunt also believed that there was one added benefit: its staff really enjoyed the experience (see *power play 4*).

The only real limits to unconventional tactics like these are the imaginations and fortitude of companies that might be thinking about venturing into these otherwise uncharted business waters.

Another thing activists rarely experience is an attack by the news media, or by one of their own. When Greenpeace founder Dr Patrick Moore started criticising Greenpeace members and their fellow activists for contaminating the environmental agenda with leftist politics, the activists did not know how to react.

According to an article about Dr Moore by Anthony Browne, published in the *Observer* on 21 May 2000, 'Greenpeace has declared that he has gone off the rails'. The Forest Action Network has even dedicated an Internet website (http://www.fanweb.org/patrick-moore/index.shtml) to proving that 'Patrick Moore is a big fat liar', featuring pictures of him with a Pinocchio nose.

Browne quotes Chris Genovali, of the Western Canada Wilderness Committee, on his reaction to Moore's criticisms: 'Each time I read something by this megalomaniacal [sic] crackpot, I get the urge to hurl' (Browne, 2000).

The activists appear to react badly when the spotlight is put on them.

Power play 3: Exploit your strengths. Offset your weaknesses.

Many people in corporations have been brought up with a decision-making model that is slow, methodical, incremental and, above all, risk-averse. This model works well when managing complex technical issues, or developing new products. It falls apart when a firm is under attack and decisions must be made rapidly.

Asking people engrained in the zero-risk culture to make rapid, high-risk/high-gain decisions in response to an activist attack will always be problematic. Ordering them to execute tactics that are confrontational rather than collegial will go against everything they believe in.

That does not mean that business should submit. What it means instead is using people from outside the company who know how to fight back. There are organisations, companies and highly credible people available who understand the motivation and tactics of the activists and can, therefore, assist in the business fight back.

Power play 4: If you are forced to plunder and pillage, make sure your offensive works and your people enjoy it

Activist attack groups often stage media events that involve circus-style antics. Real-life examples of these antics include unfurling banners on chemical plant smoke stacks, placard-wielding demonstrators disrupting a stockholders meeting on roller skates, and activists in funny costumes chanting anti-business slogans while scaling the walls of a corporation's headquarters. Why do this? Because activists understand *power play 4*. These stunts not only secure great media coverage, but are also satisfying for the protesters themselves.

Similarly, business people responsible for executing tactics should also find them enjoyable. If the tacticians do not enjoy their work and the execution of the tactics, this will ultimately undermine them and cause them to fail.

Those who are for giving in to the activists will say that outlandish, confrontational tactics like those used by activists could never be pulled off by corporate executives in suits. But company managers can turn the tables.

In 1999, environmental activists converged in Louisiana to protest against the state's chemicals industry. Their tactic was to confront the governor with a plate of 'toxic' fish and catch the state's top executive on camera refusing to eat the fillets.

Thanks to effective intelligence gathering, the tables were turned on the attackers. The activists were met by an aide to the governor who graciously accepted the plate of fish, and right on camera proceeded to eat it for lunch. The activists were dumbstruck while bystanders laughed. The news media had a field day. The activists had been defeated.

Power play 5: Keep sending in new plays from the bench

The average human being can only remain interested in an activity for a certain period, but attacks on industry have lasted for decades. For example, environmental activists have been seeking to eliminate chlorine chemistry and the industries that depend on it for more than a decade. They have maintained their enthusiasm for this long-standing campaign by developing new tactics and by moving to different targets.

The activists attacked paper companies who use chlorine to bleach their products. They lobbied governments to stop using chlorine to disinfect drinking water. Then they discovered that chlorine is used to make vinyl (polyvinyl chloride) plastic, so they attacked vinyl. They claimed that vinyl is not recyclable, that it produces dioxin, that it contains heavy metals. They also alleged that compounds used to soften vinyl are dangerous. The activists have attacked vinyl toys, medical devices, containers and construction materials. The picture has constantly shifted and evolved.

Moving targets and changing tactics have prevented boredom in the ranks of the activists. This has also had the effect of keeping industry off balance and on the defensive. But the same rule applies to corporations, their allies and the activists' grassroots opponents.

Not surprisingly, many of the allegations against chlorine are not supported by science and real-world experience. Companies have argued that the real health threat appears to be linked to the advice offered by the activists, not to the products under attack. It is claimed that in 1991, Peru experienced its first cholera outbreak in 100 years and thousands of people died, after government officials decided to stop chlorinating Peru's water supply (*Lancet*, 1991; Anderson, 1991; Malkin and Fumento, 1996).

If businesses adopted a more aggressive stance and countered the 'facts' produced by activists, this would have shifted the focus of attention. It does, however, have to be recognised that this would be a dramatic change of pace for any business executive. The Peruvian disaster offers an important lesson for businesses: that activists are not always right. But will businesses challenge them?

Another example is that the US Competitive Enterprise Institute (CEI) and the chemical industry challenged the claims made about dioxin by activists. In 1999, the CEI took a robust approach when the environmentally conscious Ben and Jerry's ice cream company announced that their products would in future be sold in dioxin-free packages. Ben and Jerry's are an example of a company that attempts to make a selling point of its environmental/activist record and often pushes the activists' agenda forward, giving credence to their claims.

ABC network television reporter John Stossel and the CEI argued that there were two problems with the ice cream company's move. First, few people eat the packages. Second, according to the CEI, that the ice cream itself contains dioxin, at levels higher than the US Environmental Protection Agency (EPA) considers safe (CEI, 1999).

The facts pushed by activists may not always be accurate.

Power play 6: Make them sweat your threat

When protestor Saul Alinsky sought to gain concessions from Chicago Mayor Richard Daley, Sr., he threatened to send protestors to tie up the toilets at what was then the world's busiest airport, O'Hare International. The operative word here is 'threatened'. The tactic was never executed because, within 48 hours of the threat being delivered, America's most powerful mayor capitulated.

When past attacks on industry are analysed, it becomes clear that marketplace damage is usually inflicted by a target industry's customers, not by government regulators or consumers in general. Customer decisions that translate into damage are often made in response to mere threats from the attackers, not the actual carrying out of those threats. In other words, an activist is not simply trying to cause a reaction from consumers but from other corporations, others in the business' supply chain, who may choose to protect themselves.

When activists attacked phthalates (softeners in plastics) used in vinyl baby toys, damage in the form of lost markets was inflicted on toy companies such as Mattel. The toy makers gave in to the activists' threats. Consumers did not panic. US regulators concluded that the amount of phthalates ingested by small children 'does not even come close to a harmful level' (Mayer, 1999). But some corporate bodies found the threat of reputational damage too difficult to stomach. They capitulated.

The application of *power play 6* is, in fact, a form of psychology. The objective is to create risk in the mind of the target; to force a reaction that will undermine the target's tactical position, allowing the attacker to take new ground.

There is only one effective defence for business against *power play 6*. Do not react; do not capitulate.

Power play 7: Turn your opponent's rules into your weapons

Professional activists are exceptionally effective at forcing companies to abide by 'the rules', as they see them. They are also very skilled at applying political pressure, through media pressure, political pressure and the like, on the regulators responsible for developing and enforcing the rules and regulations that companies are required to follow.

But how well do the professional activists follow their own ethical guidelines and standards, or the basic rules they expect corporations and the rest of society to follow?

In its 1998 Annual Report Greenpeace stated that: 'Our core, immutable values are shared not just with staff and activists, but with supporters. They include independence, non-violence, bearing witness and commitment to peace and the well-being of the natural world. These are our principles' (Greenpeace, 1998).

The organisation's public commitment to non-violence attracts many of its youthful supporters and liberal donors to the movement.

If businesses adopt a more combative approach, then it could be argued that Greenpeace should be challenged on any dishonest, unethical or immoral behaviour it is connected with. It could also be 'forced' to condemn other groups for their violent acts, which Greenpeace says it opposes.

Highlighting the disingenuous and violent activities of environmental and animal rights activists may have the effect of driving their natural allies away. For example, Lord Melchett, the one-time Greenpeace director in the United Kingdom, was arrested in 1999 for vandalism and property destruction aimed at field trials of genetically modified crops. His actions and calls for attacks on crops embarrassed other environmentalists and led to him being criticised by Friends of the Earth (FSN, 2000).

Businesses should always look for opportunities to use *power play 7* against their activist adversaries. The activists may not play by the accepted corporate rules, but they can be forced to play by rules that often conflict with their public actions, rules the public generally expects everyone to live by, business or activist.

Power play 8: Heap scorn and ridicule on those who deserve it

Humour is almost impossible to defend against. If your adversary becomes the target of jokes by high-profile comedians and satirists, you've probably won the war. Funny counter-protests can be even better.

Anti-business activist groups are not very good at using humour to scorn their targets directly, so ridicule is often a very effective tactic against activists because it is likely to elicit an irrational, angry response. That is good from the business' perspective. Humour also appeals to the public at large.

The problem for corporate executives is that it is hard for them to follow this path, as few CEOs are known for their comedic abilities! But that does not mean companies under attack are incapable of subjecting their attackers to a stinging dose of humour or ridicule if justified. It just means the company may have to recruit some outside help. Lets consider some examples where businesses could turn the tables.

'Let them burn dung.' Critics argue that intense opposition to hundreds of hydroelectric dams throughout the developing world has forced peasant women and girls to collect wet cow dung with their bare hands, then dry and burn it in cooking fires, as they are forced to do without alternative sources of power and new technologies.

Critics argue that activists' intense opposition to dam building ignores the needs of the world's poorest regions. Nearly 10 million people – half of them infants and children – die every year from dysentery and other water-borne diseases. Tens of millions of others contract lung diseases like tuberculosis every year from breathing the infected air, according to the World Health Organisation (Channel 4, 1997).

Some have criticised activists for supporting policies that protect the status quo and do not 'move with the times' by taking advantage of new technologies.

'Making the world safe for mosquitoes.' Malaria was eradicated in the United States in the 1950s, and from the rest of the developed nations and much of Asia and Latin America by the mid-1960s. But the disease is making a ferocious comeback in the developing world.

The disease has spread, in part, as a consequence of a reduction in the use of DDT as a weapon (see Tren and Bate, 2000). 'In many parts of the world', a report in *Science News* notes,

> this toxicant remains the best hope for reining in malaria. According to the World Health Organisation (WHO), each year another 400 million

people come down with the parasitic disease. This newly infected group equals the combined populations of the United States, Canada and Mexico.

(Raloff, 2000, p. 12)

In response to the exploding epidemic, WHO, UNICEF, the World Bank and several humanitarian groups began tackling the disease, advocating the retention of DDT for malaria control in poor areas, because DDT is far less expensive and far more effective than substitutes.

However, when countries began using DDT once again, a vocal and powerful consortium of environmental groups issued an 'urgent call' for a total, permanent, global ban on the use of DDT. Developing countries and anti-malaria groups argued that DDT was effective and safe and persuaded some groups to moderate their original proposal (Tren and Bate, 2000).

The anti-DDT activists refused to moderate their other demands and consequently many American donor groups refuse to fund any humanitarian efforts that include DDT.

Arguments like these, however, do not always persuade environmental activists to moderate their demands. A comment made by Dr Charles Wurster, former chief scientist for the Environmental Defense Fund, is illustrative and also highly offensive. Asked if he thought a ban on DDT might result in the use of far more dangerous chemicals and an explosion of malaria cases in Sri Lanka, he replied: 'Probably – so what? People are the cause of all the problems. We have too many of them. We need to get rid of some of them, and this is as good a way as any' (quoted in Whelan, 1985, p. 67; Ray with Guzzo, 1993, p. 67, citing hearings before the House of Representatives Committee on Agriculture).

Scornful humour is a largely untapped opportunity to turn the tables on the radicals, challenging their views and providing the world with the facts behind the impact of their demands.

Power play 9: Never let up. Keep the pressure on.

When activists apply constant pressure on industry, the effect is often devastating. Business executives want the conflict to end as quickly as possible, so that they can return to their normal day-to-day business. When activists sustain their attack for a long period of time, the target often capitulates.

How can companies subjected to constant attacks avoid tedium and the urge to retreat? They need to develop new tactics, involve new people and devise new messages.

Many of those in industries under siege remain in place for years, under constant bombardment, with no relief in sight. Nothing to look forward to but the constant threat of attack. It is necessary to ensure a turnover of people facing the activists and also a flow of new ideas. Only in this way will the industry maintain a fresh approach.

People involved in those industries will need to devise new weapons and tactics and launch counterattacks against the activists. If they do not, defeat will be sure to follow.

Power play 10: Locate your target. Lock onto it. Villainise it. Strike hard. Don't let up.

In marketplace conflict, there are certain commandments that are universal. *Power play 10* is one of them. There is no point in crafting strategies and tactics unless there is a target upon which to focus the attack. Activists understand this commandment and usually live by it.

Take the case of biotechnology. When European activists initially attacked agricultural biotechnology, they targeted Monsanto and the company's top leadership. If the attack had been aimed at the entire industry, the activists' forces would have been spread too thin. Monsanto was singled out and attacked. Other companies and their customers became targets only after the attack gained momentum, and the coalition to kill 'Frankenfoods' expanded its membership and its ability to strike multiple targets.

A key criterion for target selection is the target's vulnerability. Despite its size and reputation, Monsanto was vulnerable in the early days of the European genetically modified food fight. Critics have described its weaknesses as the '3As': ambitious; arrogant; American. Monsanto set out to take Europe by storm with its marketing of biotech. This was not welcomed.

The attackers could not have asked for a more inviting target. Once the company was fast-frozen into the villain role, it was not difficult to frame the issue. The issue became 'Monsanto'. The caricature was put in place: this 800-pound Yankee gorilla was not only trying to force Europeans to eat alien food, but was also trying to destroy Europe's small family farms. And what if this gene-tinkering got out of hand and destroyed the environment as well? These were the images developed by the activists.

The activists' success in exploiting Monsanto's vulnerabilities to frame the issue also had a polarising effect. European companies with a stake in advancing agricultural biotechnology concluded that this was Monsanto's fight alone. They kept their heads down, rather than risk consumer outrage.

By the time they discovered that their future was also in jeopardy, the first major battle of the Frankenfoods war had been lost.

When faced with this type of attack, businesses who want to fight back should locate the target, lock onto it, villainise it, strike hard and not let go. Coalition building will increase their fire power and staying power. Industry could use this approach against the activists effectively in the same way activists use it against them.

The anti-biotechnology activists had the tables turned on them at the 2002 'Earth Summit' in Johannesburg, South Africa, when US AID Administrator Andrew Natsios accused environmental extremists of endangering the lives of millions of famine-threatened Africans by pressuring their governments to reject genetically modified US food aid. In a comment to the news media, Mr. Natsios said, 'They (the environmentalists) can play these games with Europeans, who have full stomachs, but it is revolting and despicable to see them do so when the lives of Africans are at stake' (Martin and Itano, 2002).

Conclusion

If businesses choose not to focus on the damage being inflicted on them by activists then they will be faced with constant retreat and new demands. Appeasement is failing. Corporate cowardice needs to be replaced by corporate courage.

While many of the above actions may seem extreme, when a company is under attack it is forced to consider all options, all the power plays. Companies need to be creative, in many instances learn from how the activists behave and the tactics they employ, and turn the tables.

In summary businesses should be prepared to:

- Defend themselves and their products.
- Mix-up the tactics to confuse the activists.
- Make the most of their strengths.
- Ensure that those involved in executing the tactics find them enjoyable.
- Constantly change tactics.
- Force the activists to deliver on threats.
- Use the activists statements and positions against them.
- Use humour to show up the activists.
- Keep the pressure up.
- Be clear about their targets and keep focused on them.

It is time for businesses to fight back.

CHAPTER 9

The Evolution of the Business Lobby

Charles Miller

Introduction: A Brief History of The Business Lobby in the United Kingdom

Anthony Sampson, in the second of a set of perceptive analyses of the way Britain works spanning three decades, drew an implicit comparison between the mechanics of influence of the 1960s and 1970s with that of Bagehot's day a century before (Sampson, 1971). Walter Bagehot, you will recall, revealed the 'secret' of the British Constitution: that while most people thought that power resided in the legislature, it had in fact passed to the Cabinet (Bagehot, 1867). He cautioned, however, that it was better not to 'let light in on magic' than to disabuse those outside the system of their belief in the way it worked. What Sampson described, a world in which business saw no great need to deal with parliament or external pressures because power was focused on negotiations with civil servants, was a system of interaction that followed logically from developments since Bagehot's day (an era in which government was tiny relative to its present size): the growth of the civil service and Whitehall, 'whipped' backbencher Members of Parliament financially dependent on executive patronage, and an economy run by officials during wartime.[1] It made the skill of working the system a natural requirement for most corporations.

The Second World War and its immediate aftermath were particularly significant in this process of change. War brought business and industry, which had accustomed itself to working with government through the twin channels of its own representation on the back benches and the natural identity of its ruling class with that within the system, closer to Whitehall. Production and planning required its co-operation and involvement at ministerial and official level. War had conditioned organisations to doing without parliament. As a result, come 1945 it was Whitehall, not parliament, that increasingly provided the focus for business and industrial consultations on policy. And the Labour Government's back benchers,

enjoying an outright majority for the first time in the party's history, acqui-
esced in passing what were left of the reins to the system of committees
established to prepare decisions for endorsement by cabinet and to a civil
service made more dynamic by the responsibilities of wartime planning.
The turn of the twentieth century definition by the constitutional analyst
Lord Bryce of a lobbyist as someone, not a member of the legislature, who
is employed to lobby parliament with the aim of changing legislation, had
been made redundant within 40 years. For business, parliament had
become, more often than not, the gift wrapping around a more important
system that awarded contracts, handed out aid, and – often more important
than legislation – formulated commercially damaging or beneficial policies
that had to be monitored, protected or shaped.

The executive had long since ceased to be a committee of parliament.
Moreover, extensions of the franchise, the proliferation of interest groups
and a decline in their desire to be represented in – rather than by – the
House of Commons robbed parliament of much of its consultative function.
Government ministers increasingly felt the need to bypass MPs and consult
on policy direct with interest groups. But industry could do what pressure
groups – antibodies, as Sampson called them – could not: lobby Whitehall,
often by invitation:

> But most of the very biggest business interests do not bother much about
> parliament, and few of the big corporations now maintain their own
> members in the House. They have seen where decisive power lies, and so
> they deal directly with Cabinet Ministers or Civil Servants.... 'It's so much
> easier here', a senior manager in one big corporation once told me: 'We
> don't have to organise great formal expeditions as in Washington. Whitehall
> is only two tube stations away: we have a Permanent Secretary to lunch from
> time to time'. The chairmen of big companies do not need to stir up
> Members of Parliament; they are on speaking terms with Cabinet Ministers
> and senior Civil Servants, and can urge their views there. The more Civil
> Servants who go into industry, the closer the industry, the easier such infor-
> mal pressure becomes.... The really important lobbying – about tax conces-
> sions, locations of industries, trade agreements or subsidies – takes place in
> the recesses of Whitehall long before and Bill reaches parliament.
>
> (Sampson, 1971, p. 16)

Sampson's last word on this subject was delivered a decade ago in *The
Essential Anatomy of Britain*, the fifth and final volume in the series. Reiterating his observation of business lobbies bypassing parliament in favour
of direct liaison with ministers and their advisers, he said that:

The ministers like to conceal the fact that they are influenced by these secretive meetings; but lobbyists can be much more persuasive than members. . . and they have more patient long-term objectives which can steadily wear down ministers. . . . The interests of producers – centralised, close-knit and well-funded – inevitably win over the consumers who are scattered and fragmented; and the most powerful pressures of all, like the road-and-car lobby, change the face of the country through backstairs pressures which are concealed from any public debate. Gradually non-commercial lobbies have become much better organised, including major bodies such as Friends of the Earth or the Child Poverty Action Group, some with hundreds of thousands of paid-up members. . . . They have done much to counter big-business pressures with the help of effective publicity; but they cannot take account of grievances of the individual who can only appeal to his Member of Parliament.

(Sampson, 1992, p.13)

The Challenge

Why, you might ask, should we dwell on an analysis of the way things were ten, still less 30 years ago? Because this book challenges us to conclude that even Sampson's most recent analysis is merely historic. The corporation is under siege. It is suggested that government is no longer the most frequent obstacle in the path of corporate strategies. Now it is new forms of radical activism that are destroying corporations and shareholder value. The forces with influence are now the grassroots and the corporate lobbyists need to change their focus from looking up to looking down. Today's technology and campaigning techniques give even poorly resourced and disparate lobbies the power to sway policy and inflict corporate damage. And Sampson's antibodies have become too respectable. It is new activists who count.

A few years ago, we might have concluded that there was a grain of truth in this. Perhaps today that has become a kernel; but while it is true that non-establishment lobbies have steadily increased their power and some corporations and sectors have been exposed to pressure from NGOs, the reality of influence still conforms more to the Sampson model.

It would be understandable if academic commentators were to concur with the thesis of the large impact of radical activists on corporations, as they are often dependent on source material rather than first-hand experience. In this area the source material is press coverage, inevitably geared to the highest profile issues, or lobbyists'/NGOs' versions of case histories, inevitably geared to promoting their claims of their role in a successful campaign. Corporations have no interest in crowing about their lobbying tactics so their side of the story often goes unheard. In addition, the system of government (including official and elected elements) does not talk about how it actually makes decisions, and nor do the media; it is understandable that there is a tendency to exaggerate the persuasiveness of pressure group activity. They certainly understate the significance of administrative decisions, decisions shaped by legal advice, legal necessity (for example, the constraint on European Community institutions to act within the terms of the Treaty of Rome) or inter-departmental liaison, or the sheer toughness of ministers inured to pressure by years of knock about politics, dissatisfied constituents criticising the government through them, or criticising them for failing to deliver the impossible in their capacity as councillors, backbenchers or special advisers to ministers.

This chapter seeks both to explore academic contentions about the role and influence of activists on corporations, and to consider how close they are to the reality of business dynamics. It will examine four principal challenges that are forwarded for the impact of activism on business and concentrate its analysis on the Summer 2002 World Summit on Sustainable Development, touted by many as the most significant demonstration yet of corporate and NGO interests operating within the same forum. It will argue that business has adapted its operations and has coped well with the rise of activism. Indeed, governmental decision-making processes have altered little and business has retained its influence.

New Activism is Destroying Corporations

It is difficult to see how this contention can be justified. Even the most aggressive European activist campaign of recent years did not destroy Huntingdon Life Sciences. It is true that significant damage was inflicted on the company's shareholder base and brokers were systematically deterred from dealing in its stock, but in the absence of alternatives Huntingdon's work was too valuable for it to be allowed to fail.

Take the case of genetically modified crops. Environmental activists (principally those larger groups such as Greenpeace) have had considerable success in selling scare stories to the media. Those doubts have seemed sufficiently plausible to enough consumers to force most major European retailers to refuse to sell products containing GMOs, and there is no question that GM food manufacturers have lost revenue as a result. Monsanto, the leading target of activist campaigns, conceded in August 2002 that widespread opposition to GMOs meant that it would be another three years before it might win approval for sale in Europe. A moratorium on new GM crop authorisations has been in place there since 1998, undoubtedly as a direct result of those campaigns. But in the United Kingdom, the trials continue despite damage to crops; and one ironic result of the anti-GM lobby may have been to strengthen the resolve of governments to rely on objective science in making their regulatory decisions on GMOs.

What about tobacco? There is probably more of a gap between appearance and reality here. Without the drive of anti-smoking campaigners, the scientific research that has persuaded millions to avoid the habit and has led to regulatory restrictions such as advertising bans would certainly have had less impact. But the most significant financial damage to the industry has been sustained through concerted US legal challenges, not normally considered a form of activism, and even then the tobacco companies have found new markets and their shares still hold 'Buy' ratings because profits remain high.

What is true is that companies in certain sectors now have to devote considerable resources to countering the activities of consumer, environmental, health or ethical groups. Friends of the Earth, for example, has claimed that oil companies spend more on marketing their green credentials than on cleaning up their operations (*Financial Times*, 31 August 2002). Around 700 corporations attended the World Summit in 2002. Hundreds of millions are spent on environmental audit reports, corporate responsibility videos and political and public information programmes. Do corporations genuinely want to be green? Does corporate social responsibility (CSR) really matter to them? In the main, no. It is the price they are having to pay for being caught on the back foot by lobbies that have steadily grabbed and shaped the public mood. But apparently similar corporate reactions have been conditioned by more complex factors. BMW may have justified its enormous investment in a high-profile presence at the World Summit on the basis that 'we firmly believe that sustainability is more than just a vision of a distant future. Sustainability is the core of our corporate strategy' (*Financial Times*, 31 August 2002). In reality, however, rising fuel prices, which have shaped motorists' perception of consumption efficiency, as much as environmentally driven emission-based taxes and the threat of regulation, have been the principal drivers of the automotive industry's environmental strategy. Altruism is often no more than the public response to a practical problem.

But has this eroded shareholder value? In general, the investment community does not think so, even though finance directors fret at the cost and corporate financiers nowadays are conscious of a greater range of factors in assessing project risk, including the possibility that their own operations might be targeted if they are associated with unpopular schemes or industries.[2] A prominent analyst told the author that;

> while the market is sensitive to unanticipated regulatory costs or things such as product recalls and bad press coverage, in the main the companies prepare us for it, so there are no surprises, and underlying value is the real issue. Look what happened when Big Tobacco took a $1bn hit in the US courts. Their share price hardly moved, because however dramatic these things look in the press, their impact on overall revenue is usually limited.

In other words, whatever it costs to augment the PR department, establish an environment team or hire a lobbyist is little more than a minor irritant to the typical corporation.

Consider, to take one instance, the lobby over deep vein thrombosis (DVT). In little over two years, an organisation called the Aviation Health Institute (AHI), in reality the vehicle for a highly committed individual, was able to make a large proportion of air travellers both aware of and concerned about the risk of contracting DVT as a result of flying. Through canny promotion of minor medical studies and occasional leaks from aircrew, the DVT campaign secured thousands of column inches, a House of Lords inquiry, a Department of Health study and a new attitude to long-haul air travel. But what did the AHI actually achieve? The Lords report damned the Institute, condemning it as an unreliable witness. Transport officials, despite a brief knee-jerk by their ministers, agreed with the airlines that only better and clearer information was needed. Cabin staff reported few enquiries or expressions of concern about DVT. Even though superficial analysis might brand the campaign a success, in reality it may have achieved little more than the dissemination of scare stories. There is no evidence that demand fell as a result.

New Activists as the Way Forward

This supposed challenge stems from a lack of first-hand business experience and an over-reliance on media coverage. As the longer-established interest groups have grown, both in membership and in available resources, they have learnt how to work the system, developing the skills prized by policy makers. The UK Consumers Association, for example, frequently produces economic analysis that reads the mood of regulators more accurately than the giant companies do, even with their immense internal and consultancy resources. Some of these groups are becoming institution-alised: note, for example, how the Consumers Association now has a formal role as adviser to the Office of Fair Trading; and now legislation has created a special category of 'supercomplaint', vesting in bodies such as the CA, National Consumer Council and sector consumer watchdogs the power to bring what are in effect class actions on behalf of the public constituencies they represent.[3]

Others are also learning the system's tricks. A senior environment official told the author that an environmental activist network, which had made a name for itself through high-profile campaigning and well-publicised attacks on government and industry, began to exert influence on regulatory policy when it toned down its stridency and started to produce soundly based research rather than mere claims. Small, relatively poorly funded interest groups either do not want to be seen to go native or are unable to deploy the evidential tools that build winning cases.[4] It is just as likely that a negotiated approach to policy change simply does not suit such organisations, whose techniques may in the final analysis be more geared to keeping their members happy than to applying effective pressure.

In other words, pressure groups have to strike a delicate balance between the generally low-profile, unpublicised methods required to sway policy-makers and those that are most effective in mobilising grassroots action directed at corporations. In the same way that Labour Party activists, after many years of masochistic campaigning, lost a degree of interest once their party was finally elected in 1997, it must be conceded that pressure groups can become tired in the eyes of those who demand antibodies; but that should not be equated with lack of punch.

The Focus Should be Downwards

Once again the picture, as seen by those outside UK Government circles, is distorted by government's enduring lack of keenness to allow the media to peer over the walls of Whitehall or European Community institutions. As a result, outsiders know more than ever about the decisions of government but are no wiser about the way they are reached.

Today, more money and time is devoted by organisations – corporate or activist – to lobbying than at any time in the past. But it is as true today as it was when Attlee took power that for every instance in which government is forced to maintain or amend policy through pressure, hype or parliamentary embarrassment, there are several hundred where decisions are made or influenced purely through the undramatic submission of a well-researched, well-argued and representative case. Although commentators associate lobbying with high profile campaigns, in practice most corporate dealings with the system are quiet and businesslike. And while it is important that some policy decisions carry public opinion with them, the British policy and lobbying process is less of a downward activity than it is in the United States.[5]

On most issues, success still goes to those who best marshal evidence, understand which part of the system is driving the issue and assemble coalitions; only then is it about isolating opposition, which is rarely consumer/grassroots-based. The opponent is still, in most cases, the system itself or other corporate interests. Most grassroots lobbies make little headway. And in any event, citing Roosevelt may do no more than indicate that little has changed over the best part of three-quarters of a century.

Moves by government toward introducing greater transparency – which can be read as sensitivity to the public and a need to inform – into decision making, with the appearance of more meaningful involvement of those outside the major lobbying blocs, can also be a chimera. To take two examples, the policy developed by bodies such as UK sector regulators and the European Commission of publishing consultation responses online could be interpreted as making life easier for NGOs who would not otherwise have had access to the views of major players. But in practice it has merely led to more diplomatic public submissions by the more strategic organisations, who do not want to give away their true positions to their competitors and who reserve confidential data and more sensitive views for private briefings. The public hearings recently introduced by the UK Competition Commission carry less weight with the Commission, which will have heard the most important arguments beforehand, than with City analysts and institutional investors, to whom participants in the know primarily direct their remarks. The apparent inability of these modern developments or of more traditional consultation exercises to change political or official views that are still in a high proportion of cases crystallised early in the process and then publicly tested ('show me I'm wrong' rather than 'what should we do?') may persuade NGOs that playing the game is of little value compared with direct action or media pressure.

Business understands this reality, although even the largest organisations are:

- Thinly resourced. One person (likely to be a government or public affairs executive) having trouble keeping track of all the consultation papers landing on his or her desk. NGOs, in contrast, have nothing else to do but focus on their prey. And many NGOs can be surprisingly well funded. Note, for example, the vast attendance at the 2002 World Summit on Sustainable Development, with over 60,000 delegates

including, as the *Guardian* described it, 'a massive turnout from environmental and development lobby groups . . . the average delegate will
be spending at least £1000' (21 August 2002). It mystifies many corporate executives unable to secure approval for attendance at conferences
and other events where the case against them may be raised that their
activist opposite numbers can afford to travel the world without any
apparent means of support other than occasional journalism.

- Poor at internal communication. Those responsible for lobbying government often find that they cannot get co-operation from those in charge
of the evidence. Links between government relations, regulatory affairs,
legal and PR departments are often disjointed.

- So government-oriented that they have not learnt the tricks of pressure
groups: stunts, media timing, use of technology such as satellite linkups between news conferences around the world (many do not realise
how well funded some of these organisations can be) and Internet
campaigning.

That does not mean that the corporate lobbyist's sights are still, as
suggested by Sampson, more or less permanently trained on Whitehall.
Business is more pragmatic than NGOs. It forges alliances with trades
unions where it is expedient (Freedom To Fly, as one instance, lost no time
in co-opting the unions, going so far as making former SOGAT boss
Baroness Dean its chairwoman), with environmental groups where it can
emasculate them or create the impression of greater 'stakeholder' involvement, and with the Consumers Association and other grassroots bodies
where their approval might benefit it or where lack of opposition might get
them off its back.[6] That's the game. It is not about altruism or being
communautaire; it is about doing what you have to do to achieve your
corporate strategy.

To return to the World Summit, Greenpeace and the World Business
Council for Sustainable Development joined forces to issue a public call
for governments to act on climate change concerns. Is this evidence that
business is being forced to look down? That is doubtful. There is no love
lost between either organisation but they are experienced enough to use
each other when it suits them. There is nothing new in this: twenty or more
years ago, US corporations started to invite Ralph Nader's campaigners
into their boardrooms to advise on addressing consumer activism.

Environmental reporting makes for a good case study in this respect,
reinforcing the conclusion that NGOs are consistently faster out of the
blocks in changing the boundaries of public opinion but that business
quickly catches up, sacrificing a little ground but spending money it can

afford in order to restore the status quo. The latest (Summer 2002) triennial survey from accountancy firm KPMG, examined reporting among the top 100 companies in 19 countries in addition to the 250 leading firms in the Global Fortune 500. Of the top 100 firms in the nine countries on which KPMG reported both for 1999 and 2002, the overall proportion producing some form of sustainability report rose from 25 to 29 per cent. The motives for this trend are mixed. Some companies believe that these reports improve their public standing, and the plethora of awards on offer for them spur organisations to invest in presentation of their performance. Others do it to forestall or anticipate regulation (the number of companies producing environmental, social or sustainability reports rose fastest in France, where there was a more than fivefold increase to 21 of the top 100 companies ahead of the introduction in 2002 of a reporting requirement) in an area where governments, seeing such reporting as harmless and inexpensive, have easily been persuaded by NGOs.

The steady spread of this 'communication culture' and its impact on the balance of business's focus between looking up and looking down can be seen in another two areas. The first is the all too common scientific or health scare. The DVT and other lobbies (GMOs and nuclear power are two further prime examples) involving communication of complex scientific evidence illustrate a common theme in modern lobbying. Business (the defender) initially caught off guard, failing to grasp the need to pre-empt opposition or reluctant to dumb down its arguments, comes under pressure from the media (to which it is easier to sell simple half truths than complex scientific fact). This forces the issue into the political arena, where corporations are more comfortable because evidence is more thoroughly tested and press coverage is more often than not treated with suspicion; the business lobby improves its public relations; and, sooner or later, the problem stabilises.

Look at the often-cited Brent Spar case, a classic example of NGOs being faster and better at understanding how to use the media to influence public opinion and cause economic damage. What should business have done?

The pressure groups used techniques familiar to political parties (for example, the Conservative Party's notorious 'double whammy' campaign in 1992), based on the reality that it is easier to get air time for a simple distortion than a complex truth.[7] They were not constrained by corporate lawyers nervous at the exclusion of any relevant detail.

The case showed that first mover advantage is considerable. Rebuttal has to be rapid and sharp. But pre-emption of NGOs' arguments is far more effective.

The real lesson, however, is to wrap truth around PR: with perfect hindsight, great play should have been made with the establishment of a committee of acknowledged experts which Friends of the Earth and others should have been invited to join. The NGOs, knowing they would be outgunned in any objective assessment, would have been forced to reject the offer, handing the advantage back to BP.

The next step in this change in balance, gathering pace steadily over the past three decades, has been the rise of the 'corporate communications' cadre of lobbyists and public relations consultants and the growth in broadcast media with a never-ending requirement for attributable comment. Together they persuaded organisations to look again to parliament, where the former found a plentiful supply of politicians prepared to meet their clients and the latter could always rely on a flow of talking heads. The corporate lobby therefore went back to some extent to fighting in same arena as NGOs. Solving political problems became allied (even subordinate) to concern over what politicians thought of organisations; but that may itself be an indication of the impact of those who seek to attack corporate reputation.

This may, however, be no more than a sideshow. NGOs may have increased their influence and PR budgets have expanded, but the real power balance may have changed less than might be apparent. The United Kingdom and other government delegations to the World Summit included business, not NGO interests. While the media, prompted by the persuasive media machine of the activist lobby groups reported that 'campaigners warned that the decision to include multinational companies as part of the UK delegation designed to help save the planet seriously risked undermining their green credentials' (*Observer*, 11 August 2002), in the end it is the ability of major business sectors, not of activists, to comply with policy change and deliver its objectives that counts. Moreover, policy makers will always look to the technical expertise and advice on deliverability that business can offer, even if NGOs are increasingly finding themselves able to seed politicians with the questions that governments ask business to answer.

Technology Gives People More Power

This thesis divides itself into two parts: the proposition that it is media and external pressures, not access, that count these days; and the more obvious observation that technology has expanded the lobbying franchise, creating powerful tools that many can afford and use easily.

To a degree, the former argument has been given currency by the myth that the Labour Governments elected in 1997 and 2001 were uniquely both sensitive to media criticism and set on communicating direct with the electorate to the exclusion of political institutions. Of course, it does not require lengthy analysis to see that this is a phenomenon common to all governments of recent years; Labour simply took it to another level and the next government can be expected to take it further still (the ultimate objective being spin without the appearance of spin).

That is not to deny that there has been a steady increase in media power. However, attempts to analyse NGO or corporate attempts to make or reinforce a case through press or broadcast channels tend to be quantitative. In reality, most coverage bounces off the system. Ministers believe they can articulate a case or promote a message more effectively, and usually do. The best message retailers in the private sector have learnt the techniques of political parties, but they are in a small minority. Most find it harder; for one thing, the media seeks out politicians or party views whereas corporations have to fight for attention. The media campaigns that have made a noticeable difference have all been able to find enough new angles to sustain pressure over a period long enough to make decision makers feel they cannot get rid of the story. NGOs, with their simpler, more aggressive agendas, tend to be more successful at this than their business counterparts.

The second contention appears easier to prove. Websites, text messaging and e-mail are a rapid and relatively cheap means of distributing information to current and potential campaign supporters, allowing direct action such as product or site boycotts to be coordinated with a fraction of the effort previously required. Information that might have taken several people some hours to fax to worldwide media can now be e-mailed to a massive list at the touch of a button. Desk-top publishing enables campaigns to give the impression of being more professional and better funded than may actually be the case. More sophisticated technologies, such as satellite linkups and video news releases, are the province of better-funded bodies, but once again, the larger NGOs do seem to have been better at embracing them and understanding how to use them to best effect.

Electronic mail can also count in the numbers game. Most consultation responses can now be made online and some government departments and agencies encourage it. Corporations or sectors, which may have slaved at their careful, data-rich submissions, are often caught flat-footed by the old mass campaigner's trick of the Parliamentary Question about the number of responses for and against. And, although MPs regard e-mail as undifferentiated and easily deleted, as few as 20 genuine constituency messages sent to an MP's office will command attention.

None the less, the potential of these resources does not necessarily translate into ability, still less influence. Companies often find out about websites of campaigns directed at them before momentum can be generated by the organisers, who quickly realise that creating awareness of a site address is much harder than getting on line. Departments and other government bodies rarely monitor websites and discount mass pro-forma e-mailings. So do parliamentarians. A 2002 survey found that only 10 per cent of politicians conduct a quarter or more of their correspondence via e-mail.[8] The vast majority still prefer to use post; many respond to electronic messages with a written letter and 75 per cent prefer their constituents to communicate the old-fashioned way – by letter – because to them it indicates genuineness and commitment. So, although the demographics of our political community have changed, their receptiveness to modern channels of communication is not aligned to the desire of campaigners (not to mention many of their constituents) to use them. The same, it should be said, goes for a large part of the corporate PR work – the glossy brochures, videos and contact programmes – directed at them.

Conclusion

This chapter set the relative ease with which scare stories can be spread against the difficulty of communicating accurate rebuttals that are clear, simple and concise enough to be assimilated by the public, politicians and the media. It is difficult within the confines of a single chapter to counter what is evident to academic and other external observers of lobbyists' (both corporate and NGO) activities with an explanation of what actually works. But even a truncated analysis of the principal contentions leaves five clear conclusions:

- More often than not, the business lobby has played catch up, responding to rather than pre-empting pressure groups, whose lobbying techniques have advanced more rapidly.
- However, the business lobby has shown itself well able to absorb and head off the bulk of pressure group activity, admittedly at a cost – principally increased PR, lobbying and research budgets – but there is little evidence that even the most aggressive and apparently successful public campaigns has badly damaged corporations.
- While corporations now have to devote greater attention to monitoring and dealing with NGO activity, and while the rise of the corporate communicator has to an extent changed organisations' focus from that assessed in Sampson's earlier analyses, their principal concern is still the institutions of government. However nowadays it is necessary to have regard to a secondary, increasingly important objective: to insulate those

institutions from other external pressures. In other words, business is having to work harder in order to maintain its traditional relationships of influence: it is having to force itself to look down in order to continue to look up.

- As the longer-established, better funded pressure groups have learnt more of the tricks of effective influence, an increasing part of their work has brought them inside the system, with a consequent change in their profile. The ability of 'New Activists' to command public attention should not be equated with a conclusion that better known campaigners have had their day.
- While today's communication technology facilitates campaigning, it is a mistake to assume that because more people are speaking, their ultimate targets are listening more closely.

Notes

1. In the UK Parliamentary system backbench MPs are subject to 'the whip', a system that subjects them to party discipline; all MPs are expected to vote in the way their party wishes them to.
2. A UK Department of Trade and Industry minute of a mid-2002 meeting with project financiers commented on banks' concerns over public opposition to energy projects such as wind farms: 'Public opinion also influences the lending policy of the banks – with risk to reputation forming part of the environmental risk assessment for projects, even for banks that have no retail base' (*The Business*, 18/19 August 2002).
3. Enterprise Act 2002.
4. Look, for example, at the difference between the impact of the PR activities of HACAN (the Heathrow Airport Campaign Against Noise) – lots of column inches, which arguably made little difference to policy on airport noise – and the impact of its Judicial Review and European Court actions, which have noticeably concentrated ministerial and official minds.
5. Take, for example, the vexed issue of airport expansion in the southeast of England. Ministers were consistently deterred from taking action to address growing pressures on capacity because of the ability of local grassroots groups to generate a considerable level of publicity. It was only when all the interests on the other side – aviation, unions, tourism and business organisations – combined into the Freedom To Fly Coalition that ministers felt it would be safe to decide that a positive decision had to be taken. Even then, however, they went no further than identi-

fying appropriate sites and leaving it for prospective developers to manage public opinion as one of the critical requirements in securing planning permission.

6. SOGAT is a print trades union, of which Brenda Dean (now Baroness Dean) was General Secretary. SOGAT was involved in a long running dispute with Rupert Murdoch's News International.

7. A poster run by the Conservative Party during the 1992 General Election showed a pair of boxing gloves, one saying 'more taxes', the other 'higher prices'. The poster, headed 'Labour's double whammy', tried to play on fears of the Labour Party's perceived inability to run the economy and its profligate spending plans. The poster came, in many ways, to symbolise the whole election campaign.

8. International survey of corporate sustainability reporting 2002, KPMG.

CHAPTER 10

The Corporate Takeover

George Monbiot

Introduction

There has been a corporate takeover of Britain. Corporations, the contraptions we invented to serve us, are overthrowing us. They are seizing powers previously invested in government and using them to distort public life to suit their own needs. The provision of hospitals, roads and prisons in Britain has been deliberately tailored to meet corporate demands rather than public need. Urban regeneration programmes have been subverted to serve the interests of private companies, and planning permission is offered for sale to the highest bidder. Superstores have achieved pre-eminence in Britain, by closing down competing stores and controlling their suppliers.

There are curious discrepancies between the duties of business people appointed to government posts and their former activities. Biotechnology companies have sought to turn the food chain into a controllable commodity and there is an extraordinary web of influence linking them to government ministers and government agencies. There has also been a corporate takeover of British universities, and a resulting distortion of the research and teaching agendas. There are many examples of the corporate takeover but it also includes schools, a neglect of health and safety enforcement and a deregulation of business coupled with the increasing regulation of the citizen. *Captive State: The Corporate Takeover of Britain* (Monbiot, 2000), showed how corporations have come to govern key decision-making processes within the European Union and, with the British Government's blessing, begun to develop a transatlantic single market, controlled and run by corporate chief executives.

This chapter seeks to support the assertion of the corporate takeover and show how corporations look to extend their power and influence. It also suggests some of the means by which corporate power might be contained and accountable, democratic government protected from its excesses. This places a heavy emphasis on the role of activists and activism, expecting them to grow as a reaction to corporate power.

The Political Setting

This is not the first time that corporate power has threatened democracy. Gladstone's efforts to regulate the rail industry, for example, were obstructed by 132 MPs who held directorships in railway companies. Abraham Lincoln wrote: 'I see in the near future a crisis approaching that unnerves me and causes me to tremble for the safety of my country. . . . Corporations have been enthroned and an era of corruption in high places will follow.'[1]

These powers have re-emerged, yet the government shows few signs of trembling for the safety of its country. New Labour, its leaders often remind us, is 'the party of business', which aims to establish 'the most business friendly environment in the world'.[2] There is, Tony Blair told the Confederation of British Industry, 'great commitment and enthusiasm, right across the government, for forging links with the business community'.[3] 'We want a society', the former cabinet minister, Peter Mandelson, announced, 'that celebrates and values its business heroes as much as it does pop stars and footballers'.[4]

Parliamentary opposition to the corporate takeover of Britain is muted. The Conservative Party, which initiated many of the intrigues to which the Labour Party has succumbed, calls only for the needs of business to be better served. Some Liberal Democrat MPs have spoken out against the corporate threat to parliamentary sovereignty, but they have, for the most part, been ignored. Though many Labour backbenchers are apprehensive of the implications for democracy, most have been stifled and silenced.

This is not to suggest, however, that the appeasement of corporations by the British Government is either consistent or comprehensive. Some ministers, such as David Clark, Nigel Griffiths and Michael Meacher, have sought to resist the delegation of their powers to unelected business people. As (former) Secretary of State for Trade and Industry, Margaret Beckett established a reputation, only partially deserved, of treating applications for takeovers and mergers with caution. Most of the resisters have, however, been sacked, in Clark and Griffiths' case for the cardinal sin of keeping the promises in Labour's manifesto.

Some policies have been approved which displease corporations: the introduction of a minimum wage, for example, of energy taxes, limited working hours and the recognition of trades unions. But in every case, the impact of the new legislation has been cushioned until it meets only the minimum demands of the unions, or the minimum standards required by European Union directives or international treaties.

The trades unions were dismayed when their members failed to secure a right to bargain collectively with employers. They found the minimum wage levels disappointing, especially as a lower band was established for 18–21 year-olds. The government's energy tax proposals have twice been downgraded to allow major rebates for the most energy-intensive industries. There is, it has assured corporations, no more to come. The new employment legislation, Tony Blair insists, 'seeks to draw a line under the issue of industrial relations law. . . . Even after the changes we propose, Britain will have the most lightly regulated labour market of any leading economy in the world'.[5]

It is not hard to see why corporations might wish to infiltrate government. Their demands and those of the electorate are frequently in conflict. By bypassing the electoral process, communicating directly with ministers and officials, they can pre-empt legislation that might be popular but would restrict their ability to make money. Many businesses see government as an opportunity as well as a problem. It has long been a source for funds: relocation development grants, research money and training costs, contracts, R&D grants, for example. It also controls that part of the economy that some firms have identified as their means of future growth. In the 1980s, corporations lobbied for, and secured, a widespread privatisation or part privatisation of state-owned assets. It continues, through the private finance initiative, to this day.

Opportunities for privatisation are now more limited than they were in the mid-1980s, however, as the most accessible possessions of the state have already been procured, and public resistance impedes more ambitious schemes. Now many of the worlds biggest companies have chosen a new route to growth: consolidation. By engineering a single, 'harmonised' global market, in which they can sell the same product under the same conditions anywhere on earth, they are hoping to extract formidable economies of scale. They are seizing, in other words, those parts of the global economy still controlled by small and medium-sized businesses.

To succeed, big business has to push government out of the way. It must extract politics from the national domain and move it into the international sphere where the electorate, faced with the failing health, safety and the environmental protection standards that accompany harmonisation, cannot intervene. A compliant state, willing to assist in its own redundancy, is an indispensable asset.

At first sight, it is hard to see why a government should wish to allow the corporations to usurp it. However on closer examination there may be several reasons.

The most obvious is that the simplest means of obtaining power is to appease those who possess it already. The Conservative administration, whose links with big business could fairly be described as organic, built up the power of corporations in Britain, placing their representatives on official committees or even in Cabinet, handing over control of key sectors of the economy, deregulating business practices and harnessing the civil service to their advancement. International bodies such as the World Trade Organisation and some sections of the European Commission have also succumbed to corporate control. Confronting big business now means confronting all the institutions it has captured and co-opted.

Consolidation in the print and broadcast media industries has also enabled a few well-placed conglomerates to exert a prodigious influence over public opinion. They have used it, unsurprisingly, to campaign for increasing freedom for business (and, incidentally, reduced freedoms for everyone else). Globalisation, moreover, has enabled companies to hold a gun to governments' heads: if a government refuses to meet their demands, they threaten to disinvest, move their plant to Thailand, and damage its credibility by making thousands of workers redundant. The sheer size of the new trans-national corporations also enables them to swing an unprecedented weight.

The Labour Party, in other words, like left and centre parties all over the world, was presented with a brutal choice. It could continue to oppose the massively increased forces of corporate Britain, with the result that it would face a hard and painful struggle to be elected, and the possible disappearance of the party if it failed. Or it could bend to the power of business, promising that it would deliver not only what the corporations wanted, but also, in the absence of an official anti-corporate opposition, a pliant parliament and a discouraged electorate.

The problem with appeasement, of course, is that it makes the appeased more powerful, which makes the needs to appease them still greater. As the Labour Government was confident of winning a second term in office (which it did in June 2001), it appeared to have worried less about the electorate than about business, which seems more likely to switch its allegiance back to the Conservatives. Finally, not all the opportunities provided for corporations are provided deliberately. Their ability to exploit every ambiguity and uncertainty offered by legislation borders, sometimes, on genius. One cannot blame them: enterprising companies will always seek to maximise their opportunities. But a government that allows them to do so at the public's expense is a government that has surely lost its way.

The Historical Background

The corporation is an ingenious device for acquiring rights and shedding responsibilities. This was not, however, how the institution was conceived. The solicitor Daniel Bennett has written a brief history of corporate emancipation (Bennett, 1999). He notes that the first corporations in Britain were charitable institutions such as churches, schools and hospitals, which used incorporation to avoid the legal and financial problems – for example, death duties – encountered by a body which outlived its founders. These organisations were licensed by the Crown, which determined what they could and could not do. Engaging in profitable commercial activities was forbidden.

By the end of the sixteenth century, the monarch granted 'charters of incorporation' to trade associations. The associations were granted a royal monopoly in certain economic sectors, but did not buy and sell in their own right. Businesses had to join an association in order to trade. This closely regulated system began to break down after a trade association called the East India Company was chartered. It slowly and unlawfully transformed itself into a profit-making company of shareholders, jointly owning the stock previously belonging to its member businesses.

Other trade associations swiftly followed suit, and soon the Crown and then parliament began to licence them as commercial corporations. They were stifled after the bursting of the South Sea Bubble in 1720 but began to re-emerge towards the end of the century. Gradually they acquired many of the legal rights hitherto granted only to individuals. Governments lost the ability to destroy them if they exceeded their powers.

Throughout the twentieth century, companies learnt new means of discarding their obligations: establishing subsidiaries, often based offshore and in possession of no significant assets, for example, to handle contentious operations. In 1998, a leaked letter from the Lord Chancellor's office revealed that the government was planning to protect British-based multinationals from legal claims made against them by workers in developing countries (*Observer*, 8 November 1998). In 1999, the Court of Appeal forbade 3000 South Africans suffering asbestos poisoning to sue Cape plc, the corporation alleged to be responsible, in the British courts, even though Cape is a British Company. While they appear able to exempt themselves from national law, multinational companies also remain immune from international human rights law, which applies only to states. At the same time, however, corporations in Britain are able to sue for libel, to call the police if their property is threatened, to take out injunctions against protestors or workers. They may use the law as if they were human beings but in key respects they are no longer subject to it.

The Growing Power of Corporations

Defenders of corporate power have argued that the companies' freedom of action is crucial to the survival of a competitive economy. If their operations were restricted, they would leave the country, moving to places in which they could trade more freely. The result would be widespread unemployment and a collapsing tax base. Business, some argue, being more efficient and better organised than the state, is better placed to manage public life than government.

It is true that some companies might leave the country if the climate for investment becomes less favourable, although the threat has often been exaggerated. There is no question that greater corporate freedom worldwide puts pressure on every nation to undercut its neighbours by relaxing its standards. But it is important to determine precisely what conditions are required to encourage corporations to stay, and which gifts are superfluous, and whose withdrawal would be met with grumbling but no action. More importantly, as nation-states negotiate international treaties, they surely seek to arrest the race to the bottom that some of these compacts appear to encourage. The World Trade Agreement, for example, sets maximum standards for the protection of workers, consumers and the environment, but not minimum standards. Were states to negotiate higher global standards, they would be able to protect their citizens without fearing the loss of capital and jobs.

It is also true that many corporations are efficient and well managed. But they are, by definition, managed in interests at variance with those of the public. Their directors have a 'fiduciary duty' towards the shareholders: they must place their concerns above all others. The state, by contrast, has a duty towards all members of the public, and must strive to achieve a balance between their competing interests. Interestingly, the former minister Peter Mandelson, regarded by many as the most amenable to corporate power, appears to recognise this conflict. 'It is not practical or desirable', he wrote in 1996 'for company boards to . . . represent different stakeholder interests. Boards should be accountable to shareholders' (Mandelson and Liddle, 1996).

We hear plenty about the economies of scale, but there is a politics of scale as well: the bigger business becomes, the more we, as consumers and citizens, shrink by comparison. As businesses grow, the power of customers becomes blunt and diffuse. The diffusion of consumer power makes markets less responsive to demand. They may be sensitive to price, for example, but they are likely to be less able to respond to narrower requirements. This is why, when people who work outdoors want a pair of trousers that will last for years, they do not go to the outdoors shop in the high street, but to the army surplus store, whose products will give them three or four times the use. This is because, inefficient as it is, the initial purchaser, the Ministry of Defence, wields power in the marketplace. Big enough to be heard by the supplier, it can fine tune its demand until it obtains precisely what it wants.

Nor is it always true that prices will fall as businesses consolidate. While the companies may reach significant economies of scale, they may experience less pressure, as they grow, to pass them on to consumers. This appears to have been the experience, for example, of Britain's superstores. The vertical integration and *de facto* cartels in some sectors are likely to make the market less competitive.

Most importantly, however, big business means big politics. The bigger companies become, the more power they accumulate. As they grow, their concerns become ever further removed from those of the citizens they dwarf, until the world is run not for the benefit of its 6 billion poor or merely comfortable inhabitants, but for that of a handful of remote billionaires.

In Britain, small business in some sectors appears to be threatened with extinction. Independent butchers, bakers, fishmongers and greengrocers have all but disappeared from many high streets. Small farmers are swiftly being absorbed by large units, many of which are run by city-based management companies and investment firms. Car dealerships, filling stations, hotels and restaurants, breweries, local newspapers, television companies and publishers are concentrating in ever fewer hands. Even the Internet, which spawned thousands of small companies in the 1990s, now appears to be consolidating.

The death of small business is accompanied by the emergence of giga-corporations: companies who shares are valued in the many billions of dollars. Though the value of mergers and acquisitions in Europe broke all records in 1998, it doubled again in 1999, according to the *Financial Times* (23 December 1999). The United Kingdom is the most acquisitive nation in Europe, responsible for US$386 billion worth of takeovers in 1999, in comparison with second-placed Germany's total of $261 billion (ibid.). The corporations appeared determined to beat their own record within the first few months of 2000. The Royal Bank of Scotland overcame National Westminster Bank's resistance and bought it for £21bn. The drugs companies SmithKline Beecham and Glaxo-Wellcome – themselves, as their name suggests, the products of recent mergers – agreed a union that would create a single, £114bn company. Vodafone Airtouch seized the German mobile phone company Mannesman for £113bn. In America, Time Warner and the Internet company, AOL, concluded the biggest corporate deal in history, worth, according to some estimates, almost $300bn.

One result of this consolidation is that we are faced with a profusion of minor choices and a dearth of major ones. We can enter a superstore and choose between 20 different brands of margarine, but many of us have no choice but to enter the superstore. Were we to tell the corporations dominating some sectors that, dissatisfied with their services, we shall take our custom elsewhere, they would ask us which planet we had in mind. Employees blessed with certain skills and qualifications have more management opportunities to grasp than ever before, with the promise of vast bonuses and share options for the most fortunate. But the opportunities to enter business on your own account are, in many sectors, limited. The opportunity to drop out altogether and survive, for example, as a small farmer or craftsman has been all but eradicated.

The struggle between people and corporations will be the defining battle of the twenty-first century. If the corporations win, liberal democracy will come to an end. The great social democratic institutions that have defended the weak against the strong – equality before the law, representative government, democratic accountability and sovereignty of parliament – will be toppled. If, on the other hand, the corporate attempt on public life is beaten back, then democracy may re-emerge the stronger for its conquest. But this victory cannot be brokered by our representatives. Democracy will only survive if the people in whose name they govern rescue the state from its captivity.

Regulation

For the past 15 years, people seeking to challenge corporate power have been increasingly regulated. The 1986 Public Order Act restricted the right to demonstrate. The 1992 Trade Union Act criminalised many previously legal union activities, among them such grave threats to public order as carrying insulting banners. The 1994 Criminal Justice Act empowered the police to break up most public protests. The 1996 Security Service Act and 1997 Police Act include in their definition of serious crime 'conduct by a large number of persons in pursuit of a common purpose': peaceful protestors were thus exposed to state endorsed bugging, burglary and arbitrary searches. MPs warned the government that the 1997 Anti-Stalking Act could be used against non-violent demonstrators. The warnings were ignored with the result that several campaigners have been served with injunctions or arrested for protests outside company premises.

The Terrorism Bill, debated in parliament in 2000, expands the definition of terrorism to include 'the use of threat, for the purpose of advancing a political, religious or ideological cause, of action which . . . involves serious violence against any person or property'. Anyone found in possession of 'information' that might indicate a 'reasonable suspicion' that it could be used for such purposes is identified by the bill as a terrorist. This definition would reclassify, for example, both the activists tearing up genetically engineered crops and the sympathisers receiving their literature.

Business, on the other hand, has been released from many of its obligations. When Labour came to power, David Clark, the former Chancellor of the Duchy of Lancaster indicated that he would drop the Conservative policy of removing as many restrictions on business as possible. He replaced the Conservative Government's Deregulation Unit with a Better Regulation Unit, explaining that:

> A fair, safe and prosperous society depends on good regulation. People look to government to ensure benefits such as fair terms of employment, a cleaner environment and safer products. In many cases, statutory regulations are the only or best way to pursue such aims.
>
> (Clark, 1997)

Nigel Griffiths, the former Minister for Consumer Affairs, appeared to share his views. In May 1998, to the fury of corporate lobbyists, he refused to water down Britain's implementation of the European Union's Consumer Protective Directive. In July 1998, both ministers were sacked.

David Clark had been obliged to appoint as chair of the Better Regulation Taskforce Lord Haskins, who is the head of the wholesaling company, Northern Foods. He was also a member of the Hampel Committee on Corporate Governments, which did nothing to disguise its contempt for regulatory burdens on business. The report he helped to compile for the committee declared, 'The emphasis on accountability has tended to obscure a board's first responsibility . . . to enhance the prosperity of the business over time'.[6] Unsurprisingly, his taskforce argued that there should be fewer rules for British business. It suggested that state regulation be replaced by self-regulation, economic incentives and codes of practice, such as those 'operated by the Advertising Standards Authority' (Haskins, 1998).

By September 1998, the government had entirely reversed its initial policy. There would, it announced, be fewer government inspectors, enforcing fewer regulations. The inspectors would cease to be industry police, and become advisors instead. In June 1999, Stephen Byers, the then Secretary of State for Trade and Industry, told the British Chambers of Commerce that the government 'will be applying the following key principles to our work from now on: . . . a presumption against regulation. Regulation will only be introduced where absolutely necessary and where all other avenues have been pursued.' Regulations would 'automatically lapse' after a certain date. Enforcement, he promised would be 'business friendly'.[7]

In April 1999, the Better Regulation Unit was replaced by the Regulatory Impact Unit. Rather than balancing the interests of the public and corporations, as David Clark had proposed to do, the new unit would 'help government reduce the cumulative burden of regulation' and ensure 'greater consultation with industry'.[8] It would, it promised, seek out any regulations it deemed unnecessary and eliminate them.

The business-friendly press campaigns stoutly against regulation – or red tape, as its opponents always call it – and it is true that some rules have fallen too heavily on small businesses in Britain. But regulation is all that prevents companies from dumping their costs on society. If corporations are allowed to encourage smoking by advertising cigarettes, for example, more people are likely to contract smoking-related diseases. If car manufacturers are not prevented from attaching bull bars to the front of their vehicles, then more of the children hit by cars will die. If pollution control measures are abandoned, the environment will be destroyed. Deregulation, in other words, can become a subsidy for careless or greedy companies. Its effects are felt most keenly by workers in hazardous industries.

There appears to be a direct inverse relationship between the vigour with which companies are prosecuted for endangering their employees and the number of people killed, maimed, blinded or disabled. If companies are treated gently, workers are treated harshly.

In Britain, money is officially more valuable than human life. The directors of British companies are individually responsible for keeping the price of their shares as high as they can. If they neglect this 'fiduciary duty', they can be prosecuted and imprisoned. If, on the other hand, they neglect to protect their workforce, with the result that an employee is killed, they remain, in practice, immune from prosecution. At present the company, if it is unlucky, will suffer an inconsequential fine, which will not touch on the lives of the directors.

If governments are not prepared to regulate, they must, as Lord Haskins suggested, use 'economic incentives' to amend corporate behaviour. Compliance, in other words, must be bought. There are already plenty of means by which money is transferred from the state to corporations.

Corporations have learnt that by threatening to move elsewhere, precipitating the loss of thousands of jobs, they can ensure not only that the regulations they dislike are removed, but also that governments will pay vast amounts of money to persuade them to stay. By playing nations or regions off against each other, the companies can effectively auction their services, securing hundreds of millions of pounds of taxpayers' money that might otherwise have been spent, for example, on hospitals or schools. While taxpayers' money is being given to corporations, corporations are required to contribute ever decreasing amounts of tax. Even before the Labour Government came to power, corporation tax in Britain was the lowest of any major industrialised country. The Conservatives had reduced it from 52 per cent to 33 per cent. In 1997, the Labour Government cut it by a further 2 per cent. In 1999, it cut it again to 30 per cent. The Chancellor, Gordon Brown, boasted that this was 'now the lowest rate in the history of British corporation tax, the lowest rate in any major country in Europe and the lowest rate of any major industrialised country anywhere, including Japan and the United States'.[9]

Yet, while these corporation taxes have withered, personal taxation in Britain, as the Conservatives have pointed out, rose by some eight pence in the pound during the first three years of Labour's term in office. This reflects a long-term trend. Corporation tax in the United States, the *Economist* magazine reports (31 May 1997), brought in a third of the total federal revenues before the Second World War. Now it accounts for just 12 per cent, a quarter of the amount delivered by personal taxation. More mobile than ever before, big businesses can bully governments into relieving them of their responsibilities. If a state will not cut the taxes it levies, they threaten to disinvest, and move to somewhere that will. The highly paid, like the corporations which employ them, can also play one state off against another, driving down the top rates of income tax. The tax burden, as a result, has shifted to those who cannot get away: the poor and middle-income earners.

While businesses devise ever more ingenious ways of escaping taxation, they also lobby to ensure that the rest of us pay our dues. In October 1999, the Confederation of British Industry told the government that it should not reduce taxes on consumers, but spend its surplus money, instead, on public infrastructure (which would, incidentally, provide more revenue for corporations, especially those hoping to secure more contracts under the private finance initiative). In the same statement, however, it suggested that corporation tax should continue to be reduced (*Observer*, 31 October 1999). The corporate takeover of Britain is to be financed not by the corporations, but by you and me.

Corporations, it has to be remembered, will do anything to protect their position. Included in this is the creation of 'fake citizens' to try and change the way we think. Persuasion works best when it is invisible. The most effective marketing worms its way into our consciousness, leaving that perception that we have reached our opinions and made our choices independently. While, in the past, companies have created fake citizens' groups to campaign in favour of trashing forests or polluting rivers, now they create fake citizens. Messages purporting to come from disinterested punters are planted on list servers at critical moments, disseminating misleading information in the hope of recruiting real people to the cause. Detective work by campaigner Jonathan Matthews and freelance journalist Andy Rowell has recently showed how a PR company contracted to the biotech giant Monsanto appears to have played a crucial but invisible role in shaping scientific discourse. Following the publication of an article in *Nature* magazine, which claimed that native maize in Mexico had been contaminated across vast distances by GM pollen, Monsanto let loose fake citizens to undermine the credibility of the article. These messages stimulated hundreds of others, some of which repeated or embellished the initial accusations. This activity persuaded the journal to do something it had never done before, and retract a paper it had published.

Such activities do not stop at the creation of false citizens or citizen's groups. There are also websites that coordinate movements against environmentalists, lobby groups and even a fake scientific institute called the 'Centre for Food and Agricultural Research'. We have been confronted, in truth, by the crafted response of corporations without emotional attachment.

There is also infiltration. Even organisations established to defend citizens are opening themselves to the power of the corporations. The genius of capitalism is its ability to capture the genius of everything else. The National Consumer Council, established with UK Government funds in 1975 to safeguard the interests of consumers, has launched a 'Friends' initiative, which for £10,000 a year allows companies to 'inform our thinking on consumer policy'. The Council has promised its new donors that it 'will recognise the legitimacy of your perspective when we select work', which seems to mean that corporate sponsorship of the Council will influence the scope of its research.

Forum for the Future, the environment group set up by Jonathon Porritt and Sara Parkin, takes money from BP, ICI, Tesco and Blue Circle. All these companies, according to the Forum's magazine, 'have a demonstrable commitment to the pursuit of sustainable development'. I would challenge this. The World Wide Fund for Nature has moved even closer to its new friends, by appointing as its boss the former chief executive of one of Britain's most controversial quarrying companies. In Papua New Guinea, it struck a deal with the oil firms Chevron and BP. The oilmen gave a WWF conservation project $1 million. In return, leaked documents from Chevron revealed, 'WWF will act as a buffer for the joint venture against . . . international environmental criticism'. Going for Green struck a deal with McDonald's to print environmental messages on the company's sugar sachets. An environmental group, in other words, was helping McDonald's to create the impression that it was protecting the environment, without changing any of its practices. All these organisations insist that taking money from business doesn't change the way they work.

Conclusion

Big business has seized so much of the economy that when large corporations leave the economic consequences can be disastrous. By bidding against each other to attract companies, countries undermine each other's standards and expose their populations to predatory practices. We need, in other words, global trade agreements that set harmonised minimum standards, rather than only harmonised maximum standards.

Multinational firms must be forced to conform to the international rules binding those states that have joined the United Nations. They should be legally obliged, for example, to protect their employees from accident and neglect wherever they operate, and to refrain from harming consumers or the wider community and damaging the environment. They should be subject to human rights laws, enforceable anywhere on earth, whose neglect would result in prosecution at international tribunals.

Global taxation measures – harmonising corporate taxes, preventing companies from shifting their monies to tax havens, and levying a tariff on all international currency transaction – would forestall one of the world's gravest impending problems: the erosion of the tax base as states offer ever more generous terms to the ultra-rich in order to attract money. These would not be easy either to implement or to enforce, not least because they would hand a formidable advantage to countries playing outside the rules. Whether we intervene or not, however, corporate taxes will converge worldwide, but downwards, rather than upwards. It is possible to conceive a system of sanctions against tax havens, rather like sanctions imposed today upon countries seeking to protect their markets. Perhaps there should also be a worldwide cap on executive pay, tackling inequality by ensuring that mangers and directors cannot be given more than a certain multiple – eight or ten perhaps – of the salary of the lowest-paid member of their workforce, including subcontractors. If bosses wanted to raise their wages, they would have to raise everyone else's as well.

Corporations will never be subject to meaningful international rules while the negotiation of global agreements is opaque and undemocratic. We need to democratise international decision making, so that it remains within the public domain rather than being removed to the murky world of corporate lawyers and unaccountable committees. This might involve, for example, prior parliamentary approval of all national negotiating positions. We should consider holding referenda on the most important international decisions, just as the UK Government proposes a referendum whether or not to enter the European single currency.

The corporations are powerful only because we have allowed them to be. In theory, it is we, not they, who mandate the state. But we have neglected our duty of citizenship, and they have taken advantage of our neglect to seize the reins of government. Their power is an artefact of our acquiescence.

Governments will reassert their control over corporations, in other words, only when people reassert their control over governments. If political participation could break the bars of totalitarian state communism, it can certainly force elective governments to hold corporations to account. The real crisis for progressives, indeed for social democracy in general, arises from the gradual atomisation of society.

This reassertion of control will only happen through the peaceful mobilisation of millions of people in nations all across the world. Globalisation, in other words, must be matched with internationalism: campaigning, worldwide, for better means of government.

We have little powers as consumers. Consumer democracy is an illusion, not least because some have more votes than others. Those with the most power in the market are disinclined to use it to change the system that has rewarded them so well. There are, moreover, few parts of the economy from which we can withdraw our custom: we might dispute the merits of the Private Finance Initiative, for example, but if we fall ill we have to go to hospital. At present, many people have no choice but to shop at supermarkets or eat food containing the products of genetic engineering.

Nor is there a political system that, if we were open to embrace it, would solve all our problems. There is no utopia, no perfect state. A political system is only as good as the capacity of its critics to attack it. They are the people who enforce the checks and balances that prevent any faction – the corporations, the aristocracy, the armed forces, even, for that matter, trade unions or environmental groups – from wielding excessive power.

Our strength, in other words, lies in our citizenship, in our ability to engage in democratic politics, to use exposure, enfranchisement and dissent to prise our representatives out of the arms of the powers they have embraced. We must, in other words, cause trouble. We must put the demo back into democracy.

Troublemaking is the means by which both dispossession and the laws enforcing it are challenged. It is a costly nuisance, a drain on public resources, an impediment to the smooth functioning of government. It is also the sole guarantor of liberty. It forces our representatives to listen to those they have failed to represent. There are signs that agitation is already beginning to extract a few concessions. The World Trade Organisation has been forced to take note of some of the concerns of developing countries, after their sustained objections and demonstrations in Seattle. Some trading relationships are also beginning to shift. While governments have been attempting to engineer a single, harmonised global trading system, citizens' groups throughout Europe and the United States are breaking the market up. Organic box schemes and local farmers' markets have begun to restore some balance to commercial encounters, reducing the scale of business until the power of producers and consumers is roughly equivalent, reintroducing accountability to the food chain, curbing the environmental impacts of production and transport. In some sectors, such as farming, forestry and fishing, some companies have been obliged to seek a licence to trade, submitting their products to independent certification by a body such as the Soil Association or the Forest Stewardship Council. Though the power of consumers is, as I have suggested, limited, such constraints are likely to spread to other sectors. While governments are ever more reluctant to regulate, citizens seem to be able to force corporations to shoulder a few of their responsibilities.

It would be a mistake, however, to assume that big business will be easily subjugated. The corporations' grip on the state is firm, and most of the citizens' movements resisting it are, as yet, weak. Those seeking to contain corporate power will be forced to confront not only the corporations themselves but also the states that have succumbed to their dominion. They will suffer privations, vilification and, as the law is further distorted to accommodate business demands, even imprisonment. But the struggle for freedom was ever thus.

No one else will fight this battle for us. There will be no messiah, no conquering hero to deliver us from the corporate Leviathan. Most of our representatives have either been co-opted or crushed. Only one thing can reverse the corporate takeover of Britain. It is you.

Notes

1.   Abraham Lincoln, 21 November 1864, letter to Col. William F. Elkins.
2.   Peter Mandelson, then Secretary of State for Trade and Industry, 2 November 1998, speech to the Confederation of British Industry's annual conference.
3.   Tony Blair, 11 November 1997, speech to the Confederation of British Industry's annual conference.
4.   Peter Madelson, op. cit.
5.   Tony Blair, May 1998, foreword to the *Fairness at Work* white paper, Department of Trade and Industry.
6.   *The Hampel Report on Corporate Governance*, cited in *The Times*, 5 February 1998.
7.   Speech to the British Chambers of Commerce, 3 June 1999. http://www.dti.gov.uk/Minspeech/byers04-699.htm
8.   http://193.128.244.178/regulation/index.htm, May 2000.
9.   Speech to the CBI conference, 1 November 1999. http://treasury.gov.uk/press/1999/p179_99.html

CHAPTER 11

Food Protest and the New Activism

Martin Caraher

Introduction

There is a long tradition of food being at the forefront of popular protest. Fernández-Armesto (2001 and 2003) contends that food was the basis of the 'first class system'. Yet the focus of food historians has been on the gargantuan appetite and the development of surplus, which for many is seen as socially functional. The scraps from the tables of the rich were seen as feeding the poor, and grateful they should be! Yet food as an element of protest is a fact of life. This protest takes two forms, which are not mutually exclusive but sit at opposite ends of a continuum of protest. The first occurs where there is a huge disparity in food intake between the rich and the poor, the second where food is a metaphor for other ills that are occurring in the world. The former type of protest is in many instances difficult, as populations when they reach this stage, as in a time of famine, may not be capable of formal protest, lacking the means to protest (both the physical and practical means, such as finance). The latter use of food as a metaphor and target for protest representing wider issues such as the globalisation of the neoliberal economics is now the more common form of protest where food is concerned. The targeting of McDonald's or Starbucks as symbols of corporate globalisation (and/or Americanisation) is thus common. While some protestors may not understand the intricacies of the General Agreement on Tariffs and Trade (GATT) or Trade-Related Aspects of Intellectual Property Rights (TRIPS), food stands in as a useful metaphor for the ills that the above agreements represent. From this it is but a short step to using food as a rallying call to protest against the new world order.

Food itself, its production and its trade links demand our attention due to the inequalities inherent in the processes. Bygrave (2002) highlighted the strength of the protestors, which was the broadness of the alliance, and the same strength was also identified as a potential weakness. My contention is that the use of food as a rallying call is useful as it embodies both the physical and the metaphorical and is an issue that all can identify with, because of our shared biological need for and social engagement with food. But the diverse nature of, and understanding of, the global food system by various interests also provides potential sources of division. For example, there is a tension between whether to adopt an approach forwarding reform or revolution; what the exact focus of food protests should be; whether inequity in the global food system or the targeting of the visible symbols of the global capitalism should be the focus.

Food itself is a unifying issue that can be both a public good in that it can be seen as contributing to the health of a population, but also a private good in that it is subject to the law of supply and demand. It can also be regulated to create a middle ground between the public and private; in the United Kingdom food is zero-rated for VAT thus placing it within the category of a utility that contributes to health. In some developing countries, the World Food Programme school-feeding initiative provides another example of how food is regarded as making a contribution to the public health of a community. The entitlement to food occupies the realms of citizenship, where people and communities have a right to an adequate amount of safe wholesome food; and at the same time food is a consumer good where the entitlement may be mediated by trade and financial rights (Sen, 1981).

Even though food changed over the last hundred years, as we enter a new century it retains a fundamental truth at its core. As well as being essential for bodily health, food also represents a view of society. The nicknames we give to various nationalities are often tied in to different eating styles (e.g. the Swiss and Germans called Italian seasonal railway workers 'macaroni gluttons', the French were called 'frog eaters' by the English and the Germans were known as 'krauts', i.e. sauerkraut eaters). The metaphors used to describe the globalisation process come from the area of food such as McDonaldisation or Coca-Colaisation.

While the new generation of NGOs (such as Greenpeace and Friends of the Earth) are developing sophisticated ways of dealing with the new global order, other activists become disenchanted and seek ways of direct action. Those protestors who through their violence gain media attention may be less concerned with the issues of reform of the system then with its overthrow, and may in fact be helping divert attention from the real problems. Some NGOs devise ways of using both approaches by tackling policy and encouraging a boycott of products (see Box 11.1 for an example of Baby Milk Action, which combines policy and direct action).

Box 11.1 Baby Milk Action

Baby Milk Action is a non-profit organisation that aims to save lives and to end the avoidable suffering caused by inappropriate infant feeding. It works within a global network to strengthen independent, transparent and effective controls on the marketing of the baby feeding industry.

The global network is called IBFAN (the International Baby Food Action Network) a network of over 150 citizens' groups in more than 90 countries.

The World Health Organisation (WHO) estimates that 1.5 million infants die around the world every year because they are not breast-fed. Where water is unsafe a bottle-fed child is up to 25 times more likely to die as a result of diarrhoea than a breastfed one.

That is why a marketing code was introduced in 1981 to regulate the marketing of breastmilk substitutes. Companies continue to violate its provisions.

Taken from www.babymilkaction.org/

Food Riots and the Underlying Moral Economy

E. P. Thompson (1993), in his review of the 'moral economy' of the English crowd in the eighteenth century, noted that food riots were often a flash point for the anger of the populace. They were aimed at a more fundamental truth, which was the erosion of traditional liberties and privileges, and food offered a convenient focus for dissent and social protest rather than a protest merely against food or hunger. The riots coincided with the demise of the medieval economy and social order, and the growth of the pre-industrial and early industrial economy. Riots were social calamities and engaged the energies of the 'mob'; the response of the civic authorities was muted. For some this was seen as collusion with the mob; for others it was a way of absorbing the mob's energies and attention so that structurally nothing much changed. Hence the constant round of riots throughout Britain (see Box 11.2).

The economic dogma espoused by Adam Smith (*The Wealth of Nations*), in the eighteenth century, claimed that free trade and a self-regulating economy would result in social progress. He advocated that government needed only to preserve law and order, justice, defend the nation and provide for a few social needs that could not be met through the market. This philosophy

Box 11.2 Food riots in Britain

The demands of the crowd generally focused on two issues:

- grain riots (because of the importance of bread in the diet) to stop the movement of grain out of a region usually in years of poor harvest and
- price fixing.

The Swing Riots in the 1830s were influenced by the poor harvest of 1829 and the introduction of thrashing machines in Kent, Sussex and Hants. They were named after letters signed by 'Captain Swing'.

The Plug Riots of 1842 were a phase of the 'hungry forties'. They took their name from the rioters attacking the mills and removing plugs from the boilers. The movement was related to Chartism.

of free trade was used to justify non-intervention in the Irish famine of 1845–7 and the great Bengal famine of 1943 (Sen, 1981) and more recently in the Ethiopian famines of the 1970s and 1980s. Yet food is one of the goods that, as well as being necessary for physical development and the maintenance of health, also fulfils a social need. This can be seen in the development of public health policy related to food in the eighteenth and nineteenth centuries (Hamlin, 1998). Today we see a re-emergence of Adam Smith's dogma in the global economy in the policies of the World Bank and the International Monetary Fund and global regulatory bodies such as WTO, through the doctrine of neoliberal economics (Hertz, 2001). The new economic juggernauts are not the imperialist nation-states of old but the new order of large multinational or trans-national corporations (TNCs).

Thompson's (1993) analysis that direct protests (in his case food riots), if not actually encouraged by those in power, were tolerated as ways of distracting attention from the real forces of change (i.e. changes in the political and economic order) can equally be applied to the riots in Seattle and subsequent protests. The Seattle riots attracted a lot of publicity but achieved little in terms of bringing about change (Cockburn *et al.*, 2000; Thomas 2002). However, the negotiations of the various NGOs around the table have probably achieved equally little (see the comments from Vandana Shiva in Box 11.3).

Box 11.3 Extract from press release from Vandana Shiva following the World Summit on Sustainable Development 2002

The World Summit on Sustainable Development (WSSD) organized in Johannesburg from 26 August–4 September 2002 was supposed to have been the Earth Summit II – ten years after the Earth Summit organized in Rio de Janeiro in 1992. Instead of Rio + 10, WSSD became Doha + 10. Ten months ago, the Ministerial Meeting of WTO was organised in Doha to salvage the WTO negotiations for a new enlarged round which had failed in Seattle due to citizen protest and a walk out by smaller countries who had been marginalized and excluded in the negotiations. The implementation document of WSSD mentioned Doha and WTO 46 times at one stage and Rio only once. The draft had been introduced undemocratically by the United States and European Union, and with minor modifications was reintroduced by South Africa. There was no rebellion by governments against the surreptitious substitution of the sustainability agenda of Rio with the commercial and corporate agenda of WTO.

While the struggles of the poor in the South are related to their access and rights to natural resources – land, water and biodiversity – and hence are intrinsically environmental and ecological struggles, WSSD was artificially presented as being about 'poverty', not about the 'environment'. Globalization was then offered as the solution to poverty, and decisions that were aimed at robbing the poor of their remaining resources and hence making them poorer such as privatization of water, patenting of seeds and alienation of land, were being offered as measures for 'poverty alleviation'. While the landless people and the movements against privatization marched for environmental and resource rights, globalization pundits kept repeating the mantra that the poor could not afford the 'luxury' of their natural capital – they needed globalization. Globalizers do not see that globalization would rob the poor of their resources, make them the property of global corporations who would then sell water and seeds at high cost to the poor thus pushing them deeper into poverty, and over the edge of survival. During PBS/BBC debate in which I participated, [an] industry spokesman clearly said that imposing private property rights to natural resources was their first priority. Globalizing the non-sustainable, unethical, iniquitous systems of ownership, control and use of natural resources was the main agenda at WSSD.

> Only the governments of Norway and Ethiopia spoke up against attempts to make the multilateral environment agreements (MEAs) of Rio subservient to the trade rules of WTO and to dilute the proposals on corporate accountability that the Friends of the Earth campaign had successfully introduced in the text.
>
> ('The Great Betrayal', press release by Dr Vandana Shiva, 13 September 2002; reproduced with her kind permission)

Globalisation, Food and Health in the New World Order

In the present world order there are many similarities with the past. The nature of the globalisation project is not new, but the scale, direction and control of it are. Colonial powers in the seventeenth and eighteenth centuries transported new foods around the globe through, for example, the so-called 'Columbian Exchange' between the new world of the Americas and the old world of Europe (Sokolov, 1991). The British Empire in the nineteenth century was the epitome of a global economy (Davis, 2001). What is different today is the scale and pace of globalisation, and the shift of control and influence to the TNCs. This is accelerated by new means of communication, the decreasing time gap between the development and the use of new technologies, and the easing of global trade barriers (Castells, 1996). The developed world has always had an imperialist perspective, seeing the developing world as its 'granary'. For decades, the neoliberal economic perspective had promoted a view that health would gain from greater wealth, which in turn would be unleashed by trade liberalisation, restriction or privatisation of the state, and encouragement of private enterprise. While many campaigns and campaigning organisations developed their expertise in relation to national governments and the rights of citizenship, the new world order of TNCs demands a new way of dealing with the issues.

Amyata Sen (1981) sees the issues related to food as about the entitlements people have; famine he argues is rarely the result of a lack of food but of a lack of entitlement. This raises issues of the new and old food poverties. Famine, according to Sen 'is the characteristic of some people not having enough food to eat. It is not the characteristic of there not being enough food to eat'. Famine is a consequence of people lacking the entitlement to access the available food. This is an important distinction, as in the old global order the nation-states had some commitment to their citizens and to ensuring entitlement, however this was manifested (e.g., food welfare schemes). The new order owes no such allegiance to its customers.

How does Globalisation Apply to Food?

Globalisation has a number of meanings. The first, for our purposes here, is the economic process of trade liberalisation of food markets (Barris and McLeod, 2000). Globalisation also possess a cultural and ideological aspect, sometimes referred to as 'McDonaldisation' or 'Coca-Colaisation' (Ritzer, 2000). People are being encouraged to think of food and drink as coming not from farmers or the earth but from giant corporations (Klein, 2000). A study by opinion pollsters Gallup has found that 65 per cent of people in China recognise the brand name of Coca-Cola, 42 per cent recognise Pepsi-Cola and 40 per cent recognise Nestlé (Gallup, 1995). This is a deliberate moulding of taste, with the large corporations now the primary drivers in dietary change, controlling production and distribution chains. The eating habits of whole populations are changing fast. Globalisation of the food chain introduces more opportunities for breakdowns in the safety system and for more people to be affected by any such lapses (WHO, 1999).

People in the developed world eat a different and better diet than their predecessors a hundred years ago. They live longer, are taller and do not suffer from diseases of deprivation associated with food. On the other hand, more of us are affected by food-related diseases such as coronary heart disease (CHD) and cancers, and more are obese.

The developing world is also experiencing a so-called 'nutrition transition' (Popkin, 1998; Drewnoski and Popkin, 1997) with diseases, such as type II or late onset diabetes and obesity, previously associated with middle age and lifestyle factors, now skipping a generation and occurring among younger members of society. The nutrition transition is occurring at a faster rate then we previously thought possible using conventional public health modelling. Instead of change occurring across generations, we are seeing changes within one generation related to food and lifestyle factors and the consequent impacts on health care systems. Many of these changes are being driven by the globalisation agenda. Estimates from WHO for the costs of poor nutrition, obesity and low physical activity for Europe, calculated in DALYs is 9.7 per cent, which compares to 9 per cent due to smoking (WHO, 2000). Recent analysis suggested strategies to promote healthy eating and dietary change were among the most cost-effective of methods of preventing cardiovascular disease (Brunner *et al.*, 2001).

Popkin's (1998) analysis of the dietary shifts associated with globalisation – the 'nutrition transition' – shows that fat consumption increases in low-income nations with resultant increases of obesity and chronic diseases: the 'diseases of affluence'. Partly responsible for this shift is the greater availability of cheap fats as a result of global trade. The first indications of the shift are differences in the urban/rural populations, and the urban affluent classes adopting the food habits of the 'developed' world and the consequent diseases of affluence. Later stages of the transition are characterised by the adoption by the remainder of the population of First-World food habits and diseases, while the urban rich return to healthy eating based on peasant diets. An example of this is the adoption of the so-called 'Mediterranean diet' in Europe by the rich of the northern climes as the peasant classes of the Mediterranean shift to a diet high in fat and sugar.

The nutrition transition demonstrates how diseases cross national borders; the causes are not infectious agents but the new agencies of culture and behaviour, different mechanisms from communicable diseases. Whereas the latter usually spread by infection, the former tend to spread in other ways (Lang and Caraher, 2001). For example, diet-related diseases are spreading globally through lifestyle and social changes. Obesity and CHD have until relatively recently been seen as a diseases of affluence, less of a problem in developing countries than in rich, industrialised ones. This is no longer true (Drewnoski and Popkin, 1997). CHD and some food-related cancers (e.g. bowel) (WCRF, 1997) are on the increase in develop-ing countries, where the more affluent social groups are tending towards a more 'Western' lifestyle: eating different foods, taking less exercise and not just aspiring to, but achieving, western patterns of consumption. In devel-oping countries obesity now exists alongside more traditional problems of under-nutrition. As in developed countries, abundance exists alongside people going hungry. Food poverty is a phenomenon not associated only with developing countries or with differences between nations. It can be observed at a sub-national level as we shift our conception of want and scarcity and move away from traditional approaches to food and nutrition based on knowledge and skills to one of access and financial resources. These 'old' and 'new' inequalities are summarised in Table 11.1.

Food security is a case in point (Lang, 1996). Whereas the post-Second World War policy vision was for efficiency and output to be raised at national level and for countries in food deficit to increase their own supplies, by the end of the twentieth century a new vision was for food security to be achieved through imports. The goal of food self-reliance has been replaced by one of achieving food security through trade. Yet the unequal terms of trade mean that the gainers are purveyors of high value-added foods – the Western brands – rather than those who need the exchange most – the commodity-selling developing countries (Watkins, 2002; Madeley, 2000). The case of coffee provides a good example: the global market is dependent on world supply and recent over-supply resulting from intensive production in Vietnam has resulted in a collapse in

Table 11.1 The new and old food inequalities/poverty

The old food poverty	The new food poverty
Lack of food	Overabundance of processed foods
Undernutrition	Lack of balance
Cost of food	Relative cost of food
Removal from the norm	Socially and culturally isolated
Underproduction	Overproduction
Non-availability of food	Poor access to available food

global prices to the lowest level for 35 years. This has left 10 million large and small-scale coffee growers in Uganda, Tanzania, Central America and Southeast Asia destitute. Coffee production in Vietnam was supported by the World Bank and the International Monetary Fund. The main beneficiaries of this are trans-national corporations who do not necessarily pass on savings to the consumer.

Campaigns by growers and development NGOs have heightened awareness of unfair coffee and tea terms of trade, and have sparked a fast rise in ethical or fair-traded commodities. For coffee, the added value between leaving the farm and reaching the checkout has increased by 7000 per cent. Such NGO niches are supported but may do little to help bring about long-term changes in the system. They are major steps forward in bonding consumers to producers in a less exploitative relationship (Hines, 2001; de Selincourt, 1997). One counter to globalisation's control by a handful of coffee companies has been the fair-trade movement, a kind of 'virtual' localization. If the consumer cannot have local coffee, at least s/he can have less coffee that entails less exploitation and that reduces supply chain profiteering.

Privatisation of food products through biotechnology and patents provides further evidence of globalisation. Southern Africa has become a victim of drought and famine under the joint impact of climate change and structural adjustment programmes. World Bank policies and IMF policies have encouraged countries to destroy and dismantle their food security systems and the growing of local indigenous crops, resulting in nearly half a million people facing starvation. This 'manufactured' catastrophe and its consequences are now being used to market GMOs through food aid, which Zambia,

Zimbabwe and Mozambique have refused to accept. At the time of writing Lesotho is one of the countries in Southern Africa facing famine. This has resulted from poor weather conditions but also the restructuring of a local food economy along the lines recommended by World Bank and IMF policies. The growing of maize as the local staple crop has been replaced by the growing of potatoes as a cash crop for export. The underlying principle was to give more 'cash-in-hand' to growers, who can pass on the benefits by spending money in the local community. Maize is meant to be sourced from the world market, to take advantage of economies of scale. All of course a house of cards, with those who could previously fall back on foodstuffs grown on their smallholdings (ownership entitlement) in the times of scarcity now losing this option as the growing of local indigenous crops has been replaced by cash crops for export. In 2002 Argentina offered an example of this scenario: while children starve, massive amounts of foodstuffs are exported. And this in an economy that was once held to be a model for South American economic development.

This process of trade liberalisation at a global level regulated by the World Trade Organisation is allowing wealthy consumer societies to source elements of their diet globally. Developing countries, with cheap land and, importantly, cheap labour, are encouraged to grow food for the global market, resulting in the demise of local systems of agriculture. This can lead to a situation where food is exported when there is need locally, something akin to the Irish famine in the nineteenth century, (Tóibín, 1999, Woodham-Smith, 1962/1991) and repeated at the height of the famine in Ethiopia in 1984–5, with green beans still being exported to UK supermarkets (Athanasiou, 1996). Sen (1981, 1997) says that the principle of 'social choice' often overrides the provision of famine relief, the belief being that hard work brings financial rewards. The neoliberal economic rationale is that the 'cash-in-hand' resulting from such trade enables people to buy food: the 'trickle down effect'. Cheap food for the consumer in the developed world does not necessarily equate with fair prices for the producer (see Box 11.4 as an example).

Nestlé (2002) notes that 80 per cent of the US food dollar goes to categories other than the 'farm value' of the food itself. As food systems get more complex and value is added to the food, so variations emerge in who makes money from food: the farmers' percentage declines as the processors'/retailers' rises. This is a situation repeated the world over. It is in stark contrast to claims that food liberalisation will bring the benefits to the grower/producer of cash crops. In reality nearly 80 per cent of food expenditure goes on the so-called 'added value' to the food itself such as processing, packaging, transport, advertising and taxes. Moreover, the

---

Box 11.4 Control of world banana trade

Three trans-national companies (TNCs) control 80 per cent of the world banana trade with:

- 2 per cent of the retail price of a banana going to the fieldworker
- 5 per cent to the farmer, and
- 88 per cent to intermediaries in the food chain such as the importer, wholesaler, freight companies and the retailer.

(Based on Paxton, 1994)

---

growers/producers of *healthy* foodstuffs are less likely to receive their fair share of the retail cost of the food. The producers of foods such as beef receive 50–60 per cent of the retail cost of the food, as opposed to vegetable producers who receive as little as 5 per cent.

The Drivers of the Globalisation of Food Consumption

In his study of consumer patterns, Durning (1992), of the Worldwatch Institute, concluded that new, global consuming classes were emerging. He suggests a categorisation of the world's 5.4 billion people into three consuming classes, for which food is a key characteristic (see Table 11.2).

Similarities of lifestyle bond the rich of North and South, as well as the poor (Gabriel and Lang, 1995). This reflects the nutrition transition described earlier; Durning's rich consumers, eat well and with a wide choice. They – we – can chose from 20,000 items on the hypermarket shelves, drawn from around the world in an efficiently run system of production and distribution. This delivers fresh, green beans in mid-winter, flown in from Kenya or the Gambia to London. Biodiversity on the shelves is not necessarily reflected in the contract fields whence this abundance comes (Feder, 1997). And the poor continue to starve. According to the United Nations Children's Fund:

> one in five persons in the developing world suffers from chronic hunger – 800 million people in Africa, Asia and Latin America. Over 2 billion people subsist on diets deficient in the vitamins and minerals essential for normal growth and development, and for preventing premature death and such disabilities as blindness and mental retardation.
>
> (UNICEF, 1993)

Table 11.2 World consumption in three classes

Category of consumption	Rich consumers	Middle	Poor
Population	1.1 billion	3.3 billion	1.1 billion
Diet	Meat, packaged food, soft drinks	Grain, clean water	Insufficient grain unsafe water
Transport	Private cars	Bicycles, buses	Walking
Materials	Throwaways	Durables	Local biomass

Modified from Durning, 1992, p. 27.

While such facts are sobering, inadequacies of income affect dietary intake in affluent countries too (Dowler and Rushton, 1993). The Food and Agriculture Organisation (FAO, 1999 and FAO website www.fao.org) estimates that, for the period 1995–7, 790 million people in the developing world did not have enough to eat. The same report points out that in the industrialised countries of the First World 8 million people were undernourished and suffering serious food deprivation. In Eastern Europe this figure is estimated to be 4 million and in the newly independent states of the former USSR 22 million (7 per cent of the population). These figures refer to undernourishment rather than the availability of culturally and socially appropriate foods. The emergence of global consuming and under-consuming classes is accompanied by a globalisation of inequalities. All this leads to confusion in the mind of the public who are bombarded with messages about the abundance of food and are then told that there are many in society who do not have access to culturally sufficient amounts of food and who regularly go hungry.

Although icons such as McDonald's tend to hog the headlines, it is important to recognise that a long and powerful transformation of society is underway. Ritzer has called it McDonaldisation (Ritzer, 2000). Others have called in Coca-colonialism (Levinson, 1979). Aspirations for a lifestyle are translated in dietary form; they may be driven by the affluent but copied by the less well-off. This pattern includes, for example, an emphasis on meat eating as an indicator of progress, and a disregard for more local foods. Globalisation results in a number of different and contradicting perspectives. This is what Barber (1995) calls the *Jihad vs McWorld*. Large multinational companies want the efficiency of global systems and food chains while trading on the multiculturalism of food. In essence the aim is to standardise production and to diversify consumption as a marketing tool (Heer and Penfold, 2003).

Table 11.3 shows the top global food trans-nationals. The assets of the largest 300 firms in the world are now worth approximately a quarter of the world's productive assets (*Economist*, 1993). Trans-national corporations (TNCs) account for 70 per cent of total world trade (in all goods, not just food). Of those TNCs, the top 350 account for around 40 per cent. In food, such power is common, according to research by the United Nations Centre on Trans-national Corporations (1981), and high levels of concentration are common in the food system. Cargill, a family-owned commodity trader, has 60 per cent of the world cereal trade (Lang and Hines, 1993). The biggest five corporations control 77 per cent of the cereals trade, the biggest three have 80 per cent of the banana market, the biggest three have 83 per cent of cocoa, the biggest three have 85 per cent of the tea trade (Madden, 1992).

Table 11.3 Largest food trans-nationals, by turnover, 1998

Company	Sales (US$ bn)	Profits (US$ bn)	Chief products
Philip Morris	56.11	6.31	Tobacco, cereals, beverages
Cargill	51.00	4.68	Cereals, seeds, oils, beverages
Unilever	50.06	7.94	Oils, dairy, beverages, meals
Nestlé	49.96	4.11	Beverages, cereals, infant food
Pepsico	20.92	1.49	Beverages, snacks
Sara Lee	20.01	−0.53	Meat and bakery
Coca-Cola	18.87	4.13	Beverages, foods
McDonald's	11.41	1.64	Restaurants

Source: adapted from the FT 500, *Financial Times*, 28 January 1999.

To return to the earlier distinction of food in terms of cultural icons, as per the case by Klein (2000) the public protest tends to be directed toward the well-known cultural icons such as McDonald's or Coca-Cola. The reason for the attacks are that, notably, some of these TNCs are no longer selling goods but themselves as brands. Many of these large companies do not themselves produce goods; they sell ideas and images. A product is something grown on the farm or produced in the factory; a brand is something that is bought by the consumer (Klein, 2000). The supermarkets' marketing of brands such as 'Safeway's organic food' further succeeds in isolating the consumer from the growing and production of that foodstuff, so people are being encouraged to think of food and drink as coming not from farmers or the earth but from giant corporations. In the post-Fordist economy (marked by flexible specialisation systems of production), the distributor not the consumer is sovereign.

The Hidden Costs of the Globalisation of Food

In Europe, increases in fruit consumption can be largely accounted for by the very sharp rise in purchases of fruit juice, which does not provide equivalent nutrition to its fresh counterpart. This fruit juice consumption, however, is often of juices from far-distant fruit, notably oranges from Brazil. A study by the Wupperthal Institute in Germany calculated that 80 per cent of Brazilian orange production is consumed in Europe. Annual German consumption occupied 370,000 acres of Brazilian productive land, three times the land down to fruit production in Germany. If this level of German orange juice consumption was replicated worldwide, 32 million acres would be needed just for orange production (Kranendonk and Bringezau, 1994). The increasing range of fruit available throughout the year also contributes to this rise in consumption. Such developments result in:

- an increase in food miles with food travelling greater distances
- an increase in pollution
- a reduction in local indigenous crops as they are replaced by foods for export.

These are the indirect costs of the global food market, which we pick up in other arenas such as health, pollution or road accidents.

This hypermarket food economy is built on state-funded motorways and cheap oil, allowing the same amount of food to travel further, up and down motorways. Giant stores demand regularity of supply, which in turn necessitates large factories, tight contracts and monoculture from growers.

A German study of strawberry yoghurt found ecological absurdities in the system of processing, packaging and distribution, such that a theoretical truckload of 150 gram yoghurt pots would travel 1005 kilometres (Boege, 1993). By contrast, independent small retailers, partly due to their lack of logistics and bulk purchasing power, tend to source their food more locally. The average European weekend shopping trolley contains goods that have already travelled 4000 km before we take them home (Griffiths, 1993). In the United States, one study calculated, each individual food item in a trolley now travels an average 2000 kilometres (1,300 miles) between grower and consumer (Clunies-Ross and Hildyard, 1992). The European Commission's Task Force on the Environment calculated that there would be a 30–50 per cent increase in trans-frontier lorry traffic from 1993 following the opening of national borders within the Single European Market (European Commission, 1992)

This change in distribution not only gives retailers power over the entire food system, but also affects what the farmer grows and how she or he grows it, by the use of contracts and specifications, and also affects poor consumers. They have to pay for transport that they can ill afford. Shops sell vegetables that can and used to be grown locally, but are now brought thousands of miles. In this way, the consumer gains an illusion of choice while monoculture spreads on the land.

Discussion

The above paints a complex picture of food globalisation, showing that the system is controlled by a small number of TNCs with budgets, resources and influence greater than that of many national governments, see Box 11.5. It also shows that approaches based on protest, and particularly violent protest, are unlikely to be successful. It partially explains why activists can get frustrated and begin to look to short-term solutions to a situation that has been long in the making. The TNCs have had free rein since the 1960s to develop and control the global food market, basking in the glow of trade liberalisation and the demise of national borders as barriers to trade. The restructuring of this agenda needs to be seen as long-term project not an overnight one.

Many of the debates tend to get transmogrified into arguments on consumer rights, as these are the ones that are most easily won and that the current regulatory systems recognise (GMOs provide an example). The issues of public good/public health and citizenship are harder to argue. GATS and the freeing up of trade in goods and services are examples of this. The lack of a clear citizenship/public health rights debate is not

---

Box 11.5 The banana wars

The European Union decided to impose a quota of 10 per cent of European banana imports on the US-based company Chiquita. This was done in order to protect the livelihoods of small producers in the former French and British colonies. The company complained to the US Government, who lodged a formal complaint with the WTO claiming that the European Union approach was discriminatory. The WTO found in favour of Chiquita, and the subsequent refusal of the European Union to comply resulted in sanctions being placed on unrelated EU goods such as bath salts.

---

surprising given the shift in power from national governments to TNCs (Lee *et al.*, 2002). However, this ground needs to be reclaimed in the light of the global economy and the role of food in promoting the health of nations. Box 11.6, which outlines the activities of Consumers International, shows how a group primarily concerned with matters of consumer rights can also play a part in the public health approach by dealing with key committees and alliances that cross national boundaries.

In developing a public health approach, the role of national governments as advocates of the health of their citizens should be encouraged. In the past they have perhaps been unwilling to adopt this approach as free trade and the establishment of fluid national boundaries were considered essential for economic growth. National governments, while encouraging agricultural representation at WTO groups such as the Codex Alimentarius Commission, saw little value in the health departments being represented, although the impact of the Codex committee on health was far reaching (Lee *et al.*, 2002).

Civic society has arguably been eroded by corporate society. If we adopt Naomi Klein's approach and look at the role of brands, or take an approach that looks at the influence of corporate players, the fact is that citizens now more readily identify with corporations in their everyday lives. They believe corporations and brands to be important, and therefore they are important. This raises problems for those involved in developing responses to the globalisation of food. Alliances are often based on flimsy relationships and the competing ideologies of members. For some the issue is one of anti-globalisation and the dismantling of the system; for others it is reform of the system to make it fairer. The inaudibility of a coherent approach can be seen in Klein's (2002) book of essays, which includes a range of approaches and philosophies. None the less, the way forward is to

Box 11.6 Summary of activities of Consumers International

History and purpose
Consumers International (CI) is an independent, non-profit organisation. It is not aligned with or supported by any political party or industry. It is funded by fees from member organisations and by grants from foundations, governments and multilateral agencies. CI supports, links and represents consumer groups and agencies all over the world. It has a membership of more than 260 organisations in almost 120 countries. It strives to promote a fairer society through defending the rights of all consumers, including poor, marginalised and disadvantaged people, by:

- Supporting and strengthening member organisations and the consumer movement in general.
- Campaigning at the international level for policies which respect consumer concerns.

The organisation was founded in 1960 as the International Organisation of Consumer Unions (IOCU) by a group of national consumer organisations that recognised that they could build upon their individual strengths by working across national borders. The organisation rapidly grew and soon became recognised as the voice of the international consumer movement on issues such as product and food standards, health and patients' rights, the environment and sustainable consumption, and the regulation of international trade and of public utilities.

Areas of interest: food and health-related issues
Consumers International closely follows the Food and Agricultural Organisation (FAO) in its work on sustainable agriculture, nutrition and food standards. It is actively involved in the Codex Alimentarius Commission. It also campaigns strongly on genetically modified organisms (GMOs) and food security issues. It has a long tradition on working on many food and health related issues. These have included:

Codex Alimentarius Commission
Food safety
Genetically engineered food

Food irradiation
World Food Summit
Advertising
Food alerts

Regional and international representation
Consumers International has official representation on many global bodies, including:

UN Economic and Social Council (ECOSOC) and related UN agencies and Commissions
World Health Organisation (WHO)
Codex Alimentarius Commission
International Organisation for Standardisation (ISO)
UN Educational, Scientific and Cultural Organization (UNESCO)
United Nations Children's Fund (UNICEF)
International Electrotechnical Commission (IEC).

At the regional and sub-regional levels it represents consumers at, among others:

UN Economic Commissions
Economic Community for West African States (ECOWAS)
Organisation for Economic Cooperation and Development (OECD)
Latin American Parliament (PARLATINO)
Pan American Health Organisation (PAHO)
Association of South-East Asian Nations (ASEAN).

develop alliances that can tackle the underlying issues of the global food system and bring about permanent change. For 30 years the belief has been that free trade and a self-regulating economy would result in social progress. There was a simple equation: free-trade + economic liberalisation = social liberalisation. This mantra is in danger of being repeated as the events of September 11 make any protest against the global food system seem like an attack on social liberalisation. Social liberalisation has many benefits, including the provision of education and the emancipation of women. Noreena Hertz (2001) points out that an anti-global stance does not necessarily have to be an anti-capitalist stance and is certainly not an anti-internationalist approach. In addition, social liberalisation does not equate directly with economic liberalisation and there is a need for food protestors to recapture the high ground. Global capitalism and the global food supply chain carry the danger of killing democracy. The current focus of protestors on brands such as McDonald's or Coca-Cola also has imbued within them an anti-American perspective (Bové and Dufour 2001). This is a gross simplification of a complicated picture where large trans-national companies almost unseen by the public eye continue to trade freely and unhindered.

Violent protest is tolerated, although punished (sometimes violently), as it diverts attention from the underlying issues of power and control of the food system, and may even help alienate some sections of the community from identifying with the issues. Campaigns to change the global food system need to harness the desire for direct action of certain groups but this needs to be constructive and hit companies where it matters, namely, in their profits.

It is unlikely that major TNCs will be moved to action by a concern with global inequality, but if a campaign succeeds in a boycott of their products then they are probably more likely to pay attention to the concerns of protestors. Baby Milk Action, whose activities are described in Box 11.1, provides an example of combing high-level advocacy work with direct action. The various practices that Starbucks are alleged to engage in demonstrate the complexity of the issues; there are so many represented above that it is hard to know how to start unpacking them. Starbucks will respond that they are in business to make a profit, and ironically the new protestors can help them in this by making their business more socially responsible. The problem for the new generation of protestors is that many of the issues they are concerned with run the risk of becoming part of the socially accountability agenda of the 'globalisers' and part of the marketing strategy of the large corporations. Where do protestors begin with Starbucks? Emphasis on fair-traded coffee, which it has committed to, ignores the fact that the majority of coffee is drunk in the home and is not 'fair-trade' in origin. So again the icons of the global change are targeted as opposed to the real determinants of food inequalities. Starbucks has made a commitment to sourcing fair-trade coffee through the Fairtrade Foundation. In addition it has introduced its own 'Commitment to Origins' initiative which has as its driving principles

- using only quality (Arabica) beans
- respecting the environment
- respecting people
- paying and investing fairly.

This initiative is an attempt to develop a purchasing policy for the majority of its coffee and not just a small percentage of fair-traded coffees. Yet the real crises with coffee trading can be located in the policies of the World Bank and the International Monetary Fund and their support for the development of coffee growing in Vietnam. The global market is dependent on world supply and, as discussed earlier, the recent collapse in global prices resulting from intensive production in Vietnam has left 10 million coffee growers in developing countries destitute, benefiting the large TNCs but not the consumer. The globalised market does not benefit growers or consumers but the large companies who control world supply. The major TNCs that deal in coffee are as set out below in Table 11.4.

On the supermarkets shelves the roasters' profits emerge as $26.40 (£17.11) per kilo; the growers sell the original green coffee beans to a middleman for 14 cents (9p). Between the farm gate and the time that coffee reaches the shopper's trolley, the price has inflated by 7000 per cent. The bulk of this goes to the so-called 'added value' of the coffee, which includes transportation, packaging and branding. Those who influence the global trade in coffee are the World Bank and the International Monetary Fund policies, and the major TNCs mediated through the International Coffee Organisation (ICO). Starbucks is in reality a small player in the overall scheme of things, and while there are advantages to tackling high profile companies such as Starbucks and McDonald's, not the least of which is the resulting publicity, the reality is that such corporate social responsibility (CSR) issues are of minor concern and are rarely discussed at board level.

Table 11.4 Major coffee TNCs, 2000

Name	Where based	Global sales	Profits	Brands
P&G	US, Cincinnati	$39.3bn	$2.92bn	Folgers, and more than 250 brands
Nestlé	Switzerland	$50.2bn	$3.96bn	Nescafé, Gold Blend
Sara Lee	US, Chicago	$17.7bn	$2.27bn	Douwe Egberts
Kraft	US, Illinois	$33.9bn	$4.88bn	Maxwell House, Café Hag, Carte Noire

CSR is in many companies lumped under the banner of public relations or marketing, resulting in little, if any, major change to the way in which business is conducted. The post-Seattle focus on CSR also relied on the involvement of the NGOs. Such 'partnerships' had the advantage to the TNCs of silencing the NGOs' advocacy role. Many NGOs concerned with food found themselves confused as to their focus: advocates, protestors or partners with major TNCs? The time is ripe for a review of the role of NGOs in relation to food (Ollila, 2003).

The events of September 11 2001 have provided an opportunity for a review of global systems of both food governance and protest. We need to address them so that they contribute to global equality and address the root causes of food inequality, while at the same time ensuring that the various interested parties in the movement can find enough common cause to stay together and pursue a common agenda. Hari (2002) notes that the anti-globalisation movement is not a coherent force and exists despite conflicting agendas. The core issue for food is that of inequality, and the way forward may be the creation of global systems of government that serve the interests of citizens as opposed to those of the large TNCs. Naomi Klein (2001) similarly notes that the movement is 'a movement of many movements – coalition of coalitions'. The focus should be on justice and not trade as the unifying concept. The appropriate stance is one that helps reform the global food system so that it becomes more sustainable, equitable and regionalised. The challenge for both national governments and the NGOs will be to find ways of reconciling these within a broad alliance of interests, ranging from those want reform to those who want to overthrow the system. An interesting future awaits. The following lines from a song by Richard Thompson called 'Fast Food' from his 1994 CD *Mirror Blue* sums up the problems for many engaged in the day-to-day reality of eking out a living:

Small Mac, Big Mac, burger and fries
Shove 'em in boxes all the same size
Easy on the mustard, heavy on the sauce
Double for the fat boy, he eats like a horse
Fry them patties and send 'em right through
Microwave oven gonna fry me too
Can't lose my job by getting in a rage
I've gotta get my hands on a minimum wage
Shove it in their faces, give 'em what they want
Gotta make it fast, it's a fast food restaurant.
(© Beeswing Music, used by permission)

CHAPTER 12

Activism: Behind the Banners

Duane Raymond

First they came for the Communists,
but I was not a Communist
so I did not speak out.
Then they came for the Socialists and the Trade Unionists,
but I was neither,
so I did not speak out.
Then they came for the Jews,
but I was not a Jew
so I did not speak out.
And when they came for me,
there was no one left
to speak out for me.

(Pastor Martin Niemoller, 1945,
commenting on Nazi incarcerations)

Introduction

On the morning of 18 December 2002, executives at Nestlé woke up to a surprise: headlines and talk radio were asking 'Does Nestlé know it's Christmas?' Nestlé was trying to claim $6 million from the Ethiopian Government at a time when 11 million Ethiopians were facing a famine two or three times worse than in the 1980s. Not only was their claim questionable, it was unnecessary, since Nestlé earns that amount every hour. The money would be better used to feed a million Ethiopians for a month. Oxfam and others were asking Nestlé to drop the claim.

Within three days, 15,000 e-mails from outraged individuals had been sent to Nestlé – Oxfam's most successful e-mobilisation to date – and in the next few weeks the total climbed to more than 40,000. Meanwhile the media around the world had picked up the item and some used it as their lead story. Letters to editors and comments on media chat sites streamed in. On scores of Internet 'web logs', people started actively calling for a boycott of Nestlé products. The company scrambled to respond. They first offered to invest the money in Ethiopia. Then they changed their position and offered to donate the proceeds of the claim to a humanitarian organisation for famine alleviation. Unsatisfied, Oxfam continued its campaign. On 24 January, 35 days after the story hit the headlines, Nestlé and Ethiopia settled and the money was immediately given over to famine relief in Ethiopia. Activism had succeeded again.

Who was 'in the right' in this situation? Have you already made your mind up? If so, you are reading this chapter and book from a set corporate or activist position. How can you expect others to change if you are unwilling to? How can you help find new common ground between activists and corporations if your mind is already made up? This is the biggest challenge we all face: suspending our stereotypes and genuinely listening to each other. This chapter will help you understand activism. It demonstrates – in relation to corporations – what activism is, how activists think, what is happening in activism and where activism is going. You role as reader is to suspend your judgement and empathise with both activists and business people. If you cannot do that, you may as well stop reading now.

Activism keeps governments, corporations and the planet healthy. It is a natural part of being human and provides insight into the public's evolving concerns. Understanding this is critical for anticipating and addressing these concerns before they have negative social, environmental and economic costs. Twenty-first century leaders need not only to comprehend the value of activism, but to embrace it early as a key part of their decision making.

The Job of a Citizen

> The Job of a Citizen is to keep his mouth open.
>
> (Günther Grass, author and Nobel Literature laureate)

Activism is our human duty. It is the obligation each of us have to ensure that everyone – including future generations – is able to live the fullest life possible in good health, just conditions and fair prosperity. It is also a sign of a healthy democracy that people can participate, dissent and influence their society. When this duty is forgotten, we become ruled by economic and political tyrants who use people for their own profit. When it is exercised, we create a society of equals: 'of the people, by the people, for the people'. This is activism's legacy.

Activists are society's most active, committed citizens. They take risks by questioning the status quo – including themselves and each other – every day. Collectively, they are highly influential and trusted in affecting and creating societal change. They provide insight into future values and hopes of societies, since they are the ones shaping that change. They do this by highlighting – and trying to close – the gaps between the current reality and expectations. To ignore them is to ignore the future.

Activism as a duty is not a modern concept. It has been called different things, but the act of standing up for a just cause is as old as humanity itself. Faiths in all corners of the planet have a version of the 'Golden Rule': do unto others as they would have them do unto you, the world's most universal moral code. For instance in Hinduism it is: 'This is the sum of duty; do naught onto others what you would not have them do unto you'.[1] In Islam it is: 'No one of you is a believer until he desires for his brother that which he desires for himself'.[2] Judaism even emphasises this rule's primacy over all others by decreeing: 'What is hateful to you, do not to your fellow men. That is the entire Law, all the rest is commentary'.[3] Even atheists and 'freethinkers' have the Golden Rule as the base code of their philosophy of life (Carrier, 1999). This rule stresses that every person has a duty to strive the common good. This is the essence of activism. Without activism, the golden rule would be replaced with 'those who have the gold make the rules'.

Activism is fuelled when ordinary people's concerns are not heard or addressed. It is a normal, natural ways for human beings to pursue change, especially since politicians and corporations are not trusted. The latest research (Gallup International, 2002) reveals that 'across the world, the principal democratic institution (i.e. parliament, congress etc.) is the least trusted [institution]'. It also reveals that 'fully two-thirds of those surveyed worldwide disagree that their country is governed by the will of the people'. Corporations are also trusted poorly, ranking second last to parliaments/congresses. Given the public's massive disillusionment with political parties and corporations and their 'declining trust that the world is moving in the right direction', it is no wonder activism appeals to growing numbers of people.[4]

Critics pointing to the 'unrepresentativeness' of activist groups have therefore utterly missed the point. Currently, 'non-governmental organisations (NGOs) including environmental and social advocacy groups enjoy the second highest trust ratings' of people around the world and are almost twice as trusted as elected assemblies (Gallup International, 2002). Even senior politicians acknowledge this when they observe that 'all of Britain's political parties together have less than a million members. But there are over five million paid-up supporters of environmental groups in Britain'.[5] Activism as 'democratic participation' is different from the concept of representation, but it is as least as significant. Electing a representative is a rudimentary – but key – democratic process. Yet if left to voting, democracies would fail. It is the participation of independent groups of citizens – activists – that sustain democracy. Activists are 'citizen diplomats' who articulate people's concerns and negotiate with governments and corporations to find a satisfactory resolution. While informal, this is a form of democracy that is highly trusted by the public (Edelman, 2002a), giving it moral legitimacy.

Frederick Douglass, a leading figure in the abolition of slavery in the United States, said that 'those who profess to favour freedom, and yet depreciate agitation, are men who want rain without thunder and lightning'. Similarly, those who think activism is unnecessary or unwanted are greatly mistaken. The freedom upon which free enterprise is based was created and is sustained by activists: people who stood up for ideals that were initially rejected. This process continues today with a growing movement that is pushing society towards responsible business practice. Some people do this by scrutinizing or altering existing corporations, some by changing the rules under which corporations operate, and others by founding new businesses founded on ethical principles and practices. It is through this agitation by activists that societal values shift and change occurs. In the language of economics it could be considered 'citizen competition'.

Every person has human rights. These rights are inalienable: we have them from the moment we are born and as long as we live, and arguably before and after. In ensuring our rights are more than just theoretical, we need to do something for ourselves and for others – these are our duties – to uphold and defend human rights. We also have a duty to uphold and defend the rights of future generations and of other forms of life. Our ancestors did this to ensure we are here; now it is our turn to ensure future generations of all life have a right to exist. When individual rights conflict, we also have a duty to ensure that the solution is fair, yet favour universal human rights over all legal rights. Activism is the practice of these duties and is not bound by religion, ethnicity or nationhood. It is global and is everyone's job for life.

'If you think you're too small to be effective, then you've never been in bed with a mosquito' (Anita Roddick, founder of The Body Shop).

Twenty-first Century Activism

There may be times when we are powerless to prevent injustice, but there must never be a time when we fail to protest.

(Elie Wiesel, Nobel Peace laureate)

Activism's essence is the same today as it has always been: an expression of genuine public interest in participating in and shaping society. Yet significant changes are happening as activism enters the twenty-first century. Activism is globalising: growing in every corner of the planet, expanding the range of tactics and connecting up in worldwide alliances. The global media and Internet are making activism more accessible and inclusive today than it has ever been. Activist attention to corporations has also gone from peripheral to a key focus in the last decade. Overarching these trends are the shared values on which twenty-first-century activism is shaping: participation, diversity, transparency, accountability and fairness.

Activism is spreading. When the powerful met at the 2003 World Economic Forum in Davos, they noted that:

> the numbers [of people] indicate concern that comes not just from protesters and activists in the street, but runs deep and broad throughout society. It's unfocused, but there is a lot of angst in the world. We can learn from it. The questions is, what?[6]

Unlike past movements, today's activists represent a wide range of issues and perspectives: hence the movement seems unfocused from the outside. The world is in a state of rapid change triggered by the collapse of the Soviet bloc, and most people now believe the primary threat to the planet is a blend of social, environmental and governance problems. What particular concerns these are depend more on the actions – or inactions – of governmental and corporate leaders. Hence protests shifted focus from 'globalisation' to 'peace' after the 2001 terror attacks.

The Art of Activism

Winning the intellectual and moral arguments is rarely sufficient to achieve change. Usually political and corporate leaders need a push to get – and keep – issues on their agenda. Thus activists must also use tactics that make an issue impossible and even detrimental to ignore. When the intellectual and moral arguments fail to open the door to dialogue, activists can be quite creative in finding other ways to get their concerns across. Often this is by mobilising large numbers of people since this gives an issue added legitimacy, but it is not the only way. The range of these tactics is constantly spreading and expanding, and the Internet and other electronic media are creating whole new channels through which this can be done.

Activists usually first try to address an issue through raising their concerns directly and privately with those with the power to change things. If dialogue happens and the issues are resolved, then activism ends. All too often, these concerns are ignored, trivialised or nullified without being answered, or dialogue ends without acceptable resolution. In these cases, activists can then escalate the situation with the aim of either starting or continuing dialogue. This is 'citizen diplomacy' in action and is comparable to traditional diplomacy.

While this dialogue is rarely publicised, it is absolutely critical to achieving change. It is through this conversation and negotiation that learning and mutually acceptable solutions are arrived at. Without it, neither side would learn the deeper, more complex aspects of the situation and a win–win resolution would be almost impossible. All other tactics serve to help ensure that dialogue happens, continues and is successfully concluded either by the campaigning group or an ally. In fact, corporate responsibility managers often desire and privately advocate activist pressure to help them make their case internally, since without it top management and board members seldom take activist concerns seriously.[7]

Despite these attempts, success in activism is always uncertain. It is like the common saying 'the straw that broke the camel's back': small changes can build up and trigger a major change. With activism you never know how much effort is needed in each case, you often don't know what influence your work has, and success can come suddenly from a relatively minor incident. Activism succeeds by heaping on more 'straw' until success comes, but never knowing what will be the 'last straw'. With good research and strategy, this process can be shortened considerably, but never averted. Perseverance is thus a key factor in successful activism.

Global Citizen Alliances

On 15 February 2003 more than 10 million people in more than 600 cities and 72 countries and territories around the world spent the day protesting against the US and UK Governments' march towards war with Iraq.[8] This wasn't the first time. What is especially interesting is that global demonstrations are occurring more frequently, they are getting easier to coordinate, and they involve millions of people with diverse concerns. Activists have always existed everywhere in the world, but until recently they were not connected. The combination of a global mass media, global publishing and the Internet has meant activists can learn about and communicate with each other, forging a new solidarity around shared values. The *New York Times* calls this a second 'superpower' (Tyler, 2003).

Everyone has their own reasons for protesting. Most people are more thoughtful and complex than the media convey. They are united in the belief that the government's or corporation's approach is not the way forward. Protest is coordinated by a loose worldwide coalition that communicates via e-mail and websites to personal contacts and to coalition members. The message then ripples through the Internet and mass media to other interested parties.

The globalisation of activism is happening locally and globally simultaneously. Locally, many of the same people will attend demonstration after demonstration on a range of issues because the same shared values run through each. Each time, new people will join, growing the movement and creating new relationships among people and among groups. Globally, there are also 'parallel summits': grassroot versions of formal governmental and economic summits for activists to network and articulate a different way forward. These bind together local groups from around the world into a global movement, and they are growing fast. At the first World Social Forum in Brazil in 2001 11,000 people attended, in 2002 65,000 people attended, and in 2003 100,000 people attended. This globalisation of activism is now well established and still growing rapidly. It will probably be an enduring aspect of twenty-first century activism.

Parallel summits also allow local activists to share their successes and challenges. This ensures that good ideas travel around the world and inspire more activism. In Brazil, the 'Landless Peasants Movement' occupies unused private land to settle and provide landless peasants with a sustainable existence. Their non-violent, intelligent approach is inspiring others around the world to take up the issue of land rights and land injustice. While those in South Africa are learning about land justice from the Brazilians, the South Africans are succeeding in ensuring the poor are not cut off from electricity. They are not only reconnecting those cut off, but they are disconnecting key corporate and political leaders from electricity to demonstrate the effect of the current policy. Others, in turn, learn from the South African experience and the sharing goes on.

Global alliances of local activists have already produced some of the most important developments since the formation of the United Nations. The last few years of the twentieth century saw a global ban on landmines, the creation of an international criminal court, a biodiversity treaty, a climate change treaty and progress on debt relief for the heavily indebted least developed countries. These were all achieved with global activism, often despite the efforts of elected and corporate leaders to ignore or undermine them. Key in these alliances are thousands of established non-profit organisations, which each independently worked towards a specific common goal. These coordinated alliances were working towards a clearly articulated common goal such as a global ban on landmines, despite their differences. This focus contributed to their success but also meant that they addressed one issue at a time when often the larger issues were barely challenged.

Some journalists and writers have prophesied that established groups would lose ground to newer activists. This analysis of the situation is deeply flawed. Rather, the field of activism is expanding, creating new opportunities and new roles for old and new players alike. In fact, new generations of activists have a symbiotic relationship with the established groups, relying on their expertise and research to inform them while inventing new ways of mobilising people and influencing the key actors. While established groups are challenged by new trends in activism, most are continually adapting and evolving.

Targeting Corporations

Activists target corporations because their immense wealth and influence require democratic accountability. The corporate obsession with profits as the 'purpose' of business has created a society sceptical of corporations and their willingness to act responsibly. While rhetoric over the last few decades has tried to reduce corporate responsibility to purely economic terms, the reality is that profits are like breathing: we need to breathe to live but we don't live to breathe. Corporations exist to serve human needs, not themselves. They are largely conceptual entities. If we change our concept we can create innovative new corporations to fit these needs.

Corporations have obligations to society beyond mere wealth creation. Corporations need to contribute to human aspirations since few people are driven by wealth accumulation alone. When leaders forget this, it creates fertile ground for activism. Profit is a key part of achieving these aspirations since profit ensures the viability of the corporation to continue advancing human aspirations, but it is not the aspiration itself. The public expects corporations to be responsible to society. As long as corporate leaders persist in seeing profit as the purpose rather than the means, activists will continue to succeed by exposing their failure to meet their corporate societal responsibilities.

The focus on corporations is relatively new. Activists traditionally focused on governments as the target for achieving change. While governments continue to be targeted, corporations are increasingly seen as valid targets due to the growing economic and political power they wield. This power is vividly demonstrated by the fact that of the top 100 economies in the world, 29 are corporations (UNCTAD, 2002). The public also perceives that business is now more powerful than governments (Edelman, 2002b). With this economic power, corporate policies and practices have a real impact on billions of people. Concentrated power requires democratic accountability, and this is completely lacking in most corporations. Challenging corporations is thus necessary when formal democratic accountability is absent.

Activist Tactics

Activists must make highly effective use of their limited resources. Intelligent tactics are key to achieving the intended impact. These tactics are often misunderstood and underestimated by corporations and the media, but can be amazingly effective. Some of the more noteworthy of these are shareholder activism, copycat actions and direct action.

Shareholder activism attempts to use the shareholder accountability rules to get activist concerns raised and addressed. Corporations publicly traded on stock markets are accountable to their shareholders. They must hold annual meetings that enable shareholders to ask the board questions. These are important events for corporations since shareholders and the media are listening closely and what they hear will guide their investment decisions. These meetings can also involve votes on issues of key shareholder concern. Activists are increasingly purchasing or borrowing shares in corporations to enable them to ask questions about their concerns and introduce proposals to for a shareholder vote. The intent is to educate shareholders and board members on the issue and keep up the pressure for a satisfactory resolution.

Copycat action is the most underrated tactic, because it relies on a corporation taking pre-emptive action to avoid negative publicity. Activists apply the tactics of a successful action to a different corporation in similar circumstances in the hope that other corporations will settle quickly. After Nestlé settled their claim with the Ethiopian Government, Jubilee Debt and Oxfam campaigners in Wales discovered that the parent company of Iceland, a top UK supermarket, was trying to claim £12 million from Guyana, a country with a rapidly declining level of 'human development'. Because of the Nestlé–Ethiopia publicity and settlement, activists only needed to raise the issue with the corporation and they quickly settled the claim. Similarly, the People for the Ethical Treatment of Animals (PETA) spent a long time getting McDonald's to accept ethical practices for sourcing their meat. After they won they used the same tactic with Burger King and Wendy's. They quickly won the same commitment for each. Once an action succeeds, the media, public and corporations are more aware of the issues and potential consequences of corporate inaction. This creates the conditions not only for easier media coverage and public participation, but for faster corporate resolution.

Direct action is the least understood and most contentious tactic because it is easily misinterpreted as mindless violence. Nothing could be further from the truth. Direct action is a tactic of last resort, a last defence used when all other tactics have failed. It involves activities like locking oneself in a tree to block deforestation, tunnelling under a planned road to halt construction, disabling equipment to stop its use, jamming a website so customers cannot order any goods, or women sitting topless along logging roads to distract truck drivers from extracting the lumber. Not only does it get media attention for the issue and obstruct progress, but it also increases the economic cost for a corporation – potentially above the revenue derived from the activity, thus making it unprofitable. It can take only one innovative and determined activist to make a big direct difference and thus it is growing in popularity.

Courtroom Activism

The last decade has started to see the growth of a new approach to activism: in the courts. People are increasingly winning compensation for events that happened decades ago. For example, German companies settled salary claims owed to people used as slave labour during the Second World War, Swiss banks paid out life insurance claims to relatives of people murdered in Nazi concentration camps, asbestos claims have already bankrupted several large companies and threaten several more, and tobacco suits have won large settlements. Even if the company goes bankrupt, banks often end up owning the companies' liabilities and thus can also be held to account.

This is only the start of a process of holding companies and banks responsible for their actions, even if they happened generations ago. For environmental contamination, banks that inherit the assets of bankrupt companies are finding they are responsible for footing the bill for cleanup costs that can run into hundreds of millions of dollars. New claims are also appearing on the scene, such as suits against fast food companies for encouraging obesity, claims for reparation because of slavery, and suits to reclaim savings lost through Citibank's involvement in Enron and WorldCom.

The future will probably see even more successful claims against companies and perhaps even governments. What would be the cost if each oil, energy and car company were held financially responsible for the proportion of climate change damage its products and services contributed to? What about claiming from multinational companies the costs of poverty alleviation to offset the poverty they have inadvertently created through their activities? Why could victims of human rights abuses or families of murdered political critics not claim for compensation from corporations complicit in these incidents? Might Palestinians sue Israeli companies for theft of land? Or perhaps Swiss banks be sued over their bankrolling of apartheid. Seem unbelievable? In June and November 2002, two lawsuits were filed against corporations who did business with the apartheid regime; the future of activism in the courts has already started.

Bringing activism to the courts is an important step in getting corporations and governments to live by international laws and ethical principles. It not only demonstrates to other corporations that they can and will be held to account for unethical behaviour but, from a market perspective, it increases the financial risks they must take into account, either making them less lucrative investments or discouraging them from taking those risks. From a personal perspective, it often offers the only real hope of compensation. Governments are reluctant to pursue these demands themselves because of fears of scaring away investors. Activists and lawyers are thus the last resort for people to get justice. Regardless of the outcome, the debate these cases generate is as important as the success of the suits themselves.

The United States has a law that could be a model for the rest of the world. Elsewhere, people generally only have the right to take legal action if they have been personally affected. In the United States, people may bring to court anyone who is breaking environmental laws that authorities are ignoring by not enforcing. This means that, in cases such as a river being polluted, citizens can bring the case to court on behalf of the government and win. If this were extended to include labour laws and other laws to which corporations must comply, there would be more opportunities to ensure existing laws are enforced regardless of the mood of the current regime.

Even without legal suits, the true costs of environmental and social negligence are being brought home to companies through economic factors. Financial companies wish to minimise risk. When there is excessive risk they avoid it or allow for it in the terms of their contracts. Banks now increasingly assess environmental risks to prevent being liable for costly cleanup costs in the case of bankruptcy. Insurance companies are increasing some premiums because of the massive increase in damage due to climate change. In the nuclear industry, few companies wish to be involved because of the massive cost of decommissioning or the consequences if things go wrong. When the impact of massive claims against companies and industries is considered, insurers and bankers have a diminished appetite for picking up the costs. Increasingly, they are directly and indirectly pressing corporations to avoid unethical practices and encourage ethical ones. As many corporations are discovering, unethical practices are bad business. Activists just accelerate this discovery.

Nothing About Us, Without Us

Activists in western countries are often accused of being 'rich troublemakers' who have no legitimacy talking about problems affecting non-western countries or poor people around the world. While these are usually unfounded comments that attempt to discredit activists' concerns, they raise a valid issue. If a campaign is relevant to non-western countries or poor people, it is essential that it be carried out in conjunction with them. Each group achieves this in its own way.

Some consult relevant stakeholders to ensure their policies are appropriate. Groups like Oxfam base their campaigning on direct field experience and that of their partners around the world. Others act in solidarity with existing non-western activists. Alternatively, an indicator that a particular concern is shared around the world is the existence of a global activist alliance campaigning on the issue. For domestic campaigns, this can mean including the key domestic stakeholders; increasingly, however, there are few issues that are only local. Regardless of how it is achieved, inclusiveness is a key condition for twenty-first century activism.

While new bridges are being built between people around the world, there is a growing gap between political leaders and the public. 'Not in our name' is a slogan used in conjunction with peace marches. While leaders claim to act in the interest of the people they serve, a majority often disagree with what their political leaders are doing and feel unrepresented. The only way many feel they can be heard is to protest. This is endemic to the wider growth in activism as the gap between people and leaders, including corporate leaders, grows.

Electronic Activism

Electronic activism (e-activism) is transforming the art of campaigning, though it will never replace traditional approaches. It involves using the Internet, mobile phones, faxes and other 'electronic' methods, of which the Internet is currently the most important. While this has been the sexy side of activism for the last half decade, it is still in its infancy and is overlooked by many life long activists. E-activism has already proven it is effective at some campaigning activities such as research sharing, promotion, education, recruitment, dialogue, disclosure and mobilisation – all of which are critical for activist success. However, it is still uncertain how far one can make a direct impact through online actions like petition signing, letter writing, spoof sites or hackivism. This is partly because activists are still learning how to use e-activism effectively and partly because those targeted by activists are not using technology effectively. While there have been, and will continue to be, e-activism successes, it needs to be used in conjunction with other forms of activism.

Whenever a new technology emerges, each technology's usage changes. Initially there is usually a flood of hype about how an old technology will become obsolete. In reality this is almost never the case. What innovation does is shift the balance of using each technology so that each is used for what it is best suited for. When radio was introduced it did not replace books; when the phone was invented it did not replace travel; when television was invented it did not replace radio; when computers were invented they did not replace work or teachers; and when the Internet came into our lives it did not replace books, radio or television. So why should e-activism replace traditional activism? E-activism is reshaping the practice of activism in positive ways, but it is not replacing older forms. Today activists can reach millions of people online in a matter of days or weeks rather than years, but they still have to get them on the streets when that is needed. Anyone can find out what is happening on the other side of the world and raise their concerns with relevant leaders. E-activism has already achieved many things, and there are many more to come. Despite that, activists are still just starting to discover what e-activism can be.

Activists need to demonstrate that their concerns are credible. This is often done through research. With the Internet, activist research is shared widely and quickly. This speeds up the debate and gets the ideas into the hands and heads of journalists, analysts, academics, policy advisors and decision makers, including those whom the research may criticise and implicate.

Activists must also promote their concerns and usually have an existing supporter base. Promotion is as simple as e-mailing supporters and allies, asking them to pass the e-mail on to others. Within days a message can reach double or triple the original recipient base. A compelling message can spread even further and faster. Even for those people who don't participate right away, receiving and reading the message helps to educate them to the issues. This is important even if those people do nothing else since it may affect opinions and decisions for years to come. Others will explore the issue for a while and over a few months become convinced and then take action. Among those who take action, some wish to be kept updated and thus the supporter base grows.

Any of these stakeholders – policy makers, decision makers, journalists, supporters or the public – can connect with each other through the Internet to debate the issues. This is both a learning experience and an opportunity to share their own perspectives. Since traditionally these stakeholders would rarely, if ever, meet, online dialogue is one of the more unique aspects of e-activism.

Disclosing sensitive information is another of the more powerful uses of the Internet for activism. Even national laws and courts cannot stop disclosure. This is boosted even more when combined with interactivity. Interactivity enables people to find out what dangerous chemicals are in their local area and who spilled them, to research companies and learn how ethical they are, to discover the safety of a product or to assess their own health.

Online, activists can mobilise millions of people in less time, at less cost and with less effort than ever before. All of the large globalisation protests from at least 1998 have been promoted and coordinated through the Internet. Even when traditional media fail to spread the word, activists are finding they can still get people on the streets.

Yet online actions or protests are still less powerful than traditional approaches. A few people standing on the street with clipboards can get far more people to sign signing petitions, although paper petitions do not usually enable the activist to keep in touch with supporters cheaply, quickly and easily. Letters received by post are more likely to be opened, read, considered and responded to than e-mails, but people are more likely to write and send an e-mail letter. The real skill for today's activist is to use the strengths of each method of activism to achieve the desired goals.

Other types of e-activism are more controversial but are still in the tradition and spirit of conventional activism. Spoofing – the copying and parodying of brands, advertisements and websites – is quite widespread on the Internet. Some parodies are so convincing that they confuse even experienced Internet users. In a few instances, people have requested – and received – guest speakers from spoof sites, believing them to be officials of the spoofed organisation (Unseem, 2002). The intent is to annoy the spoofed corporation and provide education and humour for the public. When attempts are made to criticise or shut down a spoof site, the result can even be extensive publicity and thus more education about the issue.

Hackivism – the act of civil disobedience or direct action online – is the most contentious form of e-activism. It can include breaking into a target website, jamming or overloading a website or e-mail server, or other creative technical techniques to agitate and disrupt. The intent – as in traditional activism – is to bring the issue to the attention of the target and perhaps even cause loss of business to increase the economic cost of corporate inaction on activist concerns. While it has not been adopted by large campaigning groups, there have been some successes. Most likely it will remain the tactic of individual activists and small groups, just like traditional tactics such as blockading, civil disobedience and direct action.

All these tactics and impacts can be carried through without the Internet. What makes the Internet special is they can be done easier, faster and cheaper and be more inclusive. For activism, that makes a big difference.

'Never doubt that a small group of thoughtful committed citizens can change the world; indeed, it is the only thing that ever does' (Margaret Mead, pioneering anthropologist).

Learning from Activists

In the future, the successful companies will be those who work hardest to make sure that they are in tune with the needs and aspirations of society.

(Mark Moody-Stuart, Chairman, Royal Dutch/Shell)

Activism is a positive influence on corporate policies and practices. It is a 'moral barometer' providing insight into the public's concerns. When issues are resolved early, corporations can benefit from the use of that insight. Ignoring and resisting public concerns results in the negative impact that many corporations experience when faced with activism. To move constructively forward, corporations need not only to overcome the massive trust deficit they face, but also their fear of activists. Codes of conduct, corporate social responsibility programmes and triple bottom line reporting are all necessary approaches, but are inadequate to the challenge of genuinely addressing public concerns. At a minimum, corporations need to ensure their social and environmental impact is neutral, either by doing no harm in the first place or offsetting any harm, with verifiable proof that they have done so. Ideally they need to be partners in resolving society's most pressing issues in ways that benefit people, profits and the planet.

The public are on the front line of the social, environmental and economic consequences of corporations. Thus they are best positioned to recognise dangers and raise concerns. This is the root of activism. If corporations were to recognise and address these concerns early, then the public and the company would both win. Billions are spent each year on legal services to stop activists. If even a portion of this money was spent on understanding the public's concerns when they are first raised, it would allow companies to resolve them before they became critical. This would not only save them money in lost investment, but allow that investment to be directed into areas that genuinely serve both the corporations and the public. In the future, learning from public concerns will be seen to be as vital to business as customer feedback is today. Some companies are already trying to do this with mixed success. Those that continue to try may not only gain an advantage over less progressive competitors, but they will improve the breadth and accuracy of their ability to detect and learn from the public's concerns, and then resolve them quickly.

If corporations are at 'war' with activists then they will definitely lose. The bulk of the most important advances of the last few centuries were brought about by citizen activism. Human rights, women's rights, labour rights, food safety, environmental standards, property rights and even democracy in most countries came about through people uniting to work for justice. This progress continues today, partly because these rights have not been secured by billions of people around the world and partly because there will always be new areas of concern that people raise. Ignoring or resisting activists' concerns will only cause a failure to deal with the issues until the activists succeed despite everything. Thus the issue for a corporation becomes how and when these concerns will affect it. What side of history a corporation is on can affect its fortunes decades afterwards, as some corporations have already discovered.

'The court of public opinion sometimes decides before you're ready for them to decide, and I want to make sure we're ready and ahead of the curve' (Bill Ford, Jr., Chairman, Ford Motor Company).

The Trust Deficit

In Europe, activist 'brands' are already more highly trusted than any corporation, and in the United States three out of the top 11 brands are those of activist organisations (Edelman, 2002b). People – including employees, customers, shareholders and journalists – are already sceptical about corporate intentions and practices following the Enron and WorldCom scandals. The onus is thus on corporations to act ethically when dealing with activist concerns. Failing to be genuinely ethical has negative consequences on a corporations' stakeholders, its competitive position and its cost of doing business.

This trust gap is partly created by secret corporate lobbying. When the public don't know what is happening, that fuels mistrust. Research reveals that corporations and parliaments/congresses are the least trusted institutions. The primary reasons are that their leaders 'don't do what they say', act out of 'self-interest' and because of 'secrecy' or 'arrogance'.[9] Trust is more easily lost than gained: mud sticks. Being proactive about resolving activist concerns is the best way for corporations to ensure they retain the public's confidence.

Genuinely addressing their trustworthiness is the most important work leaders and institutions can do, and it will take time. Forecasts see the world shifting from a 'trust me' world, where institutions and individuals are given the benefit of the doubt until they act in a way that loses them that trust, to a 'show me' world where everyone has to constantly prove their trustworthiness.[10] Activists play a vital role in this process because they often expose institutions or leaders who have betrayed societies' trust or sense of justice. They will continue to play this role not only by exposing institutions and leaders who cannot be trusted, but by building and maintaining the trust of those who earn it.

Activists: David or Goliath?

Since activism is daily democracy, it is ultimately pointless for corporations to attempt to counter activists with PR, legal threats or other efforts to distract or discredit them. While the corporation may sometimes succeed temporarily, they just feed the fire of injustice in activists, escalating the situation. Activism as democracy means that activists cannot be dismissed as an insignificant minority, because they are not insignificant and they are creating the majority. The main choice for corporations is how early to engage with activists and resolve relevant issues.

The most ill-advised courses of action would be to try and silence, counter or undermine activist concerns because in the eyes of the public this would only serve to reinforce a corporation's guilt and do irreparable damage to its reputation. This approach tends to come from those hostile to activism who view activists as the 'enemy' and react as if at war. Unfortunately in war everyone loses: it is the one who loses the least and lasts the longest that prevails.

Some corporations to portray themselves as 'David' versus 'Goliath' activists in a desperate attempt to gain sympathy. The facts demonstrate the reality: not only are 29 of the world's largest economies corporations, but the top 500 corporations account for 70 per cent of world trade (UNCTAD, 1995)! Corporate 'Goliaths' are bigger than most realise. While there are millions of citizen groups, even the largest can only mobilise a few thousand people independently. This is why alliances are key to activist success since they help to counter the massive power of corporations.

A prime reason why corporate leaders relate to activists so inappropriately is that there are few places where one can learn to engage with activist concerns. Most business schools fail to include activism as part of the business curriculum. It is thus understandable that many business leaders are hostile. When criticised they respond as if attacked by an enemy rather than as a source of legitimate concern. A more mature grasp of the role of activism would lead them to see it as a positive force in society and the marketplace: one that creates the conditions for business to contribute to its own and society's advancement.

'All truth passes through three stages. First, it is ridiculed. Second, it is violently opposed. Third, it is accepted as being self-evident' (Arthur Schopenhauer, nineteenth century philosopher).

Cherishing Activism

Some people see things as they are and say why. I see things that never were and say why not.

(George Bernard Shaw, Nobel Literature laureate)

You have now gained insight into activism and activists. Did it change some of your perceptions of the role and intentions of activists, or did it reinforce your existing beliefs? Did you get a sense of the potential for corporations to learn from activists rather than simply react to them? Could other friends, family or colleagues also benefit from this insight? If so, share it with them. If you have seen possibilities for new ways of working, then you have already make the most important step; now's its time for action. Discuss it with others, try new ways of working, get involved in a campaign. See what a difference you can make when activism is a healthy companion to work and life. It is up to you.

Activism needs to be engaged with, learnt from and resolved by those to whom it is relevant. People need time and space to publicly discuss and engage with issues in which they are concerned. This is what activism is and does: stimulate dialogue and participation. It is a key part of human life and a natural duty to question and challenge, even at the risk of being wrong. Fighting or ignoring activism are thus losing strategies. Perhaps in a few decades it will be self-evident that activism is a source of inspiration for individuals, politicians and corporations. It can start today with you.

It is from numberless diverse acts of courage and belief that human history is shaped. Each time a person stands up for an ideal, or strikes out against injustice, he sends forth a tiny ripple of hope; and crossing each other from a million different centers of energy and daring, those ripples build a current which can sweep down the mightiest walls of oppression and resistance.

(Robert F. Kennedy, US Senator, South Africa 1966)

Notes

1. The Universality of the Golden Rule in the World Religions, Teaching-Values.com/goldenrule.html, Hinduism, Mahabharata 5,1517 (5 February 2003).
2. The Universality of the Golden Rule in the World Religions, Teaching-Values.com/goldenrule.html, Islam, Sunnah (5 February 2003).
3. The Universality of the Golden Rule in the World Religions, Teaching-Values.com/goldenrule.html, Judaism, The Talmud, Shabbat 31a (5 February 2003).
4. Results of the Survey on Trust, World Economic Forum website, 2003.
5. Robin Cook, in a speech to Green Alliance Environment Forum in February 1999.
6. 'The Future of the Anti Globalisation Movement', World Economic Forum website, Stephen J Korbrin, Professor of Multinational Management, The Warton School, University of Pennsylvania, USA (23 January 2003).
7. Personal conversations with corporate responsibility managers. Reference on case by case basis.
8. United for Peace Website at http://unitedforpeace.org/article.php?id=725
9. Results of the Survey on Trust, World Economic Forum website, 2003.
10. Theme: Corporate Challenges, World Economic Forum website, 2003.

CHAPTER 13

Swarms and Networks

New Modes of Struggle in the Alternative Globalisation Movement

Graeme Chesters

A world made of many worlds opened a space and established its right to exist, raised the banner of being necessary, stuck itself in the middle of the earth's reality to announce a better future.

A world of all worlds that rebel and resist Power.

A world of all the worlds that inhabit this world, opposing cynicism.

A world that struggles for humanity and against neoliberalism.

That was the world that we lived these days.

This is the world that we found here.[1]

This chapter describes the 'found world' of the above quote and the new geography of social movement networks that have sought to announce their presence. Populated by tree-sitters, office-occupiers, land and housing squatters, street reclaimers, *carnivalistas*, hackers, culture-jammers, independent journalists, *piqueteros* and guerrilla gardeners, this movement with no name has been saddled with plenty, this movement of many movements: the anti-globalisation, anti-capitalist, anti-corporate, 'anarchist road show'.[2]

The intention behind this chapter is not to claim some privileged overview or to elucidate any universal specifics about these phenomena, which are complex and evolving. Instead, I hope to place things in context and to trace a series of trajectories: discursive paths of ideas and action through which this movement has intersected with the social, political, cultural and economic domains. To say something about the form and substance of the movement that is not immediately obvious from either media or academic commentary, and to present in a lucid manner the challenge it poses to governance in all its forms. In doing so I hope to dispel some of the more widely disseminated inaccuracies and point out the increasingly sophisticated patterns of opposition and resistance this movement has given rise to.

Contrary to popular belief, what is commonly referred to as the 'anti-globalisation movement' did not start with protests against the World Trade Organisation in Seattle.[3] Nor is it just a product of post-material sensibilities harboured by the children of the 'new' middle class, a common and dismissive rejoinder to the debate that caricatures this movement as a product of the 'North' and 'West', categories which themselves are rapidly exploding along the variegated axes of globalisation. To address these misconceptions and contextualise this movement I begin by sketching out two case studies. These serve as examples of the ideological and situational catalysts that have sparked resistance and fanned it across the globe. The chapter then moves on to outline the organisational forms that have emerged within and between these groups and to describe how these forms have been expressed at an extra-national level in the work of People's Global Action (PGA) and other similar initiatives. This leads to a discussion of the dynamics of these movement networks and the complex characteristics they exhibit, including a brief introduction to a conceptual framework for their analysis. The chapter concludes by evaluating the outcomes of these processes and assessing the implications for the movement, its allies and opposition.

The Alternative Globalisation Movement

For the purposes of clarity and brevity, I am going to refer to the widespread opposition to capitalist globalisation as the alternative globalisation movement (AGM). However, before continuing it should be noted that the phenomena I am referring to are, in truth, far more complex than this description would suggest. The AGM is not a social movement in the traditional sense of that concept. It is best defined as a network of networks, with significant nodes and clusters consisting of social movements, social movement organisations, groups and individuals, expanding across an 'n'-dimensional space that has both real and virtual aspects. Coterminous with this network is a series of what I have referred to as 'plateaus' (Chesters and Welsh, 2002): protest events, campaigns, gatherings of one type or another which allow for a brief manifestation and stabilisation of the network, facilitating processes of identity building, the exchange of ideas, and the planning of protest actions and so on.[4]

Consequently, any neat or linear explanation of origins and context would be inappropriate. In many ways, the AGM represents a confluence of different conflictual currents originating in diverse regions of the world that have identified a common opposition and sought a shared terrain. Thus, we must proceed through examination of actors, events and above all processes that have proven on reflection to be indicative of the development of the AGM. To this end, I want to sketch out two examples of parallel processes that eventually became synthesised in the AGM: the Zapatistas in Mexico and Reclaim The Streets in the United Kingdom. The most frequently cited catalyst of the AGM in the southern hemisphere is Zapatismo, the discursively constructed 'ideology' of the Zapatista communities of Chiapas, South East Mexico, and it is to this we turn first.

Zapatistas and the Insurgent Imagination

The Zapatista National Liberation Army (EZLN) first came to the world's attention on 1 January 1994, the day that the North American Free Trade Agreement (NAFTA) came into force. In a well-planned armed uprising, 3000 Zapatistas briefly occupied seven towns in the state of Chiapas declaring 'Ya basta!' – Enough is enough! This was to be the beginning of what came to be known as the 'war against oblivion' (Ross, 2000) a war against the certitude of poverty, disease, hunger and environmental desecration that was the fate of the indigenous and their lands, a process that NAFTA was already beginning to accelerate. Free trade as interpreted in this agreement meant the reform of Article 27 of the Mexican Constitution, which had been one of the outcomes of the Mexican revolution, the catalyst for 75 years of agrarian reform and the foundation stone of the *ejido* system of communal land ownership. With this legal 'barrier' to trade removed, the way was open for trans-national agro-industries to purchase what had previously been communally held lands. Once more the familiar refrain of land, liberty and freedom was the core of resistance, but this was to be resistance in an information age, for which the Zapatistas have a particular gift.

The genius of the Zapatista uprising has been its reliance upon *symbols*, *networks* and *charisma*, characteristics that have also proven crucial to the success of the AGM elsewhere. The Zapatista message is communicated by a diverse network of activists and intellectuals and is articulated through the iconic symbolism invoked by Zapata's name and the delivery of their message through the words of the masked poet-warrior Subcommandante Insurgente Marcos. At once comic, lyrical, ironic and proud, the Zapatista communiqués have established a dignified intellectual tone that has echoed around the world, enabling commentators to cite the Zapatistas as both the first 'postmodern guerrilla insurgency' and as heralding the advent of a 'social netwar' (Ronfeldt *et al.*, 1998), a veritable siege of the signs and codes of contemporary capitalism. It appears that Mexico, which gave the world a new prototype for social revolution at the beginning of the twentieth century, has once again given birth to an imaginative leap in political form: information-age insurrection that is reflexive, dialogical and readily communicated within the discourse and activism of dissident groups of radical persuasion across the globe.

Politically and theoretically, the Zapatistas have been successful in their attempt to name, appeal to and propagate the idea of a *global civil society*. Although Marcos appears to have been heavily influenced by Gramsci, his theoretical construction of civil society is distinct from traditional understandings of that term. That is civil society as the contested terrain of nationally based institutions serving normative functions that have transformative potential because of their roots amongst both state and people: church, trade unions, civic associations and the like. The Zapatista concept of civil society is different in that it acknowledges the institutions, structures and processes of traditional civil society, but recognises them as part of a globally constituted domain that is replete with new social actors, new forces and new challenges. It also suggests that any project to capture the state through civil society is both illusory and essentially undesirable (Lorenzano, 1998).

The Zapatistas announced a project that is in some ways as old as the hills and as familiar as the praxis of the peoples of the hills they themselves inhabit. Their argument suggests that a global civil society that was networked self-aware and reflexive would seek not to capture the state but to negate it, diffuse power rather than concentrate it, and strive through a radically democratic praxis for the emergence of a global public sphere, constituted by and from struggle:

> And its result will not be the victory of a party, an organisation, or an alliance of triumphant organisations with their own specific social proposal, but rather a democratic space for resolving the confrontation of various political proposals.
>
> (Zapatista communiqué, 20 January 1994)

Such a development they reasoned might yet act as a brake upon neoliberal globalisation, a rationale for which they already have some evidence, given their successes in utilising the interventions of this ill-defined sector as a buffer against the Mexican Government and army. Once they had envisaged this global civil society, all that remained was to invite 'it' to Chiapas, to a newly constructed 'reality' in a place of that name: La Realidad. Here, in the 'First Intercontinental *Encuentro* for Humanity and Against Neoliberalism', activists from around the world – trade unionists, environmentalists, campaigners from various NGOs, sympathetic writers and intellectuals –

gathered to hear of and respond to the particular situation the Zapatistas had helped create. In Marcos' words:

> Some of the best rebels from the five continents arrived in the mountains of the Mexican Southeast. All of them brought their ideas, their hearts, their worlds. They came to La Realidad to find themselves in others' ideas, in others' reasons, in others' worlds.
>
> (Marcos, 2001, p. 121)

This gathering and the issues it addressed, like the proverbial stone dropped in water, caused ripples of recognition to rebound from many shores. The Zapatistas' paradoxical lyricism and directly democratic structure caught the mood of southern activists engaging in collective struggle against global institutions and processes. Their targets were essentially the same, the architects and architecture of neoliberal capitalism: the International Monetary Fund, World Bank and the soon to be formalised World Trade Organisation, as well as the proxy governance through multinational corporations facilitated by free trade agreements (FTAs), structural adjustment programmes (SAPs) and the rapacious conduct of the corporations themselves. The only difference was the form and type of resistance. These struggles were already global but had yet to be conceived of as such, or communicated in a comprehensive or cohesive way. Looking back now to the early 1990s and sweatshop workers rioting in Manila, Indian farmers dismantling Kentucky Fried Chicken outlets and land being reclaimed across Brazil by Movimento Sem Terra, the connections between their targets and methods of intervention are pronounced. The First Encuentro was clearly an attempt to name these struggles as one, to offer space for connections to be made, to construct an inclusive framework and to announce an alternative, albeit one which in the Zapatistas' words sought 'everything for everybody and nothing for ourselves'.

While they are significant, it is also important to avoid the construction of a narrative that eulogises the Zapatistas as the sole catalyst of the AGM. This would be to deny the simultaneous emergence of similar critiques voiced by movements and peoples struggling to find a place in and to avoid being 'switched off' from the 'network society' (Castells, 1996). These critiques subsequently found themselves mirrored in Zapatista praxis, but were not originated by, or through interactions with, the Zapatistas. These parallel patterns of resistance rooted in specific social and economic conditions occurred in many locations, and in many instances they were derived from similar and seemingly incongruous interactions between diverse constituencies. In Mexico, it was urban Marxists in dialogue with the rural indigenous, which led to a peculiarly hybrid expression of anti-capitalism. In the United Kingdom, it was a curious mixture of urban sub-culture, environmental sensibility and the criminalisation of dissent that facilitated the emergence of an antagonistic movement.

Reclaim The Streets and the New Crime of Dissent

The Criminal Justice and Public Order Act (CJ&POA) became law in 1994 and quickly became the catalyst for interaction between groups that might otherwise have taken far longer to identify a common interest, if indeed they ever would have done so. The CJ&POA set out to criminalise whole swathes of activities and people, many of who were considered to be a rump of resisters, an inappropriate blot on the copybook of 15 years of Conservative Government. New Age travellers, hunt saboteurs, squatters, environmental protesters and rave-goers were all targeted, and in turn united in common opposition to this draconian piece of legislation. Tellingly *SchNEWS*, a weekly direct action newsletter, thanked the Home Secretary for 'your inspiration' which has

> made us work closer together: networking is happening across the nation – Road Protesters and Ravers, Gay Rights Activists and Hunt Saboteurs, Travellers and Squatters and many more, as we realise the strength of our numbers. . . . Thanks to you we are witnessing the largest grassroots movement of direct action in years.
>
> (*SchNEWS*, 1995)[5]

It was from these networks that Reclaim The Streets (RTS) subsequently emerged, an eclectic fusion of politics, party and protest based in London and utilising street blockades, direct action and the reclamation of urban space for political purposes and pleasurable ends. The use of novel and confrontational tactics ensured the rapid dissemination of street reclaiming as a repertoire of collective action and RTS as a form of intervention quickly became a national and then global phenomenon. The theoretical endeavour and intent behind RTS as an organisation was also clear-cut, albeit this was sometimes lost in 'the party as protest dynamic' that by 1997 had given rise to street occupations on major thoroughfares across the United Kingdom. In form, discourse and tactic RTS were already 'anti-capitalist', explicitly deconstructing capitalist social relations, located in either the imposition of the artificial rhythms of commerce and the car upon cities, or the fractured anomic relations inspired by normative urban geography and the processes of production underpinning it.

That this was largely missed or misunderstood demonstrates something of the insurgent imagination that was at work. Art and politics had been absent from public life in all but the most sanitised of forms and interventions of this type were no longer supposed to occur; after all political discourse had for some time been following the Thatcherite doctrine of TINA: 'There Is No Alternative'. That some believed 'another world is possible' became a lot clearer when on 18 June 1999, the City of London was 'temporarily liberated' as part of 'a global carnival against capital'. However, if we are to connect the dots it is important to understand something of the emergent global processes and connections that were taking place behind the scenes.

Activists from RTS and British Earth First! were present at the Second Zapatista-inspired Encuentro held in Spain in 1997 and were subsequently involved in the founding of People's Global Action (PGA) one year later, which was perhaps the most important initiative that emerged from the Second Encuentro. Formed to coordinate actions and interventions against the global market economy, groups within PGA have been prime movers behind most of the large anti-capitalist mobilisations in recent years, including the protests in the City of London, Seattle, Prague, Gothenburg and Genoa. Their inaugural conference took place in Geneva at the same time and in the same city as the WTO were meeting to celebrate 50 years of free trade (GATT) and to announce Seattle as the venue for their next ministerial conference. This led to the most significant instance of public disorder in Switzerland's post-war history, including mass protests, clashes with riot police and property damage to the outlets of multinational corporations. This was an instance of opposition to the WTO that is absent from any of the most recent accounts of these movement networks (Brecher *et al.*, 2000; Dannaher and Burbach, 2000, Cockburn *et al.*, 2000; Starr, 2000), despite being a portentous indication of what would later transpire on the streets of Seattle.

Only days before the founding conference of PGA, the internationalist intentions of RTS became apparent during a 'global street party' involving 72 countries and timed to coincide with the Group of Eight (G8) meeting in Birmingham, England.[6] It is perhaps little wonder then that the first convenors of PGA Europe were London Reclaim The Streets, one of many groups emerging in Europe for whom an 'anti-capitalist' praxis that combined internationalism, imagination and direct confrontation was increasingly viable. This praxis was an outcome of a global synthesis of movements and organisations expressing themselves at an extra-national level organised in a network structure coordinated in small gatherings and via computer-mediated communications. This synthesis or 'structure' has since been consolidated within PGA, which functions as a framework for orientation, networking, action and communication.

Form and Meaning

In this section, I will introduce some thoughts on the nature of the dynamics of the AGM and try to account for its persistence and resilience. I will also introduce some ideas from contemporary complexity sciences that I believe can form the basis of a radically new means of engaging with and understanding the AGM. This will therefore constitute a brief overview of the analytical framework I have developed elsewhere (Chesters and Welsh, 2002).

What I have sought to outline through the two examples used above is the discursive construction of a global field of struggle, constituted by the forging of connections between social movements operating in a context defined by the hegemony of neoliberalism and the arrival of the information age. This social movement network has proliferated by using inclusive methods of organising, pluralistic patterns of intervention and the targeting of organisations, events and situations that have a global impact and as such have resonance for social movements and other sympathetic constituencies globally. An additional success of these targeted actions against the G8, WTO, World Bank or IMF has been the enormous cross-fertilisation of ideas, concepts and collective action repertoires resulting from the express desire of organisers to see politically contiguous actions proliferate in the same spatial and temporal context. In this sense, a thousand flowers have metaphorically bloomed.

The AGM gives voice to a huge range of campaigns, protests and alternatives, some of which conflict with each other and therefore arouse considerable internal debate. Campaigns have included opposition to the global restructuring of economies through instruments of neoliberal policy such as FTAs and SAPs, as well as campaigns to cancel the debt burden of developing countries and for a tax on currency speculation (Tobin Tax). They have included well-organised and concerted opposition to privatisation and the corporate control of essential services – specifically water and power – plus a whole range of other issues, including environmental deterioration, access to health care, racism and minority rights, cultural imperialism, gene modification and patenting, and the free movement of people. In all these areas the AGM has provided the means through which politically engaged people can conduct the necessarily collective work of deciphering their individual experiences of globalisation and forging from them shared understandings that can become the basis of recognisable needs and therefore political demands. This work takes place within the *shadow realm* of alternative fora and networked interaction facilitated by People's Global Action and other coordinating bodies.

The key to understanding how this occurs is not to be found among individual actors, be they groups or organisations. We must instead focus our attention upon the processes of interaction between actors. For if we are to reveal anything about how the AGM works we must look to processes and to form: it is within this hidden architecture that something of the dynamic strength of the AGM can be grasped. The AGM is a network of networks and as such, displays what are known as 'small-world' characteristics (Barabasi, 2002; Buchanan, 2002). That is to say, it is composed of clusters of hubs and nodes that are typified by having a penumbra of 'weak links'. This structure allows rapid communication across a network and resilience to all but the most focused of attacks. There is also increasing evidence that such networks demonstrate a collective intelligence that is greater than the sum of the parts of the network. A capacity that appears close to what the political theorists Hardt and Negri (2000) refer to as a 'general intellect'. To use the idiom of contemporary complexity sciences, what the AGM is demonstrating are *emergent* properties: these are an outcome of complex adaptive behaviour that occurs through self-organisation from the bottom up. This organisational form and the behaviour that structures it leads to higher order macro-outcomes such as the emergence of collective intelligence. Recent scientific endeavour in this field has demonstrated (Barabasi and Albert, 1999) that these properties are ubiquitous in complex network forms, albeit they are often unrecognised. What appears to have occurred within the AGM is that its affinity with acutely democratic forms and its flirtation with anarchism has encouraged organisational forms that encourage emergence and that the advantages conferred *have* been recognised.

Unpacking the implications of complexity theory for social movement analysis is a task beyond the remit of this chapter, although it is a project that is at the core of my work elsewhere (Chesters and Welsh, 2002). Here it should be sufficient to note that the evidence emerging from within the natural sciences supports and dramatically reinforces the point made in a seminal sociology paper by Mark Granovetter entitled 'The Strength of Weak Ties' (1973). This counter-intuitive argument suggests that it is the weak ties between people, not strong friendships, that are most important when it comes to finding a job, accessing news, launching a new enterprise and so on. This is because weak ties are crucial for our ability to communicate beyond our immediate social world. Our close friends almost inevitably move in the same circles as we do, and as such are most likely to be exposed to the same information. We need to activate our weak ties if we are to open new channels of information and maximise our potential for agency. It appears then that the instincts of the AGM – its reliance upon flat structures and network forms, its antipathy to institutionalisation and leaders *per se*, its generation of events, gatherings, e-mail lists and websites – have created a structure that is dynamic, resilient and actualises the potential of those belonging to it. The apparent disorganisation, which is so obvious a feature of the AGM that it leads to groups self-identifying as 'disorganisations', masks a deeper truth: an emergent order on the edge of chaos. This truth is hinted at ironically in the slogan 'anarchy IS order', for as Steve Johnson writes in a recent book on emergence: 'Nowhere are the progressive possibilities of emergence more readily apparent than in the anti-WTO protest movements, which have explicitly modelled themselves after the distributed, cellular structures of self-organising systems' (Johnson, 2001, p. 225).

The lessons for business and government may therefore be quite profound. The successes of this movement, its capacity to concretely intervene on the streets and in boardrooms, stem directly from its networked structure, its curious leaderless cultures and anarchic patterns of organisation and communication. These are indeed its strengths. Small-world networks are ubiquitous: the same patterns are replicated everywhere from neural connections in the brain to the food webs that underlie the world's ecosystems and on in to the apparently haphazard development of the Internet. So much so that physics itself is changing its focus; a central task in this new century will be the study of complex adaptive matter (Laughlin and Pines, 2000), in other words, the study of emergent properties. These insights and the science behind them are in their infancy, but they are already yielding important discoveries about the capacities of complex systems to demonstrate properties that exceed the sum of their parts. Small-world networks such as the World Wide Web are beginning to demonstrate the capability of collective intelligence and as Johnson points out:

> if the Web's collective intelligence is still in its infancy, think of how much room the new protest movements must have to grow. But thus far, their instincts have been sound ones. Beneath the window smashing and the Rage Against the Machine concerts, the anti-WTO activists are doing something profound, even in these early days of their movement. They are thinking like a swarm.

> (Johnson, 2001, p. 226)

Conclusion: Listening Before It Is Too Late

The outcomes of this swarming behaviour are numerous. We are reminded that the margins can speak, hold forth, and carry on a fight, that the edges may not be distant from where things are at, but might instead be leading the way. For instance, who would have imagined that capitalism would once more be discussed as if there were alternatives to it? This mode of production and set of social relations that has been so hegemonic since the break up of the Soviet Union had all but disappeared as a public discourse. The AGM has put it back on the table, to be picked over, analysed, debated and resisted. Who would have believed that ever-increasing numbers of people globally would chose to access their 'news' through independent media sites that continue to proliferate at an astonishing rate?[7] Sites that utilise open-source software and encourage participation through the unrestricted flow of stories, audio clips and video footage posted by independent journalists, activists and concerned 'netizens'. The AGM has opened a space for thought, reflection and action that will not easily be closed. Perhaps then the proponents of the 'end of history' thesis (Fukuyama, 1992), those celebrated celebrants of the omniscience of capital were a touch premature, a collection of Cinderellas masquerading as 24-hour party people.

The purpose of this book is to describe activism of various sorts at the beginning of the twenty-first century, to map origins and trajectories, and to suggest some of the implications that specific forms of activism have for governance, broadly conceived to include the state, corporate and public sectors. In this respect, it is important to note that the forces that constitute the AGM are already proving capable of innovations that can shape state-level initiatives and thus simultaneously reshape the institutional contours of modernity. The vibrancy of the initiatives present within fora convened by People's Global Action and the World Social Forum represent alternative stances on every imaginable 'policy sphere'. All of these are typically excluded by the expert-dominated thinking of technocratic decisional forms that take place within the context of extraordinary asymmetries of power, a point exemplified by the prevarication of the United States Government on environmental issues and the distortion of power through corporate lobbying that led to the failure of the United Nations World Summit on Sustainable Development in Johannesburg.

The challenge is not to bolt these insights from the AGM on to established technocratic agendas, but to work at reconfiguring organisational forms democratically and from below, in a way which reflects the unity in diversity that characterises the AGM. If we fail to do so, we will also fail to realise the hybrid aspirations of people seeking a better way to live and the self-organising capacity to generate emergent qualities that exist in network structures. For these ends to be achievable, we need to stay close to and embed ourselves within these networks. We need to learn to look for, and recognise, forms of action and agency that are generative of imaginative, just and sustainable alternatives and we need the training to hear what the AGM is saying. This means moving beyond the white noise of smashed windows, tear gas and the political posturing of elites.

Notes

1. Subcommandante Insurgente Marcos (1996), 'Tomorrow Begins Today'. Closing Remarks at the First International Encuentro for Humanity and Against Neo-liberalism. In *Our Word is Our Weapon* (Marcos, 1996).
2. Carnival has become a widely used metaphor to describe contemporary collective action (see Kennedy, 2002). *Piquetero* is a term that describes unemployed workers organising autonomously in suburban *barrios* in Argentina. Their tactics include the blocking of highways in order to disrupt the circulation of goods and to demand concessions from the government and corporations. Tony Blair has famously described the alternative globalisation movement as an 'anarchist roadshow'.
3. I am aware that labelling this movement is problematic. In activist publications and discourse the point has been repeatedly made that this is an 'alternative globalisation movement' rather than an anti-globalization movement. Other commentators have referred to a process of 'globalization from below' (Brecher *et al*, 2000). My preferred option is alternative globalization movement – AGM.
4. The term 'plateau' is of limited utility in the context of this chapter, but the concept is at the centre of the analytical framework for understanding and interpreting the AGM that colleagues and I have advanced elsewhere (Chesters and Welsh, 2002). The term originates in the work of Gregory Bateson (1973) and became widely known through its subsequent use by Deleuze and Guattari, (2002).
   The World Social Forums) held in Porto Alegre, Brazil in 2001 and 2002 and the PGA conferences held in Bangalore, India and Cochabamba, Bolivia in 2000, 2001 are probably the best examples of meetings that constitute 'plateaus'.
5. *SchNEWSreader*, 1995, No. 1 available from Justice?, Prior House, 6 Tilbury Place, Brighton, BN2 2GY.

6. 'Thousands of anarchists occupied city centre streets in defiance of the massed ranks of hundreds of police....The "green" protest was organised by the underground Reclaim The Streets movement' (Taylor and Walker, 1998).
7. See www.indymedia.org

CHAPTER 14

Scholar-Activism and the Global Movement for Socioeconomic Justice

Antonio Carmona Báez

> Ours is, in numerical terms, the biggest protest movement in the history of the world.
>
> (George Monbiot)

> Worthwhile projects and commendable programmes cannot exist in a vacuum. They need intellectual ammunition to create the context in which they can flourish.
>
> (Susan George)

Introduction

Whether or not mainstream media choose to expose it, a new form of activism is on the rise. From Chiapas to Seattle, from Cochabamba to Genoa, social activists have been mobilised at a global level. Some call it the anti-globalisation movement; others call it the anti-capitalist movement, and others, the global protest movement.[1] Throughout the 1990s and now in the twenty-first century, grassroots movements have evolved into greater struggles for peace and security, the democratic rights of indigenous peoples, economic equality through fair trade, the elimination of poverty, concern for the environment and alternatives to capitalist development. Though pluralistic in the issues they tackle, year-by-year these tendencies have drawn closer together and appear to be forming one global movement for socioeconomic justice.

Some well-known scholars have dedicated the bulk of their work to analysing and supporting this movement, among them Susan George, Alex Callinicos, Mike Gonzales, Ronnie Hall, and Barry Coates. In a publication entitled *Anti-Capitalism: A Guide to the Movement* (Birchman and Charlton, 2001), these writers together with other analysts argue for an alternative to neoliberal globalisation. They also highlight instances where groups of diverse people have demonstrated their willingness to form common agendas. References are often made to Seattle (Washington, 1999) where 70,000 demonstrators took to the streets to protest against the World Trade Organisation, and to Genoa (Italy, 2001), where 300,000 people demonstrated against the G8 Summit and eventually clashed with police.

In recent times, the media has erroneously tended to classify the struggles of those who challenge the present world order as those belonging to the 'anti-globalist' movement. Contrarily, analysts like the ones mentioned above have emphasised that those who manifest their disenchantment with current global structures are not against globalisation. Rather, they are fighting neoliberal or corporate-led globalisation and are attempting to construct a globalisation of justice from below. What the world is seeing is the building of globally concerned *counter-hegemonic alliances*. That is, a linking of diverse groups of people and organisations that oppose the world's status quo and its course of direction.

The aim of this chapter is to sketch out this global movement. Who are they? How did they come about? Who are they fighting? What do they want and, more specifically, what do they need? Furthermore, I will argue that this movement is dependent on the network of professional scholar-activists to find clear ideas, to search for viable alternatives and to arm the movement intellectually. In contrast to 'conventional' forms of single-issue social activism (street demonstrations, fax cramming, e-mail bombardment, boycott campaigns, tying oneself to a tree, throwing rocks at a McDonald's window, etc.), scholar-activism can potentially make a bigger impact upon the way people think. Scholar-activism can be described here as the intellectual force that is the cornerstone of the *counter-hegemonic alliance against neoliberal globalisation*, a permanent force of critical thinking as opposed to the activism that lives only temporarily.

What Is New About This Movement?

The roots of the global movement for socioeconomic justice can be traced back to the 1960s, when political ideas of the left dominated the minds and concerns of workers and students who found the need for solidarity in their struggles against inequality, colonialism, poverty and war (Wainwright, 2002). These ideas were mostly generated in political organisations, mostly of socialists, communists, Maoists and anarchists. But when the 'state socialist' experiment of Eastern Europe and throughout other parts of the world fell during the late 1980s, many activists became disillusioned; some of the old social activists were lost in a world with apparently no alternatives to modern day capitalism.

Between the 1960s and 1980s, most activists stuck to single-issue campaigns. Greenpeace was saving the whales, there was the anti-nuclear movement, homosexuals had their gay and lesbian pride days, trade unions concentrated on obtaining fair labour practices and pacifists opposed Western military intervention in the South. Although some political organisations understood that these were all related, few were those who saw the necessary link. During the 1990s, however, a new generation of social activists came to the fore, realising the continuous contradiction between the interests of corporate power and those of common people and the environment. This new movement of resistance against global capitalism left behind the fragmented struggles of the previous decade, found the bigger picture and now seeks to fight the structures and ideas that dominate society worldwide.

The linking of these movements did not happen in a vacuum, however. There were certain events that caused people to question the viability of global capitalism as a whole. The globalisation of the media through television and the widespread use of the Internet made people aware of the injustices committed by the powerful. It became increasingly difficult to hide the disasters that were caused by trans-national corporations (TNCs) in distant lands. Additionally, during the second half of the 1990s, global capitalism encountered numerous crises and conflicts that led people to question its legitimacy. More specifically, the neoliberal ideology was increasingly unable to persuade people of the 'necessity' of an unsustainable system of production, trade and distribution. These defects motivated thousands of individuals to seek alternatives.

The disasters brought on by structural adjustment in Africa and Latin America, the chain reactions of financial crises throughout East Asia, Russia, Mexico, Brazil and more recently and harshly in Argentina, and the massive fraud and spectacular wiping out of trillions of dollars of investors' wealth (the Enron scandal) have all eaten away at the credibility of neoliberal capitalism (Bello, 2002). Additionally, there is the crisis of liberal democracy. This is seen in all over the world. In the South, governments serve international financial institutions, regional development banks and TNCs instead of the citizens. The demise of practical democracy is also evident in the United States and Western Europe. Every election period is marked by a significant decrease in voter turnout and the institutions of multiparty democracy are found to be useless when it comes to maintaining welfare or dealing with the questions of immigration or security. Finally, the so-called 'war against terrorism', led by the United States after the events of 11 September 2001, has proven to be a strategic move on behalf of the world's only superpower to secure its economic interests across the globe: limiting human rights domestically, condoning authoritarian regimes abroad, legitimising the use of unilateral military action and pushing the neoliberal agenda in the interests of international investors.

Neoliberalism: A Hegemonic Ideology

What is this thing called neoliberalism? According to the political economist Arthur MacEwan: 'The essence of the neoliberal position on international commerce is the proposition that economic growth will be most rapid when the movement of goods, services and capital is unimpeded by government regulations' (MacEwan, 1999, p. 31). Its name comes from the experience of nineteenth-century *liberalism*, which was thought to have brought wealth and power to English and other Northern European societies, and the suffix *neo-*, meaning new or revised by contemporary conditions. To elaborate, neoliberalism is a political and economic ideology that represents the interests of market leaders (i.e., big business and finance) in its tendency to expand globally. Governmental rules and practices that prevent or hinder expanding markets are thought to be the enemy.

The term neoliberalism can be misleading in that the suffix *neo* is often interpreted to mean something new. However, the only thing new about this ideology and political, economic practice is the dominance it seemed to have had throughout the last decade. Some point to the Reagan–Thatcher era (early 1980s) as the beginning of neoliberalism, and to the fall of the Berlin Wall (1989) as the start of its global consolidation among states and international financial institutions. The truth is that, in the words of Susan George: 'The victory of neoliberalism is the result of fifty years of intellectual work, now widely reflected in the media, politics, and the programmes of international organisations' (George, 1997). George points to the establishment of think tanks in the United States and the United Kingdom during the 1940s, when liberalism was a marginal ideology in politics. Through the institutions, wealthy conservatives poured millions of dollars into research and materials for the development of anti-New Deal plans geared towards political leaders of the right. In turn, these politicians and capitalists formed an alliance to dismantle the power of the state in public spheres.

The intellectual roots of neoliberal economics can be found in the inter-war period with individuals like Richard Weaver and Friedrich von Hayek, who both started a trend of producing literature that discredited the 'transformation' from free-market capitalism to state-controlled economy (Tomlinson, 1990; George, 1997). The production of literature and ideology that fortified conservative forces eventually laid the basis for the 'conservative revolution' against Keynesian economics, which called for state intervention in the economy to regulate trade and production and to maintain welfare. Today, neoliberal ideology, as a doctrine, is reflected in the practices and formulas that are often promoted by international financial institutions when dealing with the question of development in the countries of the South (George and Sabelli, 1994). The eventual global acceptance of this ideology by state leaders and international organisations is what makes neoliberalism a hegemonic ideology in the process of globalisation.

Hegemony, coming from the Greek word *hegemon* meaning leader, is a concept that was developed early last century by the Italian Marxist Antonio Gramsci. While most Marxists during the 1920s explained global as well as state-centred phenomena by using a strictly economic interpretation of history, Gramsci added an intellectual/cultural element, which concluded that social classes could establish domination over others through promoting their ideology and culture at social and political levels (Gramsci, 1971). If there is any truth in this, the experience of the 'conservative revolution', and the neoliberal order today, which relies upon the production of liberal, economic literature makes it evident. Susan George goes as far as saying that because the progressive forces did not promote intellectual production, were complacent and did not mobilise a front based on substantial professional thinking, the conservative forces were able to step in and make their project hegemonic.

Even though most countries, both in the technologically advanced North and the developing South, and global structures fall under the umbrella of neoliberal ideology today, there are always political moments when social forces gather enough strength to resist and counter the dominating mind frame. Robert Cox calls this counter-hegemony (Cox, 1987).

Neoliberal Practice

But what exactly does neoliberalism consist of in practice? As its ideology dictates, neoliberal practice comprises the implementation of a number of tactics or policies that result in diminishing the authority of the state or public sector in society, especially in the market, and placing large, private corporations at the top of organised society. This implies that corporate leaders make a pact with certain political figures and/or organisations in governmental and international bodies, in order to lay the legal basis for this movement or transition.

The most effective way to render power to corporations is to privatise publicly owned enterprises and services. A service like transportation, for instance, will go from being a public and local patrimony funded by taxes, to a private business that will profit from the consumers of the provided service. In a democratic setting, a political party, usually funded by leading entrepreneurs, would encourage voters and legislative bodies to support the project of privatisation in return for a number of advantages. Often an incentive is the reduction of income taxes on common workers. Other neoliberal politicians might argue that a service or public industry would become more efficient, if it were free from governmental bureaucracy. These myths have been widely contested by people who have actually experienced the privatisation of industry or services, as efficiency issues after privatisation are often neglected. But the essential problem with privatisation is that, in most cases, the decisions to privatise companies are not made democratically but in most cases are made from above without a public-based consensus. In this sense, the opponents of neoliberalism argue, privatisation equals thievery from the wealth of society in order to subsidise private capitalists in their mission to expand (Petras and Velt-meyer, 2001). This is not to say that all public ownership of production and services is necessarily democratic. However, the privatisation of publicly owned enterprises does exclude the chance of democratic governance, or at least decreases the power of the people to regulate production, services and redistribution.

Privatisation might be attractive to politicians who are in the position of solving state indebtedness or government bankruptcy. By selling off national industries or public services, governmental bodies are thought to be relieved from debt and responsibility over social concerns. Those politicians interested in making governmental bodies smaller will use privatisation as a means of doing that in addition to raising funds for the government. The problem comes to the fore when non-governmental groups lobby for state monitoring over the transition to privatisation, either in defence of the environment, in the interests of workers or to deter corruption. Furthermore, fundraising arguments fall by the wayside when one realises that privatisation is not a sustainable source of government income; companies can only be privatised once. The practice of privatisation becomes even more anti-democratic and much more controversial when international governing bodies and institutions put pressure on poorer countries to privatise production domestically.

Privatisation is but one of the many practices. From the business point of view, neoliberal practice entails freeing the market from rules that hinder economic growth and profit. For instance, politicians who represent the interests of private capital might campaign against a hike in the minimum wage for workers in order to keep profits rising. Another example can be found when private companies are given the right to ignore the demands of labour unions (in other words hire and fire as they want), and move from one region where legal wages are high to places that offer a surplus of workers willing to produce for a lower and less secure income. Neoliberalists might also pressurise local or national governments to relax environmental laws in order to allow private companies to produce more cheaply rather than under 'earth-friendly' frameworks, which often require businesses to employ 'costly' production methods that crunch profits. When these ideas are put into practice, the result is that workers are employed more often on either a part-time or temporary basis, and with less job security. When it comes to environmental quality, the risks of air and water pollution logically become more pronounced.

The examples mentioned above are best demonstrated in real national case studies. However, neoliberalism, an international project, goes beyond nation-state structures and specific instances and is applied globally. That is, not only are neoliberal practices implemented by domestic politicians but also by international financial institutions that often pretend to aid countries in need of development. After the demise of the so-called socialist regimes in Eastern Europe and the fall of authoritarian political structures in Latin America during the late 1980s, neoliberal policies were followed by new governments in reaction to years of state dominance in the economy. Critical political economists have noted that international financial institutions, in the hands of neoliberal thinkers, actually forced many of the state-dominated economies to dismantle (Bello *et al.*, 1994). This was done by denying international bank loans and credits to countries that refused to privatise or to cut state subsidies in domestic agricultural, industrial or service sectors. Evidently, the purpose was to allow large transnational corporations (TNCs) to successfully compete against or buy up small domestic businesses, whether private or public. The result has been the selling out or disintegration of national economies and, in their place, allowing the TNCs to dominate almost every aspect of life. This is seen more clearly when state companies and public services – from telecommunications to water and energy sectors – in small underdeveloped countries are sold to large corporations, usually based in the technologically advanced North. The international institutions that are most known to promote these policies of privatisation are the International Monetary Fund (IMF), the World Bank and the World Trade Organisation (WTO).

For some time now, the World Bank has been the architect of the liberalisation of developing economies by overseeing privatisation programmes and implementing what are called structural adjustment programmes (SAPs). SAPs are packages that are offered either to heavily indebted countries that have experienced a sharp transition from a state-dominated to private corporate-led economies, or to those very poor nation-states that were or are in a condition of economic and political bankruptcy. In offering loans to these troubled countries, the World Bank demands that recipients meet certain conditions. The conditions for receiving loans for infrastructure or any other kind of development are set by structural adjustment programmes. Looking at the political aspect, once again, the government then responds to foreign lenders and investors and not to its citizens. This pushes the neoliberal project to its global extreme.

Most recently, in 1999 and 2000, member states of the World Trade Organisation held a number of negotiation summits that laid the basis for implementing agreements on trade in services; this was called the General Agreement on Trade in Services, or, GATS2000. The negotiations are focused on liberalising trade that affects all service sectors, from investment banking to the energy sectors, and reducing domestic subsidies for national services. Once again, the political – if not moral – issue comes to the fore when looking at the practices that are employed in these negotiations and agreements. Rich and powerful TNCs are known to lobby successfully during the negotiation rounds, whereas groups from civil society such as labour organisations are not invited to give their input or represent their interests. In the case of the European Union, the European Commission meets with corporate leaders behind closed doors (Wesselius, 2002).

What happens in this process of neoliberal globalisation is the forming of alliances between top government officials and big businesses, and the alienation of public interests in the organisation of present day society. Neoliberal politicians and political organisations, which promise their constituents in poorer countries more development by employing free trade policies and SAPs, are concerned with making their country attractive to foreign investors and technology. They argue that privatisation, the relaxation of environmental and labour laws, and the reduction in state subsidies to domestic producers and service sectors are all necessary for efficiency, in the interest of the common good and the advancement of their societies. Consequently, local or domestic governments in developing countries render up most of their power to foreign private corporations, who throughout the last decade have exposed themselves as environmentally irresponsible and negligent when it comes to human rights (Wysham, 2002).

Mutate Nomine Fabula te Narratur

The global movement has learnt a lot by looking at the rise of neoliberal globalisation and the conservative revolution. The moral of the story is that in order for the global movement to overcome current structures and impinging forces, to influence government social policy and steer the world into a more sustainable direction, it is not enough to take to the streets and challenge the police or military. It is also imperative to develop new ideas, think, plan, communicate and try to reach the masses of people who are yearning for alternatives, and join forces in solidarity with one another. In other words, form counter-hegemonic alliances. And all this is where scholar-activism and progressive think tanks come in.

Susan George often emphasises that the corporate coup d'etat and the triumph of rich over poor is not inevitable. In 'Winning the War of Ideas' (1997), she argued that in order to overcome the status quo it is necessary for the social movements to arm themselves with intellectual ammunition, just as the conservative right did before reaching hegemony during the 1980s.

A somewhat astonishing conclusion can be drawn from all of this: the right is a hotbed of Marxists! Or at least of Gramscians. They know full well that we are not born with our ideas and must somehow acquire them; that in order to prevail, ideas require material infrastructures. They know, too, that these infrastructures will largely determine the intellectual superstructure: that is what Gramsci meant by capitalism's 'hegemonic project'. Defining, sustaining and controlling culture: get into people's heads and you will acquire their hearts, their hands and their destinies.

(George, 1997)

Therefore special attention must be drawn to the think tanks that support progressive movements; without them, the new movement is lost. Just like any successful movement, the global movement for socioeconomic justice needs journalists, academics and research centres.

In the boxes below, I highlight only some of the most prominent think tanks currently at work. They foster research projects, organise conferences for left wing thinkers, publish books about real alternatives and support either in word or deed the global movement. Looking at their profiles, one can see that these think tanks are not all that new, and some of the people mentioned are not very young. This is because successfully maintaining the network of scholar-activists entails combining the young and old, learning from the experience of movements and scholars who were active back in the 1960s and 1970s.

Among the world's most prestigious think tanks is the Trans-National Institute (TNI). This is a worldwide network of scholar-activists committed to critical analysis of current global problems. According to its Mission Statement, 'it aims to provide intellectual support to those movements concerned to steer the world in a democratic, equitable and environmentally sustainable direction'. Working in the spirit of public scholarship, and aligned to no political party, TNI undertakes collaborative international research projects, hosts seminars and publishes books, booklets, policy briefings and articles. Modelled after the Washington D.C.-based Institute for Policy Studies, it was founded in 1973, shortly after the coup in Chile when the right-wing military leader Pinochet overthrew the democratically elected President Allende.[2]

At the heart of TNI lies a committed core of fellows and advisors. They include journalists, independent researchers, and senior scholars from similar institutes in Africa, Asia, Latin America, Europe and North America. Fellows are usually appointed for a three-year term, but through their work and dedication, most are locked into the broader network for life. TNI is coordinated from Amsterdam, the Netherlands, where it is registered as a non-profit organisation. It receives part of its institutional funding from the Samuel Rubin Foundation (New York) and a range of governmental and non-governmental funders supports its projects.

With the onset of the 'information age' in the 1990s, a new opportunity arrived on the shores of scholar-activism: the Internet. TNI, just like most scholar-activist institutions, went online. The Institute now uses the Internet to disseminate in-depth articles, valuable ideas and reports on interesting projects around the world in literally no time. This was not just about giving each fellow an e-mail address. It was also intended to create a picture of the institute online with a proper website, giving the world access to a wealth of knowledge.

Scholar-Activism's Challenge

Today, scholar-activism has become very expensive; the information era created the need for progressive institutions to employ full-time professional webmasters and the like to project the institutes' images to the world. Communications officers were employed; there was need for a clear division between labour and management, the hiring of professional secretaries and so on. Furthermore, there were increasing internships opportunities: not only to allow a younger generation to get experience in the scholar-activist environment, but also to keep experienced scholars up to date on the current issues.

The headraising or looking upwards of progressive think tanks has its dangers of course. Institutes are now playing the competition game for

Box 14.1 TNI profile

Trans-National Institute: A worldwide network of scholar-activists dedicated to promoting research that will assist progressive movements in their campaigns to turn the world towards a more equal, democratic, and environmentally sustainable direction. Pays especial attention to North–South relations. Maintains research programmes on the global economy, peace and security, Asia–Europe relations, drugs and democracy, alternative regionalisms, and energy; also sponsors publication series.

Research Programmes: Drugs and Democracy, Energy and Development, Global Economy, New Politics Nuclear Abolition, Militarisation, Regionalisms, Asia–Europe Relations.

Projects: Drugs and Conflict, The Energy Project, ASEMwatch, GATSwatch (http://www.gatswatch.org), The Sustainable Energy and Economy Network (http://www.seen.org), Carbon Trade Watch, Korean Unification, Missile Defence, Migrant Workers' Rights, Alternative Regionalisms.

Media:
TNI News: a biweekly electronic bulletin announcing new articles written by Fellows, publications, conferences/seminar announcements and resources for today's social activists *(2002)*
TNI Actual: quarterly news for funders, fellows, and friends of the Institute.
TNI Briefing series: 16–18 pp. booklets written by researchers in projects, geared towards influencing public policies and updating analysis
TNI Alterantiv@s: a bilingual (Spanish/English) online journal of in-depth theoretical articles written by scholar-activists in the North and South; includes book reviews and calendar of events.
TNI Drug Policy Briefing: an occasional briefing on drug and conflict related policies geared towards informing government and non government organisations on related policies and the war on drugs.
For a complete list of books and other publications, see http://www.tni.org/pubs.htm

> *Current Fellows and Associates:* Mariano Aguirre (Spain), Marcos Arruda (Brazil), Walden Bello (Thailand), Phyllis Bennis (USA), Praful Bidwai (India), Kees Bieckart (Netherlands), Brid Brennan (Ireland), John Cavanagh (USA), Daniel Chavez (Uruguay), Ophelia Cowell (Indonesia), Susan George (France), Jochen Hippler (Germany), Martin Jelsma (Netherlands), Boris Kagarlitsky (Russia), Dot Keet (South Africa), Manuel Pérez Rocha (Mexico), Joel Rocamora (Philippines), David Sogge (Netherlands), Acchin Vanaik (India), Myriam Vander Stichele (Belgium), Basker Vashee (Zimbabwe), Howard Wachtel (USA), Hilary Wainwright (UK), Daphne Wysham (USA), Pauline Tiffen (USA), Ricardo Vargas (Colombia), Saul Landau (USA), Michael Shuman (USA), Dan Smith (Norway), Miguel Teubal (Argentina).
>
> Budget: €974,454   Expenditure: €989,573
>
> Funders: European Commission, Fondation de Sauve (UK), Heinrich Boell Stiftung (Germany), HKH Foundation (USA), HIVOS (Netherlands), Ministry for Development and Cooperation (Netherlands), Ministry of Cooperation Development (Denmark), NCDO (Netherlands), NCOS (Belgium), Association for Innovative Co-operation in Europe (Belgium), NOVIB (Oxfam, Netherlands), Samuel Rubin Foundation (USA), Trocaire (Ireland).
>
> (All the data was gathered from http://www.tni.org where the TNI Annual Report is available to the public)

funding by keeping up appearances online. Think tanks also need to champion or market their writers and speakers in order to attract core-funding and sustain their networks. Some institutes have a group of 'Friends' who contribute financially. For instance, someone like Noam Chomsky may donate a couple of hundred dollars to a think tank or progressive organisation, and the director will mention the gift in a formally published annual report in order to demonstrate the seriousness or high level of activism in which the organisation involves itself; this in turn will attract new funders.

Most progressive funding institutions, however, are decreasing the amount of capital they invest in scholar-activism year by year. Unless, that is, the institutes demonstrate their ability to keep up to date with the pressing concerns of the global movement. So while social activists are seen as dependent on scholars and think tanks for intellectual support, the research

Box 14. 2 Some of the brains behind the scene

Corporate Watch (UK): A radical research and publishing group based in Oxford, dedicated to documenting the evildoings of multinational corporations.
http://www.corporate watch.org.uk

Corporate Watch (USA): San Francisco-based organisation that educates and mobilises through its website.
http://www.corpwatch.org

Corporate Europe Observatory: An Amsterdam-based NGO that mostly monitors European multinational corporate activity on the continent and throughout the world.
htttp://www.ceo.org

Focus on the Global South: Bangkok-based research centre dedicated to analysing the causes of uneven development, poverty and inequality. Builds networks among countries in the South (Africa, Asia and Latin America). Initiates campaigns aimed at governments and multinational corporations.
http://www.focusontheglobalsouth.org

Global Exchange: A US-based research and activist centre dedicated to initiating local/community projects and international exchange of information on social issues. Scholars include specialists in global economy, fair trade, labour issues and immigration, among many other fields.
http://www.globalexchange.org

Indymedia: A network of independent and collectively run media output centres in many countries around the world.
http://www.indymedia.org

Institute for Policy Studies: One of the first progressive, leftwing think tanks in the United States, based in Washington, D.C. Fellows concentrate on a variety of global issues including the environment, militarisation, and US policy in the Middle East, to name but a few. Dedicated to turning US domestic and foreign policy around to support a more sustainable and democratic world.
http://www.ips-dc.org

Oxfam International: An international organisation with national affiliates, dedicated to correcting the injustices and inequalities in the world through organising NGO campaigns, publishing reports and supporting sustainable projects and research centres in the global South. Currently concentrating on fair trade. http://www.oxfam.org

Pluto Press: Established in 1970, Pluto is one of the United Kingdom's leading independent publishers dedicated to critical thinking. Authors include Franz Fanon, Antonio Gramsci and Noam Chomsky. http://www.plutobooks.com

SEEN: A project of the Transnational Institute and the Institute for Policy Studies, the Sustainable Energy and Economy network dedicates its website to mobilising campaigns against irresponsible and unsustainable governance. Its most recent contribution has been an in-depth study of Enron. http://www.seen.org

agendas at places like TNI are defined by the political and strategic moment. This will be made clearer below when we consider the issue of new politics and the building of counter-hegemonic alliances.

What Does the Global Movement Want?

Now that the relationship between scholar-activists and the global movement has been made, it is time answer the questions: what does this movement want and how can scholar-activists support the movement in achieving its needs?

I have already discussed how activism has moved on from temporary or single-issue campaigns to a new global demand for structural changes by tackling international institutions, capitalist political economy and neoliberal globalisation. During this era of new activism and from this global movement for socioeconomic justice there arose the desire for a new type of politics. Somehow, the authoritarian or at least top-down left-wing movements typical of the 1960s were lacking something in their structure and practices. Additionally, in Western Europe, the labour parties and trade unions were thought to be selling out or being co-opted into conservative governments. The leaders of the so-called New Left have seemingly betrayed the working classes, dismantling the welfare states of Europe and proposing no real alternatives to neoliberal capitalism and the privatisation of public services like gas, electricity, water and transportation.[3] In the South, most communist parties collapsed after the Soviet Union imploded, or have reorganised themselves in joint alliances with other progressive movements. While some – especially older – activists in the global movement still adhere to the tenets of an ideology driven by radical militants below the leadership level and to sectarian attitudes, the younger generation of activists is searching for something else; namely, a people-based, globally conscious politics that links together all the issues of neoliberal globalisation and is interested in developing viable alternatives from below. In short, they are looking for new – preferably direct – forms of democracy.

In her *Notes Towards a New Politics* (subtitled: *New Strategies for People Power*), Hilary Wainwright (2002) argues for 'taking back' left-wing ideas. For some time, socialist politics has been perverted by authoritarian structures or compromising coalitions. In order to contribute to theorising about democratic, egalitarian and emancipatory politics, she points to new social experiments that were developed independently of both the hierarchical state and private corporations. She highlights the radical politics of participatory budgets in Southern Brazil, where citizens create, discuss and vote on local and provincial budgets. In this approach, control of public funds is taken away from corrupt politicians and interested parties, and placed into the hands of the people. This, in Wainwright's opinion, is driving closer towards direct democracy.[4]

In turn, this search for new politics has pushed organisations and parties to rethink their practices and agendas. A prime example of this would be Italy's Communist Refoundation Party; it has left behind the bureaucratic structure and some habits of the old Italian Communist Party, which was often plagued by compromising positions in local politics and corrupt leadership on the national level. The demands of the global movement are also reducing sectarian tendencies. It is no wonder that political organisations like the Socialist Workers Party of Great Britain constantly ask Susan George, Boris Kagarlitstky and Hilary Wainwright to attend and speak at their annual conferences and large gatherings.

The Phenomenon of Social Forums

Learning once again from the experience of neoliberal hegemony, the global movement for socioeconomic justice realised the need to meet on an annual basis. The World Social Forum (WSF), with its first appearance in Porto Alegre, Brazil, in 2000, was initially a counterweight to the World

Economic Forum where business and financial leaders meet to discuss the state of the global economy. The World Economic Forum, which has met in Davos, New York, and Salzburg had alienated most of the world's civil society groups. Its agenda was seen as undemocratic: neglecting the concerns of environmental sustainability, poverty amelioration, peace and security. In contrast, the WSF represents the most significant coming together of the groups that comprise the global movement for socioeconomic justice. In 2001, participants numbered over 60,000. They included trade unionists, peasants, indigenous peoples and a wide range of issue-based campaigners from all the corners of the earth. Under the slogan 'Another World is Possible' more than 700 seminars and workshops were dedicated to discussing strategies for alternatives to neoliberal globalisation. Although there were demonstrations on the streets of Porto Alegre on a daily basis during the forum, the WSF was more about networking and discovering the alternatives than just being 'against the system'. This positive quality was made possible by having people from the around the world meet independently of state or corporate structures.

Since 2001, social forums have blossomed all over the world on a regional as well as a local level.[5] The emphasis is on voicing the concerns of civil society. But what many do not realise is that regardless of the 'independent' character that the organisers of such jubilees want to portray, these social forums are where the counter-hegemonic alliances are being built. Representatives of environmental groups in the North agree upon what campaigns should receive priority after meeting up with grassroots movements in the South. There are testimonies; people exchange experiences, alternative networks are created and there is even talk of alternative regionalism as opposed to free trade agreements.

New Politics for a New World

One of the activities that TNI organised at the second World Social Forum (2002) was a two-day seminar on Alternative Political Visions. Speakers came from all over Latin America, Africa, Asia and Europe, and the sessions were packed out. These included representatives of large trade unions, new political parties and landless peasants organisations. TNI even prepared a booklet for the occasion.[6] But what was fascinating about the seminar was the participation from the audience. There were a significant number of young activists taking the floor to share their ideas about what kind of politics they need. Argentineans, Brazilians, Spaniards, North Americans, Mexicans, South Africans and Cubans – from all walks of life and political traditions – spoke their minds.

The seminar on Alternative Political Visions has been one of the Institute's most inspiring feats. Who dares to say that there is any need for an organised movement of social activists, who dares to suggest that the movement needs a political party to lead it? And of course, there are those who continue to maintain that there is not one but many movements for socioeconomic justice. This seminar, however, was not about suggesting that there should be a political party to lead the movement; it was not even about organising the global movement politically. The real purpose was to provide space for this new activist movement to discuss politics, think critically and exchange experiences. Here, the scholar-activists found a new role to play. Besides pointing out scientifically where neoliberal globalisation has caused harm, researchers dedicated to the global movement can also initiate discussion about social movements, offer lessons in history and debate the alternatives.

Getting Off the Defensive

Besides the human costs of the September 11 events in the United States, social activists came to know to another aspect of suffering that resulted from the airplanes that crashed into the World Trade Center and the Pentagon. That is, those socially progressive movements that perhaps in the past were linked to radical movements were put on the defensive. In the United States, even weeks prior to the launching of the so-called 'war against terrorism' in Afghanistan, human rights advocates, anti-military and peace activists were labelled as 'unpatriotic', even 'terrorist lovers'. President Bush Jr. made no qualms about his attitude towards the peace movement. 'If you are not with us, you are against us', were the words that poured from his lips, and then he indulged in the moment handed over to him on a silver platter. The mood that haunted the United States during that time cannot be exaggerated: it was entirely hostile. Child day-care centres sponsored by the American Friends Society (the Quakers) received bomb threats, the governor of Puerto Rico demanded that peace activists stop their demonstrations to oust the US Navy from their target practicing grounds on Vieques, any Arab-looking person was immediately pointed out as a potential terrorist. The question that resonated during the 1950s and 1960s was revived with only a one-word difference: 'Are you a communist?' became 'Are you a terrorist?'

The harm was not limited to witch-hunts and name-calling. It also resulted in a temporary setback for the global movement's momentum. Some social progressive groups divided over the issue of whether or not the United States should invade Afghanistan. On the one hand, opponents to the war argued that a US-installed regime would only serve US geo-political interests and big oil corporations. Moreover, the 'war against terrorism' never had any clear objectives. Was the use of military force against 'the countries that harboured terrorists' about finding Osama bin Laden, or was it more about the United States asserting its power? On the other hand, it should be quite easy to understand why some feminists, gay activists and human rights groups enjoyed seeing the last day of the Taliban regime.

Actually, the debate was not so new. The same phenomenon of dividing lines happened during the first Gulf War in 1991 and during the NATO strikes in Kosovo in the 1990s. But this time, during the 'war against terrorism', scholar-activists made a serious and successful comeback. By the time the war started to extend to Iraq, American scholars like Phyllis Bennis linked arms with other activists in trying to avert US unilateral action, demanding that the United States provide evidence that Saddam Hussein was creating or harbouring weapons of mass destruction. Bennis wrote articles, spoke at demonstrations, prepared papers for US congressional sessions and was interviewed on CNN.[7] Another example of the scholar-activist come-back was the TNI co-sponsored International Peace Mission sent to Basilan in the Philippines in March 2002. Even before Basilan was hailed as the 'second front of the US war against terrorists', TNI together with a number of civil society groups organised and sent an international delegation of scholars, parliamentarians, and peace groups to analyse the conflict between religious separatists and government and paramilitary forces in the region. Additionally, the group brought the world's attention to US intervention in the region.[8] Thanks to this sort of scholar-activism (targeted towards governments in the West) the peace movement was rebuilt, and this time connected with solidarity movements throughout the world.

Conclusions

The global movement for socioeconomic justice is on the rise. Its protagonists, just like their social activist predecessors, may have stumbled in confusing times – especially during war. With the help of intellectual and scholarly work, however, social activists have picked up the pieces and the global movement has started to grow as never before. This article has highlighted the interdependence between this new movement and what has been defined as scholar-activism. Now more than ever, the global movement is in need of dedicated, experienced professionals who have studied neoliberal globalisation and are willing to produce ideas and alternatives. Structural problems like poverty, inequality, and environmental degradation cannot be cured by demonstrations alone. The global movement also needs a lot of thinking, writing, preparing and networking.

It is also very important for this movement to monitor the trans-national corporations and leaders of neoliberal governments: watch their steps, know their history and learn from their development. Having clear ideas about future alternative scenarios and doing what it takes to strengthen the ties among potential counter-hegemonic forces is a necessary task and it takes dedicated and disciplined minds to do it.

Notes

1. In Dutch, the excellent term *andersglobalist* encapsulates the idea more clearly. Literally, it means 'other' or 'alternative' globalist. Unfortunately, there is no one word in English that accurately describes what the global movement for socioeconomic justice is all about. One can refer to the alternative globalisation movement, as opposed to corporate glob-alisation, but only in comparison to one another. Another problem is that it has become almost a cliché to say that there is not one but many movements. This matter will be dealt with further on in the text. But it suffices to say here that those unwilling to recognise a large single movement against neoliberal globalisation are mostly those who are afraid of subscribing to authoritarian or disciplined structures linked to political organisations or parties. Nevertheless, the unifying character of this new global movement for socioeconomic justice does not neces-sarily imply a single trajectory or the existence of a central ideology. As is demonstrated later on this chapter, the global movement of the left is very pluralistic and is currently in search of a new sort of politics.
2. Many social scientists actually look at this historic moment as the first neoliberal experiment. Indeed, once Allende was overthrown, the US-sponsored dictatorship immediately started reversing the reforms achieved under the short-lived democratic socialism and implemented policies known today as neoliberal: chiefly privatisation, deregulation, the opening up of local markets to international trade, and cutting governmental spending in all areas except for the military. The second TNI Director was former Chilean senator Orlando Letelier, who was assassinated in 1976 by Chilean special intelligence officers. See http://www.tni.org/letelier/index.htm
3. Here I am referring to politicians like the UK's Prime Minister Tony Blair or ex-minister Jan Pronk of the Netherlands.
4. Wainwright (2002) describes the experience of participatory budgets by saying:

PB varies from city to city but in Porto Alegre, the most developed example, it is an annual cycle of neighbourhood meetings where people identify their priority needs for new investment – pavements, schools, health provision, drainage, cooperative industries – and then elect delegates to meetings for wider districts. These delegates apply criteria and rules developed in previous years, which give priorities different weights. They then elect a budget council, which represents every part of the city. Through an open process of negotiation and reporting back, the overall budget is drawn up and then put to the mayor and municipal council for final agreement. These same bodies of direct democracy monitor the budget's implementation: officials have to report back to citizens' meetings on the progress of the projects agreed through the participatory cycle. After 12 years, direct participation has spread to every area of the city council's work.

5. For the World Social Forum website see http://www.forumsocial-mundial.org.br
    For a statement from the Asia Social Forum see http://www.tni.org/asia/docs/asmstatement.htm
6. See http://www.tni.org/newpol/index.htm
7. See http://www.tni.org/issues/iraq/iraq.htm
8. See htpp://www.tni.o

Conclusions

Steve John and Stuart Thomson

The contributions contained in this book show the depth of feeling on all sides, higher levels of aggression on both sides and a general recognition of the power of the activists. We are witnessing a generational shift in how governments, businesses, interest groups and citizens interact.

What is clear is an ever-expanding range of activist activity and corporations that are split between appeasing/working with the groups or fighting back. Both sides are learning from the other in terms of tactics and behaviour, with 'best practice' spreading. While the development of electronic communications has undoubtedly assisted activism in general, it has in particular empowered small, radical groups that are challenging the authority of the larger, more established groups.

What is much more difficult to quantify is the impact of the activist groups' activities. They are a constraint on the behaviour of companies, many of which have come to operate under more 'ethical' considerations. Those companies that find themselves under attack incur higher costs, lost sales, falling profits, falling share prices and so on. In essence, the very basis of their continued existence is put under threat. This is why some corporations work with the activist groups and in line with their agendas. Others have chosen to fight back and take the activists on, directly employing former activists to gain their insights or working with policy organisations and think tanks to set the policy agenda and pre-empt the activists.

However, the picture is not universally consistent. Some campaigns do not succeed and companies do not feel the pinch. This may be because the company employs the right tactics to deal with the campaign, because the activists are badly organised or simply because the public in not interested or motivated by the campaign.

What is much more frightening are those activist campaigns that target individuals with intimidation and violence. While still used in the minority of campaigns, if they are proven to work – which currently appears to be the case – then they become more common.

Why Activists Attack

There are many and varied reasons why activists undertake attacks but if we look at the details presented, then the following reasons can be suggested.

Corporations Matter More

Activists attack corporations because they *matter*. Activists used to focus on politicians when campaigning about such issues as the environment, race, gender and sexual and age equality. Civic society has arguably been eroded by corporate society. Whether we adopt Naomi Klein's approach and look at the role of brands, or an approach that looks at the influence of corporate players, the fact is that citizens now more readily identify with corporations in their everyday lives. They *believe* corporations and brands to be important, therefore they *are* important. Corporations have also fostered this image of importance, sometimes to help sales, or sometimes to make chief executives feel better! Often those very individuals, often high profile, come to represent and embody the company. Activists have managed to portray companies, sometimes because of the profile of chief executives, on other occasions by pushing forward the chief executive, as almost a physically, actually existing entity rather than simply a legal structure. Through this they have managed to make their image of a company stick: some 'exploit', others 'pollute' and so on.

Consider alongside this that corporations have become the most important single factor in the lives of most Western citizens. Business can now expect to be the primary target. Activists attack because they perceive that radical action is the only way open to them to achieve their objectives. The increase in power of large corporations is notable, as is the decline in economic power of national governments. We can also whisper the word 'globalisation' in this breath.

Shift in Responsibility

The evolution of power upwards to the supranational level has occurred without the requisite democratic controls. Democracy is under strain as falling rates of electoral participation bear witness to citizens' belief that politicians no longer matter. The corporatisation of society is arguably slowly dismantling democracy.

Add to that the idea advocated by some that 'all politicians are the same' – they offer the same policies, do not tackle vested interests and even look the same – and then you have an explanation for the rise of the far right. This is not a recent phenomenon, as the media have been trying to tell us, but a gradual increase since the mid-1980s.

New activists believe the way for individuals to have an impact upon important decisions today is not to lobby governments that claim to have no influence, or unelected and unaccountable supra-national institutions that are immune to pressure, but to target corporations. The new reality is that corporations define the operation and structure of modern societies. What corporations want, they get. Governments retain a role in setting the social and economic environment, but one that suits the corporate sector.

Corporations have been effective at socialising negative externalities while internalising profit. The antithesis of the 'polluter pays' principle rules. In other words, government creates a sustainable environment, subsidises employment, provides welfare: an infrastructure all for the bene-fit of corporations. Governments spend taxpayers' money while corpora-tions keep all their profits and maintain a low rate of corporation tax. Citizens pay every way.

Shift in Economic Power

We have also witnessed a changing context of economic power. Of the world's 100 largest economic entities, 51 are now corporations and 49 are countries.[1] Furthermore, the world's top 200 corporations account for over a quarter of the world's economic activity but employ less than 1 per cent of its workforce. In the United States at least, the share of taxes paid by corporations has fallen from 33 per cent in the 1940s to 15 per cent in the 1990s. The share of taxation paid by individuals has risen from 44 to 73 per cent.

> Between 1973 and 1975, CEOs' after-tax pay averaged 24 times that of the average manufacturing worker. By 1987 to 1989, the differential was 157 times the average manufacturing worker. But taxes for CEOs declined from 50 per cent to 28 per cent, while worker taxes increased from 20 per cent to 21 per cent.
>
> (Monks and Minow, 2001, p. 166)

Look also at the disjuncture between the economic performance of compa-nies and the rewards offered to senior management. New activists argue that when companies do badly, workers are laid off, but executives are rewarded with better packages for taking 'brave decisions'. Share prices rise with redundancies. If companies do well, employees are told that to remain competitive they have to have little or no increases in wages, while executives are rewarded with better packages again, for helping the company move forward.

Corporate Wrongdoing

Many activist campaigns are focused around issues relating to products or services that radicals believe are dangerous or detrimental to human and societal well-being.

Add to this perceived labour abuses, poor environmental records, accounting abuses, high corporate rewards and an undue influence on government and policy, which corporations have striven to build, and you have a recipe for attacks. In other words, the corporate sector has to take some responsibility for increased activist attacks on it.

Corporations often have great difficulty in understanding the motives of new activists. They act out of motives that are often confused and conflicting, but are rarely driven by efforts to secure material gain or an improved social standing. They are not in it for themselves but for others: collective action at its most altruistic.

Why Traditional Groups Matter Less

Long-established interest groups are being superseded by the smaller, more virulent form of activist group. The cause of the problem is that groups like Greenpeace and Friends of the Earth have become institutionalised, part of the establishment.

Companies know how to deal with established interest groups. Most have corporate social responsibility programmes to reach out to communities and stakeholders. Some energy companies even use Greenpeace to help them sell electricity.

Greenpeace has become institutionalised. an insider group, too close the companies it tries to attack and the governments it seeks to influence. Take a look at its founder's criticisms of the monster he has created. Paul Watson, the founder of Greenpeace, has called its members the 'Avon ladies of the environmental movement', and has described the organisation as a 'myth generating machine'. Another founder, Patrick Moore has also been critical in his assessment and has stated that 'environmental extremists are basically anti-human'.[2] Greenpeace in this analysis can itself be portrayed as a corporation, bent on growth. Some argue that a donation to the organisation discourages activism: give money and let the leaders and experts rectify the problem.

This book does not argue that groups like Greenpeace, Friends of the Earth, WWF or Amnesty are history, nor does it suggest companies should discount them. However, companies have hired people who know how to deal with these groups. Their agendas and tactics can be foreseen and smart companies react quickly.

It is the new world we need to be concerned about. New activists hunger for action that reflects their needs. The smaller groups are beginning to form and fight. In this new world, everything that went before is overturned.

New Forms of Activism

We need to be concerned with new forms of activism.

Just imagine this scenario. You wake up with a start in the middle of the night. There are people outside your house rifling though your rubbish and banging dustbin lids together. Your home has been broken into, your windows smashed and slogans daubed in red paid over the walls. Your car has been trashed and flipped onto its side, its tyres slashed.

Neighbours receive notes informing them you are a murderer. When you arrive at work you learn your colleagues had to pass a horde of screaming activists. Those activists take photographs of your staff and their vehicles to trace their home addresses. The workforce is trapped in their building until the police clear a route out.

Company morale plummets. Different groups within the company are set against one another and bitter recriminations fly. Your switchboard is jammed, website disabled, and e-mail servers crash because of the amount of traffic. Your customers, suppliers and shareholders are targeted and threatened. Natural allies retreat.

Imagine that this level of pressure continues over months and years to come. A photograph of your house is available on a website, and people can read that the consequence of the campaign against your company has led to your partner being on the brink of a nervous breakdown and that you face divorce. A director is beaten by three attackers swinging pickaxe handles. Terrified staff gallop to the exit door. Productivity and billings fall through the floor. Cash bleeds away and the board reduces staff benefits and pension contributions. Your company's shares are suspended.

This horror story is a summary of the campaign orchestrated against scientists at Huntingdon Life Sciences, one of the Europe's leading drug testing companies. The campaign began after a television documentary (on Channel Four in the United Kingdom) showed maltreatment of animals. It has to be remembered that HLS was going about its lawful business and undertaking research that is required by law: any new drug has to be tested before it is made available to the public. Groups like SHAC – the campaign to Stop Huntingdon Animal Cruelty – use a variety of tactics including violence and intimidation.

Tactics

These new activists are astute. Clients of banks who traded shares in HLS were targeted. It is not only the 'usual suspects' who are at risk. While tobacco, GMO and pharmaceutical companies, pesticide manufactures and companies making breast milk substitutes for developing countries are natural targets because they are perceived as regular transgressors, others are also vulnerable to attack. This new form of activism is targeting not only the companies but those who are associated with them. There is a complex web of relationships: a grid on which activists go up, down and side to side, to identify the weak points of a company.

TARGET SHAREHOLDERS

Making shareholders suffer is a most effective strategy. The names and home addresses of the directors of institutional shareholders can be placed on the Internet. Activists are well organised enough to send a biased briefing pack to all shareholders, with the shareholders being asked to sell their holdings. New activists will use information that is available to them perfectly legally, in most cases.

Protestors also lay siege to shareholders' offices for long periods of time. Publicity stunts such as office occupations and home visits to directors are successful tactics. Groups also organise technological attacks of financial backers to block websites and servers, and organise phone and mail blockades.

In the case of HLS, one bank received a bomb threat that caused its building to be evacuated and the bank to cease trading for the day. Similarly, campaigners have encouraged customers of retail banks involved to close their current accounts and to demonstrate at local branches. Militants also inserted cards covered with superglue into the banks' cash machines. The Bank of New York's London boardroom was occupied and interest groups published 80 bank accounts of its global custody department, which holds around $6900 billion of securities and assets.

The big battalions of commercial banks, pension funds, pharmaceutical companies and politicians have stayed firmly in their bunkers. In the case of HLS they did not run to the company's aid. But consider the domino effect: as soon as a chink was found in the banks' armour, the campaign moved from one to the other and the banks fell like a row of dominos. Then the activists looked for further targets.

Indeed, in the case of HLS, the banks were described by then British Home Secretary Rt. Hon. Jack Straw MP as 'pusillanimous'.[3] The government believed that the banks acted in a short-sighted manner, and were in effect laying themselves open to threats. They are now the targets of activists.

Government ministers have further argued that by giving in to the activists the financial institutions have in effect given the green light to campaigners against other companies to target their financial support as well.

Someone leaked to SHAC the direct-dial landline phone numbers, mobile telephone numbers and e-mail addresses of 135 senior managers and their secretaries in Deloitte and Touche, the auditing company to HLS. These people were targeted with letters, e-mails and calls, and the activists used phone-jamming computer software. Demonstrations took place at the homes of managers, criminal damage including broken windows was inflicted, and the company's Italian offices were spray painted. Within days of the campaign starting Deloitte and Touche stepped down as auditors. The activists won. Their tactics were successful.

SHAC is now promising to take the campaign to HLS's customers which includes such names as Bayer, DuPont, GSK and Novartis.

Brian Cass, CEO of HLS, is calling for the UK Government to introduce new laws that would help protect not just the company but also its employees. He believes that legislation is needed, and is pressing the case for three changes:

- a change to the Criminal Justice and Police Bill to make it an offence to protest outside a person's home
- secondary targeting such as that in the Deloitte and Touche case to be made an offence
- the introduction of a law similar to the American RICO (Racketeer-Influenced Corrupt Organisations) Act (*Business*, 2003).

ONLINE CAMPAIGNING

The power to engage, or to disrupt, is passing into the hands of those whose aims may not conform to the orderly processes and conventions of electoral democracy. The information revolution, which spawned these possibilities, will be the system's undoing.

Lufthansa has been the subject of an online demonstration because of its involvement in the deportation business. The campaign is largely run online and even offers downloadable Online Protest Software. The software is designed to cause maximum chaos to Lufthansa. For instance, the software optimises fast and constant requests to the Lufthansa websites in a way that could not be done manually by repeated reloads into the Internet browser.

Campaigners are making it as easy as possible for people to get involved. All someone needs is a computer with Internet access. In fact activists do not even need to own computers: the rise of public computers in libraries, shops and other places means they can be active away from their own homes.

Such an online demonstration can be looked at in a number of ways. It could be called a virtual sit-in. It is all about overloading the corporate site so that at a given time all demonstrators visit the Lufthansa websites together. Such overload slows the whole system down or may even cause it to crash.

This particular online campaign aimed to exert pressure on Lufthansa in order to stop its deportation flights. A small network sees the money it makes from these flights as 'unacceptable'. The groups aim to ensure that the money Lufthansa made from deportation was offset by the damage to their corporate reputation.

Lufthansa planned for its online business to grow to around 40 per cent of sales by 2005. These online campaigns are frustrating this corporate objective. For the company, the key questions are: What happens to the share price when this target is not met? What happens to senior management?

Telephone Campaigns

The company should not just worry about online demos: even more fundamental is the telephone. Activists recognise that employees cannot work effectively if they are on the telephone. Companies targeted in this way are forced to cancel or change internal numbers frequently because of constant phone calls: this looks bad to potential clients and investors. Activists in the United Kingdom have set the pace. Activists even offer calling tips:

- Use Payphones – there's no need for them to know who's calling!
- Buy calling cards to use at payphones.
- Call more than once – the longer they are on the phone, the less time they have to kill animals.
- Leave them voice-mails – 'Hey Barbara, this is Mike – I have an urgent question – call me, extension 2016'.
- Use Internet cafes to utilise free calling websites.

New Forms of Direct Action

The 1980s and 1990s saw marches. Now there is improvised theatre. There are new forms of direct action. Starbucks is a good example of a recent campaign that has used traditional activism but in a new way. Outside the New York Theater Festival, in a local Starbucks coffee shop new activists 'occupy' the shop, hand out scripts and perform sketches, each dramatising an issue critical of Starbucks.

But this is a twist on direct action. If you demonstrate you may get arrested or pilloried in the media. This campaigners mimic angry customers and act irate at the shop in which the action takes place.

MARKETING: VIRAL AND GUERRILLA

Viral marketing techniques involve activity such as this, but also include new technology. E-mails can spread literally like a virus. If an e-mail is sent to five new people every hour by each recipient, a campaign that starts at 8 a.m. in the morning will have reached over 9.7 million by 5 p.m. Another form of viral marketing is to get your message to many people using cheap and simple methods. Most people have seen stickers on public transport which advocate a cause.

THE USE OF DATA

New activists are adept at researching the management and funding of corporations. Corporate information is easily available. Activists start with the websites of the corporations themselves, which often provide a large amount of detail about their activities. The websites of government departments and regulatory bodies contain large amounts of data on breaches of regulation by corporations. For example, the Occupational Safety and Health Administration of the US Department of Labor lists inspections, accident investigations and their results.

It is also easy to research politicians. Numerous websites exist to provide campaign contribution data on Members of Congress that is comprehensive and easily accessible. Sites have downloadable files in database format on political action committees and individual contributions. In the United Kingdom there is now an Act that makes political donations more transparent (the Political Parties, Elections and Referendums Act). Outside interests and voting records are also easily accessible.

THE MEDIA

Add into the equation the thirst for news stories and new angles offered by an ever competitive media. The proliferation of TV stations and the rise of the 24-hour broadcaster has driven this forward. The traditional print media and online news sites push this drive still further.

Activists are learning how to highlight their activities, realising that raising the profile and publicising the actions of the corporations adds to the pressure being exerted. If the public is shown a company behaving badly and activists going out there and working against them, then this adds to the armoury of the activists.

We are beginning to enter a media environment of limitless choice, the end of scheduled programming, and much greater interactivity. The numbers of viewers of American prime time networks are a third of what they were 15 years ago. The American TV news broadcasts used to draw 18 per cent each; now they're down to 6 per cent. As television and mobile phones and the Internet merge, and the Internet and the computer get a divorce, you will lose the mystification of the media.

The media ecosystem is colliding with what technology soothsayer Manuel Castells (2001) calls *The Internet Galaxy*. Net activists believe that this frictionless communication will replace cosy elitist conversations between business and politicians. Yet, this lack of friction also can also lead to problems of accuracy and diversity that break down the border between the public and private realms. Internet news and wire services move news flows with unprecedented speed, meaning that the instant news culture of the Internet makes first impressions that much more lasting and hard to correct.

The anthrax scare is a case in point. On 17 October every American and international media outlet reported that the anthrax sent to Senator Daschle's office was 'weapons grade'; it took ten hours before it became clear that this phrase had no accepted meaning.

The same news flow also offers citizens unprecedented opportunities to filter what they see. A book by American legal theorist Cass Sunstein (2001) argues that what he calls this 'daily-me' culture will lead to people opting out of the public realm, effectively protected from information they do not want by a digital shield.

They will never again need to have chance encounters with ideas or information. It is not difficult to see how these two problems of filtering and accuracy might combine to make people even less interested in politics, and make government more difficult.

The media's influence in shaping attitudes will increase as it responds more easily and quickly to sectional interest groups.

The Corporate Solutions

New forms of protests, like those mentioned above and those discussed in the previous chapters, will continue to appear and disappear. Flash-flood protests and campaigns have the potential to wash away more established lobbying.

When companies consider new activist activity, they should not just think about office, home and family. They ought to think also where they do business and their customers. Most importantly, they should not limit their horizons to their street, town or country. They ought to think internationally.

These viral or guerrilla techniques will be adopted by business. Signs exist already that digital campaigning tends to lend itself to those who are organised already and who know what they are doing.

The Permanent Campaign: Grassroots Campaigning

The lobbying of politicians by professionals will become less important because the people will increasingly have all the power. There will need to be a change in focus within companies and in the political sphere from looking up to looking down.

Business should not worry so much about which board directors are meeting with which politicians. They need to be concerned about what people are doing on the ground. The Internet and mobile phones are giving the person on the street the abilities, access and influence of the £250 an hour lobbyist.

Communications with legislators, which now are few and episodic and largely driven by lobbyists, are likely to become routine, normal and extraordinarily extensive because the Internet will offer information, guidance and an easy way to get in touch. It is likely that the government of the day will find it exceptionally difficult not to enlarge its focus groups to a state of almost continuous opinion research across the whole wired population.

Intermediaries like public affairs companies, advisors and the rest might not disappear but they will have to change. They too have challenges to face.

Lobbying, which is an activity that is now upwardly driven, will change completely to a downward activity. Lobbying has to speak to the people and to encourage them to speak to the powers that be.

President Franklin Roosevelt acknowledged this subtlety when he said when approached by lobbyists that he supported their goals, but they needed to force him publicly to act. What he meant was that he wanted to be able to point to public support for legislative change.

Dick Morris (2000), President Clinton's former adviser draws an analogy with the sun and the sea. The sun shines on the sea, heats it and evaporates the water, which forms into clouds and then deluges the decision makers with rain. The role of corporate communications professionals is to be the sun to catalyse voter sentiments and to organise the public so that they do the lobbying for the company. This means that everything now hinges on its public position with the voters: their perception of the company, the issues they promote and their merits.

Because it is so easy, electronic campaigning lures those previously inactive into political activity. The general public is moving forward on a continuum of activism. Lobbying will become increasingly mass market. Important issues will become mass fights in the media, over the Internet, aimed at voters.

Business will need to run lobbying efforts in the same way that political parties run political campaigns, because they now have the same audiences and the same goals: to persuade people to support them to change legislation. What is being seen is the democratisation of the political process through the use of technology. It is important for businesses to pay attention to their grassroots – cultivate them and keep them involved – because one day they will need them.

Come Clean and Do It Quickly

One option is to come clean and do it quickly. If organisations have done something wrong, the best thing for them to do is put their hands up, accept they have done wrong, and promise to fix it, and fix it quickly. If the problem is handled quickly, a company can come over as transparent, responsive and accessible. But, as Nichols argues, the activists may simply come back for more.

Transparency in corporate behaviour is increasing rapidly. The range of issues on which companies are expected to behave responsibly has mushroomed in a swirling coalescence of environmental, ethical and social concerns: CSR activity.

The best defence from activists is not necessarily to build a fortress. There is no place to hide. A company should look within before someone else does, publish honestly before someone else leaks the bad news, and acknowledge problems and set out plans to deal with them.

The right way to fight a propaganda war is not with more propaganda. It is to tell the truth and the whole truth and nothing but the truth.

Promote Positive Methods

Companies under attack need to highlight the positive outcomes of their activities. The best way to deal with negativity is to focus on their own message. It is like the American football metaphor: the best defence is a strong offence. When building a grassroots campaign, a company should target those people that are likely to support them.

For example, there are millions of people in the United Kingdom whose lives have been saved or made better by drugs tested on animals. 'Seriously Ill for Medical Research' is a wonderful example. It is a group of patients with serious diseases, who have challenged activists to carry cards pledging to refuse emergency treatment with a drug tested on animals. But a nod in the direction of CSR is not enough, indeed it could even be counterproductive. The action has to be real and genuine.

For Grefe (1995), there are three categories to consider when looking to promote messages. The first group is 'family and friends': those with whom there is a close relationship. They include employees, suppliers and shareholders. The second group is 'foes': those who are fundamentally opposed to the activity. These two groups account for between 5 and 10 per cent of the body politic.

The final third group, the remaining 80 to 90 per cent of the population are 'strangers': the people, who from ignorance or apathy do not know and do not care. If organised they can give companies a majority of supporters and an opportunity for growth. Many of them have an open mind and an intellectual interest in an issue. An ongoing grassroots communications programme can be used tactically to win the middle ground.

If a company does not win over its 'family' then it cannot persuade the 'strangers'. If they go to the 'strangers' first then they have made a mistake. If a company's employees are not communicated with but instead hear something about their company from their next-door neighbour, then that company has already lost. The 'family' is the one that must carry the message for a company.

Media

The modern media is increasingly aggressive. Political parties have developed expertise in responding to it, and interest groups have picked up these skills.

Companies have no alternative other than to come to terms with the 24-hour news agenda. Just like democratic governments around the world, communications teams in companies cannot ignore the pressures that have been imposed by the 24-hour news cycle. These pressures can distort decision-making processes: there are pressures for instant results.

A range of other tactics should be considered by those companies under the glare of new activists. The media should be used to promote positive messages, and not simply for a reaction to a detractor's negative arguments. The focus should be on long-term strategies and every effort made not to get sidetracked by tactical fire-fighting.

Divide Opponents

Those under siege should consider options to divide opponents. After a critical survey of the landscape, consideration should be given to whether any mainstream groups could be won over, to further isolate attackers. Middle of the road groups may disapprove of the radicals' tactics and they should be encouraged to articulate that.

Companies should attempt to ensure it is not political disadvantageous for decision makers to support their case, and work to ensure government relations are close.

Campaign for Protection

There is a recognition of the need for coordinated action by government, the police, banks and industry. Organised illicit pressure needs to be recognised early and confronted with equally concerted action. It is not only terrorists from abroad that have the potential to disrupt personal and business freedoms. If governments do not offer sufficient protection, then companies should apply pressure and make specific demands, such as the legislative changes being called for by HLS, as noted above.

The Department of Trade and Industry (DTI) in the United Kingdom has persuaded HSBC, Lloyds and Barclays to form a consortium to provide funds to companies that cannot raise money on the markets. This came about after pressure was exerted. Acting together offers protection against attack. Collective action to attack; collective action to defend.

Regulation

One way corporations cope with radical attacks is to point to their compliance with statutory or self-regulation requirements. However, 'regulatory capture' is an increasingly common concept. Activists see regulation as rules that help shield companies from competition.

Many large businesses actively seek regulation to raise standards and thereby undercut some of their smaller competitors. The marginal cost of complying with regulation for large companies is substantially lower than the cost for small to medium-sized enterprises. This is a corporate solution but may not be the most attractive one.

The Activist Solutions

Without doubt, it is the activists who have grabbed the attention of the public and the media in recent years. They have taken hold of the agenda and have been making the running. However, as we have seen in the previous chapters, companies have now 'got wise', have learnt from the activists, and are now beginning to think of new ways to ensure their fight back. It is, therefore, important for activists to pick up on a number of developments if they are to continue to make the pace.

In many ways, activists are starting from the position of power. Many may not realise this, and many take the role of the plucky underdog to symbolise their struggle against the course they oppose. This is, however, a sometimes deliberate misrepresentation. It is a strength upon which many can play.

There are a number of lessons for the budding activist.

Use the Media

Organisations such as Greenpeace have been tremendously successful in using the media for their own ends. The use of stunts, personalities, shocking statistics or research all assist in driving the message home. Actions very often speak louder than words in the 24-hour news media. What is clear is that the 24-hour news agenda is looking to be filled, and a carefully positioned and targeted campaign fulfils its requirements. Being first to comment or having a controversial stance also assists the media-driven agenda. Journalists look to have an angle for their story, to be different from others, or to be looking at an issue that others have not yet taken up. This provides opportunities for the activists.

Corporations can be large and unwieldy. Press releases or even simple statements may have to go through a myriad of processes and committees before they can be agreed. A sharp, focused and nimble activist group is the absolute opposite of this style of decision making. Obviously a small group is more able to make decisions quickly, but even the larger activist groups are more nimble than companies, and this is the consequence of getting the structures right and streamlined reporting processes in place. This brings into sharp focus the internal decision-making processes and shapes of activist groups.

Infiltrate

There are many examples of infiltration but, in general, it can be overt or covert. Overt infiltration occurs where the organisation being approached knows that the activist group wants to get involved. Jordan and Stevenson's chapter, for instance, looks at the joint decision-making processes between corporations and activist groups; both know what they are getting into. Covert infiltration can take place on a number of levels and for a number of different reasons. Fighting the system from the inside was always a popular rallying cry for early parliamentary socialists, but care needs to be taken that one does not go native. Infiltration may offer many opportunities for activists to learn more about the position being taken by a company and what is really going on, but also makes it possible to put objects in the way of its progress. They may also leak sensitive information that can be used against the company.

Realise the Value of Activists

This may seem an extremely obvious point: however, having friends on the ground, as many mass participation political parties have realised over the years, can provide a network of information and influence. While small groups necessarily rely on the electronic media, large groups should not rely too heavily on this. There remains a very real value in hearing about issues from friends, from a number of sources and from others in the community. It has also to be remembered that fashions and tastes change, so while electronic communications are currently in vogue (and for many, the be all and end all), this may not necessarily remain the case forever. Activists will benefit if they have a range of communications options at their fingertips. With this in mind, they should give consideration to getting people involved.

Know your Enemy

It is vitally important that the activist groups understand who they are fighting and the type of fight-back they may be exposed to. Invariably, if we take the example of companies, they will have a soft underbelly. For instance, in recent years many have placed great weight on their corporate social responsibility (CSR) reports. Activists have seen the very obvious opportunities in examining these reports to see if the rhetoric lives up to the reality. If it does not, they can very obviously attack but, in addition, the CSR report in effect becomes a benchmark on which the company has to improve year on year. Again opportunities for the activists exist. As one company pushes the agenda forward, others have to do likewise. Unfavourable comparisons may be made between companies operating in the same sector. Likewise, if one sector is making a great play for its environmental credentials, why are other sectors not doing the same? One can argue that it was the pressure by activists that encouraged CSR activities in the first place, but the challenge remains to stay one step ahead of the companies.

Activists should always be prepared to be aggressive. This may not necessarily be in the physical sense, although this may of course be an option, but more in how they treat the target and what they demand. Once again, in the case of a company, or indeed a government, many do not have the stomach for a fight and adverse publicity, brand damage and adverse reputation impacts will be avoided at all costs. Activists can use this to their advantage.

If companies are seen to be too hard on the activists, then they can inflict damage upon themselves. They have to strike a balance and the balance tends to be in favour of doing little.

Public Involvement

The general public is a key resource for any activist group. Only under the more extreme circumstances – usually when groups use violence – will companies or governments take action that only a few people demand. It is much better if activists are able to catch the mood of a nation and then utilise this to the benefit of their campaign. Smaller groups especially have to bear this in mind, as they do not have the benefit of large memberships, extensive catchment areas or a wide geographical spread. Instead their best approach is to attempt to catch the mood: in this way they are much more likely to succeed.

This means engaging with the public. Understanding likes and dislikes and understanding current politics, political systems, issues and the parties becomes important. This does not, it has to be emphasised, mean becoming part of the political system or being integrated within it. What it does mean is that activists have to be clever enough to identify opportunities of working with or against political parties, of understanding how to frame their arguments and messages within the political environment. Do not forget that those that they attack also have to operate within this environment. It can help sharpen the attack.

As companies are becoming more adept at playing activists at their own games – for example by the use of viral marketing to push new products – activists have also used the traditional methods and tools of the corporation. Subverts are a prime example of this. Again, however, activists recognise the need to stay sharp. When companies issue their CSR reports, there is nothing to stop an activist group publishing an alternative CSR report. This could show the 'real' position of a company's activities or directly contradict the statements and documents issued by a company.

Build a Brand

While this may seem sacrilege to some activists, many could benefit by treating the name of their organisation as a brand. Activist groups, in line with corporations, benefit from having a strong identity and name that people recognise. It is often necessary that people should respect the organisation and what it stands for, and know that it can be trusted. Think of the problems Greenpeace faced in the aftermath of Brent Spa when it was revealed that it had been wrong in its assertions. This trust, respect and understanding for an activist group can be just as important as for a major corporation. Whereas the corporation will use it to sell more or new products, the activists need it to improve the possibility of success. For those using violence, brand is of less importance.

Conclusions

Many of these new activists achieve an impact far beyond their size or resources. They are almost always unwilling to engage with the traditional institutions. There are many subversive radical networks operating around the world. These webs of campaigners use every tool possible to hurt corporations and their associates with whom they disagree. This form of activism is no longer a remote risk for corporations and government. There is no such thing as 'business as usual' any more. The old, established pressure groups have become institutionalised; business knows how to talk to and deal with them. Business is using this opportunity, taking advantage of the accessibility of mainstream pressure groups to take the heat out of many potential campaigns by more extreme new activists. Activists have realised that businesses are 'wising up' and are looking to develop new tactics such as the use of smaller, more radical groups.

The battle lines have been drawn and the opening skirmishes completed. Neither side will win outright but it is who scores the victories that will be all important.

Notes

1. http://www.corporations.org/system/
2. Speaking at an LR Rice Conference and quoted in 'Greenpeace Founder Calls Extremists Anti-Human', *Arkansas-Democrat Gazette*, 11 December 2002.
3. In the House of Commons, 12 March 2001.

Bibliography

Andersen, C. (1992) *Influencing the European Community: Guidelines for Successful Business Strategy*. London: Kogan Page.

Andersen, S. S. and Eliassen, K. A. (1991) 'European Community Lobbying'. *European Journal of Political Research*, 20, pp. 173–87.

Andersen, S. S. and Eliassen, K. A. (1993) 'Complex Policy-Making: Lobbying in the EC'. In Andersen, S. S. and Eliassen, K. A. (eds) *Making Policy in Europe*. London: Sage.

Andersen, S. S. and Eliassen, K. A. (1998) EU-Lobbying: Towards Political Segmentation in the European Union. In Clayes, P. H.; Gobin, C.; Smets, I. and Winands, P. (eds) *Lobbying, Pluralism and European Integration*. Brussels: European Interuniversity Press.

Andersen, S. S. and Eliassen, K. A. (2000) 'Democratic Modernity'. In Beck, W. and Og van der Maesen, G. L. (eds) *Questioning the Social Quality in Europe*. London and The Hague: Kluwer Law International.

Anderson, A. (1997) *Media, Culture and the Environment*. London: UCL Press.

Anderson, C. (1991) 'Cholera Epidemic Traced to Risk Miscalculation'. *Nature*, 354, 28 November.

Arkansas-Democrat Gazette (2002) "Greenpeace Founder Calls Extremists Anti-Human'. 11 December.

Athanasiou, T, (1996) *Slow Reckoning: The Ecology of a Divided Planet*. London: Secker and Warburg.

Bagehot, W. (1867) *The English Constitution*. London: Chapman and Hall.

Balanyá, B.; Doherty, A.; Hoedeman, O.; Ma'anit, A. and Wesselius, E. (2000) *Europe Inc*. London: Pluto.

Barabasi, A-L. (2002) *Linked: The New Science of Networks*. Cambridge, Mass: Perseus.

Barabasi, A-L. and Albert, R. (1999) 'Emergence of Scaling in Random Networks'. *Science*, 286, pp. 509–12.

Barber, B. (1995) *Jihad vs McWorld: How the Planet is Both Falling Apart and Coming Together and What This Means for Democracy*. New York: Times Books.

Barris, E. and McLeod, K. (2000) Globalization and International Trade in the Twenty-First Century: Opportunities for and Threats to the Health

Sector in the South. *International Journal of Health Services*, **30**(1), pp. 187–210.

Bartholomew, M. and Brooks, T. (1989) Lobbying Brussels to Get What You Need for 1992. *Wall Street Journal*, January 31, p. 7.

Bateson, G. (1973) *Steps to an Ecology of Mind*. London: Paladin.

Bello, W. (2002) 'Coming: A Return of the 1930s?' Talk delivered at the meeting of the International Council of the World Social Forum, Bangkok, Thailand 13–15 August 2002. Available at http://www.tni.org/archives/bello/coming.htm

Bello, W.; Cunningham, S. and Rau, B. (1994) *Dark Victory: The United States and Global Poverty*, Amsterdam/London: Transnational Institute and Pluto.

Bendell, J (1999) 'Beyond the Self Regulation of Environmental Management'. Reproduced in business-NGO-relations archive, June 1999.

Bennett, D. (1999) *The Creation and Development of English Commercial Corporations and the Abolition of Democratic Control over their Behaviour, Programme on Corporations, Law and Democracy*, March. Research programme/articles on corporations, law and democracy. http://www.corporatewatch.org/pages/dan_corp.html

Bennett, R. J. (1999) 'Explaining the Membership of Sectoral Business Associations'. *Environment and Planning*, 31, pp 877–98.

Bentley, A. (1908) *The Process Of Government: A Study of Social Pressures*. Chicago: University of Chicago Press.

Beyer, J. and Kerremans, B. (2002) 'Bureaucrats, Politicians and Societal Interests: Is the European Union a Depoliticised Polity?' Paper presented at ARENA, University of Oslo, 19 November.

Birchman, E. and Charlton J. (2001) *Anti-Capitalism: A Guide to the Movement*. London: Bookmarks.

BITC (Business in the Community) (2002) 'Business in the Community'. www.csreurope.org

Blaug, R. (2002) 'Engineering Democracy'. *Political Studies*, **50**(1), pp. 102–16.

Boege, S. (1993) R*oad Transport of Goods and the Effects on the Spatial Environment*. Wupperthal, Germany: Wupperthal Institute.

Boleat, M. (2001) 'The Role of Trade Associations in Promoting Corporate Social Responsibility'. Unpublished paper.

Bosso C. J. (1988) 'Transforming Adversaries into Collaborators: Interest Groups and the Regulation of Chemical Pesticides'. *Policy Sciences*, 21, pp. 3–22.

Bové, J. and Dufour, F. (2001) *The World is Not for Sale: Farmers Against Junk Food*. London; Verso.

Boycott the Pumps (2000) *Campaign News*, 9 September. http:www.boycott-the-pumps.com/090900.php

Brecher, J.; Costello, T. and Smith, B. (2000) *Globalization From Below*. Cambridge, Mass.: South End Press.

Browne, A. (2000) "Judas" of the Eco-warriors Spreads his Gospel of Doubt'. *Observer*, 21 May.

Brunner, E.; Cohen, D. and Toon, L. (2001) 'Cost Effectiveness of Cardio-vascular Disease Prevention Strategies: A Perspective on EU Food Based Dietary Guidelines'. *Public Health Nutrition*, **4**(2B), pp. 711–15

Bryant, B. (1996) *Twyford Down: Roads, Campaigning and Environmental Law*. London: E & FN Spon.

Bryceson, S (2002a) 'British Petroleum: Case Study'. www.bryceson.com/bp.htm

Bryceson, S (2002b) 'Unilever Case Study'. www.bryceson.com/unilever.htm

Buchanan, M. (2002) *Small World: Uncovering Nature's Hidden Networks*. London: Weidenfeld Nicolson.

Business, The (2003) 'Huntingdon Life Sciences Calls for Stronger Rights Law'. 2 March.

Bygrave, M. (2002) 'Where Did All the Protestors Go?' *Observer*, 14 July, pp. 24–5.

Carrier, R. (1999) 'What an Atheist Ought to Stand For'. www.infidels.org/library/modern/richard_carrier/ough.html

Castells, M. (1996) *The Rise of the Network Society. Volume 1 of The Information Age: Economy, Society and Culture*. Oxford: Blackwell.

Castells, M. (2001) *The Internet Galaxy: Reflections on the Internet, Business And Society*. Oxford: Oxford University Press.

CEI (Competitive Enterprise Institute) (1999) 'Public Interest Groups File Deceptive Advertising Complaint with FTC Against Ben and Jerry's: Charge Ad Campaign Misleads Consumers on Dioxin Content of Ice Cream'. Press Release, 16 December.

Channel 4 (1997) *Against Nature*. Produced by Martin Durkin, London: Channel 4 Television Corporation.

Chesters, G. and Welsh, I. (2002) 'Reflexive Framing: An Ecology of Action'. Research Committee 24: Globalization and the Environment, XV World Congress of Sociology, 6–13 July at the University of Brisbane, Australia.

Childs, H. L. (1930) *Labor and Capital in National Politics*. Columbus, Ohio: Ohio State University Press.

Church, C. (1999) 'Dangers of Co-optation'. Contribution to discussion list, business-NGO-relations archive, 15 August.

Clark, D. (1997) Better Regulation Unit. Mission statement, June. http://www.cabinet-office.gov.uk/regulation

Club de Bruxelles (1994) *Lobbying in Europe after Maastricht: How to Keep Abreast and Wield INFLUENCE in the European Union*. Brussels: Club de Bruxelles.

Clunies-Ross, T. and Hildyard, N. (1992) *The Politics of Industrial Agriculture*. London: Earthscan.

Cobb, R. W. and Elder, C. D. (1972) *Participation in American Politics: The Dynamics of Agenda-Building*. Baltimore and London: Johns Hopkins University Press.

Cockburn, A.; St Clair, J. and Sekula, A. (2000) *Five Days that Shook the World*. London: Verso.

Collins, M. (1993) *A Complete Guide to European Research, Technology and Consultancy Funds: Guidelines for Successful Applications, Lobbying, Acquisition and Use*. London: Kogan Page.

Connor, T. (2002) We are Not Machines. Oxfam Community Aid Abroad. http://www.cleanclothes.org

Corporate Social Responsibility Europe (CSR Europe) (2002) About Us, www.csreurope.org

Covey, J. and Brown, L. D. (2001) Critical Co-operation: An Alternative Form of Civil Society–Business Engagement. *IDR Reports*, **17**(1). Cambridge, Mass.: Harvard.

Cox, R. (1987) *Power, Production and World Order: Social Forces in the Making of History*.New York: Columbia University Press.

Dannaher, K. and Burbach, R. (eds) (2000) *Globalize This!* Monroe, Maine: Common Courage Press.

Daugberg, C. (1999) 'Reforming the CAP'. *Journal of Common Market Studies*, **37**(3), pp. 407–28.

Davies, N. (2002) 'Cosy Relationship Keeps Corporates Happy but Could Cost £20 Billion in Taxes'. *Guardian*, 23 July.

Davis, M. (2001) *Late Victorian Holocausts: El Niño Famines and the Making of the Third World*. London: Verso.

Deegan, D. (2001) *Managing Activism*. London: IPR.

de Selincourt, K. (1997) *Local Harvest*. London: Lawrence & Wishart.

Deleuze, G. and Guattari, F. (2002) *A Thousand Plateaus*. London: Continuum.

Doherty, B. (2000) 'Manufactured Vulnerability: Protest Camp Tactics'. In Seel, B.; Paterson, M. and Doherty, B. (eds) *Direct Action in British Environmentalism*. London: Routledge.

Dølvik, J. E. (1999) The Global Challenge: Convergence and Divergence of National Labour Market Institutions? ARENA, unpublished.

Doner, R. F. and Schneider, B. R. (2001) 'Business Associations and

Economic Development: Why Some Associations Contribute More than Others'. *Business and Politics*, **2**(3), November, pp. 26188.

Dowding, K. (1991) *Rational Choice and Political Power*. Aldershot: Edward Elgar.

Dowler, E. and Rushton, R. (1993) *Diet and Poverty in the UK*. London: Centre for Human Nutrition, University College London.

Drapl, A.; Vercic, D.; Peterlind, I. and Ilesie, T. (2002) 'Slovenia and the EU: An Anti-Dumping Case'. In Pedler, R. (ed.) *European Union Lobbying: Changes in the Arena*, pp. 143–54. London: Palgrave.

Drewnowski, A. and Popkin B. M. (1997) 'The Nutrition Transition: New Trends in the Global Diet'. *Nutrition Reviews*, **55**(2), pp. 31–43.

Dudley, G. F. and Richardson, J. J. (1996) 'Why does Policy Change over Time? Adversarial Policy Communities, Alternative Policy Arenas, and British Trunk Roads Policy 1945–95'. *Journal of European Public Policy*, 3, pp. 63–83.

Dudley, G.F. and Richardson, J.J. (2000) *Why Does Policy Change? Lessons from British Transport Policy, 1945–99*. London: Routledge.

Dudley, G. F. (1983) 'The Road Lobby: A Declining Force?' In Marsh, D. (ed.) *Pressure Politics*, pp. 104–28. London: Junction.

Durning, A. (1992) *How Much Is Enough? The Consumer Society and the Future of the Earth*. London: Earthscan.

Economic and Social Committee (1980) *European Interest Groups and their Relationship with the Economic and Social Committee*. Farnborough: Saxon House.

Economist (1993) Survey of Multinationals. 27 March, pp 5–6.

Edelman (2002a) 'NGOs Now the Fifth Estate in Global Governance'. Edelman PR press release, 2 February.

Edelman (2002b) 'Rebuilding Public Trust Through Accountability and Responsibility'. Address to Ethical Corporation Magazine Conference, Edelman PR, 3 October.

Edwards, M. (2000) *NGO Rights and Responsibilities: A New Deal for Global Governance*. London: Foreign Policy Centre.

EPE (European Partners for the Environment) (2002) 'Welcome to EPE'. www.epe.be

ERT (European Round Table of Industrialists) (2001) 'ERT Position on Corporate Social Responsibility and Response to Commission Green Paper "Promoting a European Framework for Corporate Social Responsibility"'. November, www.ert.be

European Commission (1992) *The Environmental Dimension: Taskforce Report on the Environment and the Internal Market*. Brussels: European Commission.

European Commission (2001) Promoting a European Framework for Corporate Social Responsibility, *COM(2001)* 366.

European Commission (2002) Corporate Social Responsibility, *COM(2002)* 347 final.

Evans, M. (1997) 'Political Participation'. In Dunleavy, P. *et al.* (eds) *Developments in British Politics* 5. Basingstoke: Macmillan.

FAO (Food and Agriculture Organisation) (1999) Enabling Development: Policy Issues Agenda item no 4. Rome: FAO. http://www.wfp.org/eb_public/Eb_Home.html

Feder, E. (1977) *Strawberry Imperialism*. The Hague: Institute of Social Studies.

Fernández-Armesto, F. (2001) *Food: A History*. London: Macmillan.

Fernández-Armesto, F. (2003) 'Too Rich, Too Thin?' In Holden. J., Howland. L and Stedman Jones. D. (eds) *Foodstuff: Living in an Age of Feast and Famine*, pp. 19–24. London: Demos, London.

Finer, S. E. (1958) 'Transport Interests and the Road Lobby', *Political Quarterly*, 29, pp. 47-58.

FSN (Food Security Network) (2000) 'Greenpeace USA Struggles to Raise Funds'. Available on www.foodsecurity.net/news/newsitem.php3?nid=249&tnews=news (accessed 18 July).

Fukuyama, F. (1992) *The End of History and the Last Man*. New York: Free Press.

Gabriel, Y. and Lang, T. (1995) *The Unmanageable Consumer*. London: Sage.

Gaines, S. (2002) 'High Flyers'. *Guardian*, 23 October.

Gallup (1995) Financial Times Exporter, Summer, p. 4.

Gallup International (2002) 'Trust will be the Challenge of 2003'. Press release, 8 November.

Garceau, O. (1941) *The Political Life of the American Medical Association*. Cambridge, Mass.: Harvard University Press.

Gardner, J. N. (1991) *Effective Lobbying in the European Community*. Deventer: Klewer Law and Taxation.

George, S. (1997) 'Winning the War of Ideas'. Dissent, Summer. See http://www.tni.org/george/articles/dissent.htm

George, S. and Sabelli, F. (1994) *Faith and Credit: The World Bank's Secular Empire*. London: Penguin.

Gilliatt, B. (2002) 'Operating in Contested Environments: Chlorine'. Paper prepared for presentation to the conference on the Challenge of Change in EU Business Associations, Brussels, 7–10 May. www.ey.be/euroconference

Gramsci, A. (1971) *The Prison Notebooks*, London: Lawrence and Wishart.

Granovetter, M. S. (1973) 'The Strength of Weak Ties'. *American Journal of Sociology*, **78**(6), pp.1360–80.

Grant, W. (1997a) *The Common Agricultural Policy*. Basingstoke: Macmillan.

Grant, W. (1997b) 'BSE and the Politics of Food'. In P. Dunleavy *et al.* (eds) *Developments in British Politics* 5. Basingstoke: Macmillan.

Grant, W. (2000) *Pressure Groups and British Politics*. Basingstoke: Macmillan.

Grant, W. (2001) 'Pressure Politics: From "Insider" Politics to Direct Action?' *Parliamentary Affairs*, **54**(2), pp. 337–48.

Greenpeace (1998) '1998 Annual Report'. www.greenpeace.org

Greenpeace (2000) 'Gerber Parent Novartis Eliminates Genetically Engineered Food From All Products'. Press release, 3 August.

Greenwood, J. (2002) *Inside the EU Business Associations*. Basingstoke: Palgrave.

Greenwood, J. and Aspinwall, M. (eds) (1998) *Collective Action in the European Union*. London, Routledge.

Grefe, E. (1995) *The New Corporate Activism: Harnessing the Power of Grassroots Tactics for Your Organization*. New York: McGraw-Hill.

Griffiths, J. (1993) 'A Freer Flow of Goods'. *Financial Times*, 12 March.

Gupta, S. K. and Brubaker D. R. (1990) 'The Concept of Corporate Social Responsibility Applied to Trade Associations'. *Socio-Economic Planning Science*, **24**(4), pp 261–71.

Hamer, M. (1987) *Wheels Within Wheels*. London: Routledge and Kegan Paul.

Hamlin, C. (1998) *Public Health and Social Justice in the Age of Chadwick: Britain 1800–1854*. Cambridge: Cambridge University Press.

Hardt, M. and Negri, A. (2000) *Empire*. London: Harvard University Press.

Hari, J. (2002) 'Whatever happened to *No Logo*?' *New Statesman*, 11 November, cover story, pp. 20–2.

Hartman, C. and Stafford, E. (2001) 'Enviro Groups Entering the Marketing Fray'. *Marketing News*, July 30, p.15.

Haskins, C. (1998) Foreword to Principles of Good Regulation. Better Regulation Task Force, http://www.cabinet-office.gov.uk/regulation/1998/task_force/principles.htm

Heer, J. and Penfold, S. (2003) 'True Grits'. *Boston Globe*, 9 February, Ideas Section, p. D1.

Heinz, J.; Laumann, E.; Nelson, R. and Salisbury, R. (1993) *The Hollow Core: Private Interests in National Policy-Making*. Cambridge, Mass.: Harvard University Press.

Helfferich, B. and Kolb, F. (2001) 'Multilevel Action Coordination in European Contentious Politics: The Case of the European Women's Lobby'. In Imig, D. and Tarrow, S. (eds) *Contentious Europeans: Protest and Politics in an Integrating Europe*, pp. 143–62. Lanham, Md.: Rowman and Littlefield.

Hernes, H-K. and Mikalsen, K. H. (2002) 'From Protest to Participation? Environmental Groups and the Management of Marine Fisheries'. *Mobilization*, **7**(1), February, pp. 15–28.

Herring, E. (1929) 'Group Representation Before Congress'. Institute For Government Research, *Studies In Administration* No 22. Baltimore: Brookings Institute.

Hertz, N. (2001) *The Silent Takeover: Global Capitalism and the Death of Democracy*. London: Heinemann.

Hines, C. (2001) *Localisation*. London: Earthscan.

Hirschmann, A. (1970) *Exit, Voice And Loyalty: Responses to Decline in Firms, Organizations and States*. Cambridge, Mass.: Harvard University Press.

HM Treasury (2000) 'Pocket Data Book: Table 11: UK Public Finances'. www.hm-treasury.gov.uk/e_info/overview/index

Imig, D, and Tarrow, S. (2001) 'Political Contention in a Europeanising Polity'. In Goetz, K. and Hix, S. (eds) *Europeanised Politics? European Integration and National Political Systems*, pp. 73–93. London: Frank Cass.

Imig, D. and Tarrow, S. (2001) (eds) *Contentious Europeans*. Lanham, Md.: Rowman and Littlefield.

Ingle, S. (2001) 'Politics in 2000: Life in the Year of the Dome'. *Parliamentary Affairs*, **54**(2), pp. 177–89.

Islam, F. (2003) 'Lets Hear it for the Boycott'. *Observer*, 2 March.

Johnson, S. (2001) *Emergence: The Connected Lives of Ants, Brains, Cities and Software*. London: Penguin.

Jordan, G. (2001) *Shell, Greenpeace and Brent Spar*. Basingstoke: Palgrave.

Jordan, G. and Maloney, W. A. (1997) *The Protest Business? Mobilizing Campaign Groups*. Manchester: Manchester University Press.

Kennedy, P. (2002) *A Carnival of Revolution: Central Europe 1989*. Princeton: Princeton University Press.

Kewly, S. (2002) 'Japanese Lobbying in the EU'. In Pedler, R. (ed.) *European Union Lobbying: Changes in the Arena*, p. 177–200. London: Palgrave.

Klein, N. (2000) *No Logo*. London: Flamingo.

Klein, N. (2001) 'Reclaiming the Commons'. *New Left Review*, 9, May/June, pp. 81–9.

Klein, N. (2002) *Fences and Windows: Dispatches from the Front Lines of the Globalization Debate*. London: Flamingo.

Kranendonk, S. and Bringezau, B. (1994) *Major Material Flows Associated with Orange Juice Consumption in Germany*. Wupperthal, Germany: Wupperthal Institute.

Lancet (1991) 'Cholera in Peru', *Lancet*, 337, 2 March.

Lang, T. (1996) 'Food Security: Does it Conflict with Globalization?' *Development*, 4, pp. 45–50.

Lang, T. and Caraher, M. (2001) 'International Public Health'. In Pencheon, D. and Melzer, D. (eds) *Oxford Textbook of Public Health*, pp. 168–76. Oxford: Oxford University Press.

Lang, T. and Hines, C. (1993) *The New Protectionism*. London: Earthscan.

Laughlin, R. and Pines, D. (2000) 'The Theory of Everything'. *Proceedings of the National Academy of Sciences of the United States of America*, 97: pp. 28–31.

Lee, K.; Buse, K. and Fustukian, S. (2002) *Health Policy in a Globalising World*. Cambridge: Cambridge University Press.

Lenschow, A. (1999) 'Transformation in European Environmental Governance'. In Kohler Koch, B. and Eising, R. (eds) *The Transformation of Governance in the European Union*, pp. 39–60. London: Routledge.

Levinson, C. (1979) *Vodka-Cola*. London: Gordon and Cremonesi.

Lloyd Parry, R (2002) 'Nike and Adidas Have Failed to Stop Sweatshop Abuses'. *Independent*, 8 March.

Lorenzano, L. (1998) 'Zapatismo: Recomposition of Labour, Radical Democracy and Revolutionary Project'. In Holloway, J. and Pelaez, E. *Zapatista! Reinventing Revolution in Mexico*. London: Pluto.

Lubbers, E. (2002) *Battling Big Business*. Totnes: Common Courage Press.

MacEwan, A. (1999) *Neo-Liberalism or Democracy? Economic Strategies, Markets and Alternatives for the Twenty-First Century*, London: Zed.

Mack, C. S. (1989) *Lobbying and Government Relations: A Guide for Executives*. New York: Quorum.

Madden, P. (1992) *Raw Deal*. London: Christian Aid.

Madeley, J. (2000) *Hungry for Trade*. London: Zed.

Malkin, M. and Fumento, M. (1996) 'Rachel's Folly: The End of Chlorine'. Competitive Enterprise Institute. http://www.cei.org/gencon/025,01518.cfm

Maloney, W. A.; Jordan, G. and McLaughlin, A. M. (1994) 'Interest Groups and Public Policy: The Insider/Outsider Model Revisited'. *Journal of Public Policy*, 14, pp. 17–38.

Mandelson, P. and Liddle, R. (1996) *The Blair Revolution: Can New Labour Deliver?* London: Faber and Faber.

Marcos, Subcommandante Insurgente. (1996) *Our Word is Our Weapon.* New York: Seven Stories Press.

Marsh, D. and Smith, M. (2000) 'Understanding Policy Networks: Towards a Dialectical Approach'. *Political Studies*, **48**(1), pp. 4–21.

Martin, P. and Itano, N. (2002) 'Greens Accused of Helping Africans Starve'. *Washington Times*, 30 August.

Mayer, C. E. (1999) 'Toys Safe to Melt in the Mouth? Mattel Plans to Replace Soft Plastic with Organic Playthings'. *Washington Post*, 8 December.

Mazey, A. and Richardson, J. (1993) *Lobbying in the European Community.* Oxford: Oxford University Press.

McFarland A. S. (1993) *Cooperative Pluralism: The National Coal Policy Experiment.* Lawrence, Kans.:University Press of Kansas.

McKay, G. (1998) 'DiY Culture: Notes Towards an Introduction'. In McKay, G. (ed.) *DiY Culture: Party and Protest in Nineties Britain*, pp. 1–53. London: Verso.

McKean, D. (1938) *Pressures on the Legislature Of New Jersey.* New York: Columbia University Press.

Monbiot, G. (2000) *The Captive State: The Corporate Takeover of Britain.* London: Pan.

Monks, R. and Minow, R. (2001) *Corporate Governance.* London: Blackwell.

Moore, M. (2002) *Stupid White Men and Other Sorry Excuses for the State of the Nation.* London: Penguin.

Morris, B.; Boehm, K. and Vilcinskas, M. (1986) *The European Community: A Practical Directory and Guide For Business, Industry and Trade.* London: Macmillan.

Morris, D. (2000) *Vote.com: How Big-Money Lobbyists and the Media Are Losing Their Influence, and the Internet is Giving Power Back to the People.* New York: Renaissance.

Murphy, D. F. and Bendell, J. (1997) *In the Company of Partners.* Bristol: Policy Press.

Nestle, M. (2002) *Food Politics: How the Food Industry Influences Nutrition and Health.* Berkeley, Calif.: University of California Press.

Newman, D. (1990) 'Lobbying in the EC'. *Business Journal*, February.

Odegard, P. (1928) *Pressure Politics: The Story of the Anti-Saloon League.* New York: Columbia University Press.

Ollila, E. (2003) 'Global Health-Related Public–Private Partnerships and the United Nations'. Available on the Globalism and Social Policy Programme Website www.gaspp.org

Olsen, J. P. (2001) 'Organising European Institutions of Government'. In Andersen, S. S. (ed.) Institutional approaches to the European Union. Proceedings from ARENA-workshop, report 3/2001.

Olson, M. (1965) *The Logic Of Collective Action: Public Goods and The Theory of Groups*. Cambridge, Mass.: Harvard University Press.

OPEC (2000) 'Opening Address to the 111th Meeting of the OPEC Conference by HE Alí Rodríguez Araque, President of the OPEC conference and Minister for Energy and Mines of Venezuala, 10 September'. OPEC Press Release, 9/2000. www.opec.org/Newsinfo/PressReleases/pr2000/PR9_2000.htm

Panitchpakdi, S. (2002) 'Why Cancun Matters'. Speech to Second International Conference on Globalisation, Leuven, 22 November.

Paxton, A (1994) *The Food Miles Report*. London: Sustainable Agriculture, Food and Environment (SAFE) Alliance.

Pedler, R. (ed.) (2002) *European Union Lobbying*. Basingstoke: Palgrave.

Pedler, R. and Rautvuori, H. (2002) 'EU Accession and the "Acquis": Saving Nordic Monopolies'. In Pedler, R. (ed.) *European Union Lobbying: Changes in the Arena*, pp. 125–42. London: Palgrave.

Petras, J. and Veltmeyer, P. (2001) *Globalization Unmasked: Imperialism in the Twenty-First Century*. London: Zed.

Philip, A. B. (1987) Pressure Groups in the European Community and Informal Institutional Arrangements. In Beuter, R. and Taskaloyannis, P. (eds) *Experiences in Regional Co-operation*. Maastricht: EIPA.

Phillips S. (1994) 'New Social Movements and Routes to Representation'. In Brooks, S. and Gagnon, S. (eds) *The Political Influence of Ideas*. Westport, Conn.: Praeger.

Phillips, A. (1995) *The Politics of Presence*. Oxford: Clarendon.

Plowden, W. (1971) *The Motor Car and Politics: 1896–1970*. London: Bodley Head.

Pollack, A. (2000) 'Novartis Ended Use of Gene-Altered Foods'. *New York Times*, 4 August.

Popkin, B. (1998) 'The Nutrition Transition and its Health Implications in Lower-Income Countries'. *Public Health Nutrition*, **1**(1), pp. 5–21.

Public Affairs Newsletter (2002) 'European Parliament Calls for Registration of Lobbyists'. *Public Affairs Newsletter*, **8**(10), July/August, p. 5.

Rallings, C. and Thrasher, M. (2001) 'Elections and Public Opinion: The End of the Honeymoon?' *Parliamentary Affairs*, **54**(2), pp. 322–36.

Raloff, J. (2000) 'The Case for DDT: What Do you Do when a Dreaded Environmental Pollutant Saves Lives?' *Science News*, **158**(1), July, p. 1.

Rawcliffe, P. (1998) *Environmental Pressure Groups in Transition*. Manchester: Manchester University Press.

Ray, D. L. with Guzzo, L. (1993) *Environmental Overkill: Whatever Happened to Common Sense?* Washington, D.C.: Regnery.

Reinicke, W. H. (1998) *Global Public Policy: Governing Without Government?* Washington, D.C.: Brookings Institution Press.

Riccardi, N. (2000) 'Boot Camp for Roving Protesters'. *Los Angeles Times*, 28 July.

Rieger, E. (2000) 'The Common Agricultural Policy: External and Internal Dimensions', In Wallace, H. and Wallace, W. (eds) *Policy Making in the European Union*, 4th Edition. Oxford: Oxford University Press.

Risse-Kappen, T. (1995) 'Structures of Governance and Transnational Relations: What Have we Learned?' In Risse-Kappen, T. (ed.) *Bringing Trans-national Relations Back In: Non-State Actors, Domestic Structures and International Institutions*, pp 3–36. Cambridge: Cambridge University Press.

Ritzer, G. (2000) *The McDonaldization of Society: The Millennium Edition*. Thousand Oaks, California: Sage.

Robinson, N. (2000) *The Politics of Agenda Setting: The Car and the Shaping of Public Policy*. Aldershot: Ashgate.

Robinson, N. (2002) 'The Politics of the Fuel Protests: Towards a Multi-dimensional Explanation'. *Political Quarterly*, **73**(1), pp. 58–66.

Robinson, N. (2003) 'The Government and the Politics of the Fuel Protests: From Ignorance to Political Crisis'. *Parliamentary Affairs*, forthcoming.

Ronfeldt, D. F.; Arquilla, J.; Fuller, G. E. and Fuller, M. (1998) *The Zapatista 'Social Netwar' in Mexico*. Santa Monica, Calif.: RAND Corporation.

Ross, J. (2000) *The War Against Oblivion: The Zapatista Chronicles*. Monroe, La.: Common Courage Press.

Rowell A. (1996) *Green Backlash: Global Subversion of the Environmental Movement*. London: Routledge.

Rowell, A. (2001) in Maomagazine.com, 17 July. Also to be found on AndyRowell.com/articles under the title *Genoa G8*.

Rugman, A. (2000) *The End of Globalization*. London: Random House Business.

Sabatier, P. (1998) 'An Advocacy Coalition Framework of Policy Change and Role of Policy-Oriented Learning Therein'. *Policy Sciences*, 21, pp. 129–68.

Salisbury, R. (1969) 'An Exchange Theory of Interest Groups'. *Midwest Journal of Political Science*, 13, February, pp. 1–32.

Salisbury, R. (1984) 'Interest Representation: The Dominance of Institutions'. *American Political Science Review*, 78, March, pp 64–76.

Sampson, A. (1971) *The New Anatomy of Britain*. London: Hodder and Stoughton.

Sampson, A. (1992) *The Essential Anatomy of Britain*. London: Hodder and Stoughton.

Sassen, J. (1992) 'Getting Through to Brussels: Business Lobbying at the European Commission'. *International Management*, **47**(2), p. 62.

Schattschneider, E (1935) *Politics, Pressures and the Tariff: A Study of Free Private Enterprise in Pressure Politics*. New York: Prentice Hall.

Schattschneider, E (1960) *The Semisovereign People: A Realist's View of Democracy in America*. New York: Holt, Reinhart and Winston.

Schendelen, M. P. C. M. van (ed.) (1993) *National, Public and Private EC-Lobbying*. Aldershot: Dartmouth.

Schendelen, R. van (2002) *Machiavelli in Brussels: The Art of Lobbying the EU*. Amterdam, Amsterdam University Press.

Schneiberg, M. and Hollingsworth, J. R. (1991) 'Can Transaction Cost Economics Explain Trade Associations?' In Czada, R. M. and Windhoff-Heritier, A. (eds) *Political Choice: Institutions, Rules and the Limits of Rationality*, pp 199–231. Frankfurt: Campus.

Sen, A. (1981) *Poverty and Famines: An Essay on Entitlement and Deprivation*. Oxford: Clarendon.

Sen, A. (1997) *Inequality Re-Examined*. Cambridge, Mass.: Harvard University Press,

Slaughter, A-M. (1997) 'The Real New World Order'. *Foreign Affairs*, 76, pp. 183–97.

Sokolov, R. (1991) *Why We Eat What We Eat: How the Encounter between the New World and the Old Changed the Way Everyone on the Planet Eats*. New York: Summit.

Soros, G. (2002) *George Soros on Globalization*. New York: PublicAffair.

Stafford, E.; Polonsky, M. and Hartman, C. (2000) 'Environmental NGO–Business Collaboration and Strategic Bridging: A Case Analysis of the Greenpeace–Foron Alliance'. *Business Strategy and the Environment*, 9, pp. 122–35

Starr, A. (2000) *Naming the Enemy: Anti-Corporate Movements Confront Globalization*. London: Zed.

Stern, A. (1992) *European Lobbying: How to Keep Abreast and Wield Influence in the EC*. Brussels: Club de Brussels.

Sunstein, C. (2001) *Republic.com*. Princeton: Princeton University Press.

Tansey, G. and Worsley, T. (1995) *The Food System*. London: Earthscan.

Taylor, B. and Walker, J. (1998) 'Brum Shut Off by Road Demo'. *Sunday Mercury*, May 17th, pp. 1, 10.

Tenbücken , M. (2002) *Corporate Lobbying the European Union: Strategies of Multinational Companies*. Frankfurt am Main: Peter Lang.

Therborn, G. (1997)Politics and Policy of Social Quality. Research report. Uppsala: SCASS.

Thomas, J. (2002) *The Battle in Seattle: The Story Behind and Beyond the WTO Demonstrations*. Golden, Colo.: Fulcrum.

Thompson, E. P. (1993) *Customs in Common: Studies in Traditional Popular Culture*. New York: New Press. See chapters IV and V.

Thomson, S. (2000) *The Social Democratic Dilemma: Ideology, Governance and Globalization*. London: Macmillan.

Tóibín, C. (1999) *The Irish Famine*. London: Profile Books.

Tomlinson, J. (1990) *Hayek and the Market*. London: Pluto.

Tren, R. and Bate, R. (2000) *When Politics Kills: Malaria and the DDT Story*. Washington, D.C.: Competitive Enterprise Institute.

Truman, D. (1951) *The Governmental Process: Political Interests and Public Opinion*, Westport, Conn.: Greenwood,

Tyler, P. E. (2003) 'A New Power in the Streets'. *New York Times*, editorial, 17 February.

Tyme, J. (1978) *Motorways versus Democracy*. Basingstoke: Macmillan.

Tyszkiewicz, Z. (2002) 'National Members and their EU Associations'. In Greenwood, J. (ed.) *The Effectiveness of EU Business Associations*, pp 171–81. Basingstoke: Palgrave.

UNCTAD (1995) *World Investment Report 1995: Transnational Corporations and Effectiveness*. www.unctad.org.en/docs/wir95ove.en.pdf

UNCTAD (2002) 'Are Transnationals Bigger Than Countries?' Press release, August.

UNICEF (1993) *Food, Health and Care: The UNICEF Vision and Strategy for a World Free from Hunger and Malnutrition*. New York: United Nations Children's Fund.

United Nations Centre on Transnational Corporations (1981) *Transnational Corporations in Food and Beverage Processing*. New York: United Nations.

Unseem, J. (2002) Will the Real WTO Please Stand Up. Fortune.com (January 21).

Van der Storm, I. (2002) 'CASTer: Creating the Future in Steel Regions'. In Pedler, R. (ed.) *European Union Lobbying: Changes in the Arena*, pp. 229–56. London: Palgrave.

Wainwright, H. (2002) Notes Towards a New Politics: New Strategies for People Power. *TNI Briefing Series No. 3*. Amsterdam: Trans-national Institute.

Walker, W. (1991) *Mobilizing Interest Groups in America: Patrons, Professionals and Social Movements*. Ann Arbor: University Of Michigan Press.

Warshal, S. (ed.) (1996) *Brent Spar and After*. Conference papers from Greenpeace business conference, September (available from Greenpeace).

Watkins, K. (2002) *Rigged Rules and Double Standards: Trade, Globalisation, and the Fight Against Poverty*. Oxford: Oxfam International.

WCRF (World Cancer Research Fund) in association with American Institute for Cancer Research Food (1997) *Nutrition and the Prevention of Cancer: A Global Perspective*. Washington, D.C.: World Cancer Research Fund/American Institute for Cancer Research.

Wesselius, E. (2002) Behind GATS2000: Corporate Power at Work. *WTO Briefing Series No. 4*. Amsterdam: Trans-national Institute.

Whelan, E. (1985) *Toxic Terror*. Ottawa, Ill.: Jameson.

WHO (2000) *Food and Nutrition Action Plan for Europe*, August 2000. Copenhagen: WHO European Regional Office.

WHO (World Health Organisation) (1999) *Food Safety and Globalisation of Trade in Food: A Challenge to the Public Health Sector*. Geneva: Food Safety Unit, WHO.

Wilson, J. Q. (1995) *Political Organizations* (revised edition). Princeton, N.J.: Princeton University Press.

Woodham-Smith, C. (1962/1991) *The Great Hunger: Ireland 1845–1849*. London: Penguin.

Wysham, D. (2002), The Plain Dealer Commentary
http://www.seen.org/pages/media/20020811_nigerwomen_plain-dealer.shtml

Zagorin, A. (1989) 'An Expanding Game'. *Time Magazine*, 29 May, pp. 38–9.

Index

Key
b box
f figure/illustration
n note
t table
bold extended discussion or
    heading emphasized in main
    text